the birth of the Church

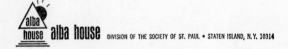

alba house DIVISION OF THE SOCIETY OF ST. PAUL • STATEN ISLAND, N.Y. 10314

the Birth of the Church

A BIBLICAL STUDY

Giblet
Andriessen
Cerfaux
Coppens
Denis
Grelot
Marle
Van den Bussche
van Unnik

translated by Charles Underhill Quinn

Original title: Aux Origines de L'Eglise, published by Desclee de Brouwer
Translated by Charles Quinn

Nihil Obstat: Donald A. Panella, M.A., S.T.L., S.S.L.

Imprimatur: † Terence J. Cooke, D.D.
New York, N. Y. January 9, 1968

The nihil obstat and imprimatur are official declarations that a book or
pamphlet is free of doctrinal or moral error. No implication is contained
therein that those who have granted the nihil obstat and imprimatur agree
with the contents, opinions or statements expressed.

Library of Congress Catalog Number: 68 - 17766

This book was designed, printed and bound in the U.S.A. by the Pauline
Fathers and Brothers of the Society of St. Paul, 2187 Victory Blvd., Staten
Island, N. Y. 10314, as part of their communications apostolate.

Contents

Contents

Jean Giblet

Foreword

Till recently emphasis in exegesis has been primarily on developments in Pauline theology. Today there is an attempt to widen the scope of investigation and to undertake a more systematic study of the Old Testament theology of the people of God and the modalities of religious organization in Judaism. On the other hand, without neglecting the Pauline teaching, the originality and importance of other New Testament currents and their extension into the second century are recognized. Finally there is a certain stress on questions dealing with the primitive organization of the apostolic communities—a point where, paradoxically enough, Catholic exegesis has been somewhat lagging. These were the influences coloring the program of the 14th *Journées Bibliques de Louvain*.

Choosing one of the most characteristic passages from the Old Testament, Msgr. J. Coppens has commented on Jeremiah 31, 31-34. The freshness of the Jeremian vocabulary goes hand in hand with the views proposed. This perfect and definitive union, going beyond the great pardon for sin, this knowledge, without intermediary, of essential religious and moral truths for which the prophet uses but one word, "knowledge of Yahweh,"—all this implies a sort of democratization of the prophetic charisms that paved the way for revolutionary perspectives. This quite thorough study will therefore underline the complexity of Old Testament theology and the subsequent possibilities that are open to New Testament theologians. Moreover it was suitable first to look into what the Jewish notions were, and particularly the views of those religious groups that we have come to know through the Qumrân discoveries. Fr. Denis, O.P., professor at the Collège Théologique of La Sarte, began by proposing a chronological classification of the various materials available, and then showed the evolution of a religious movement that emerged from a deep eschatologically colored emotion and gradually grew into a religious association on the one hand and a cenobitical society on the other. Fr. Denis was careful not to make comparisons with forms of New Testament eschatology, but his article does allow us to see where certain details converge as well as the profound differences in orientation that exist.

In my own paper, keeping within a very well defined area of the question, I examined the problems relating to the historicity and the significance of the Twelve in the original evangelical tradition. It seems to me that the Bultmann school's skepticism on this point is not well founded and that we must acknowledge the historicity of this first organization formed by Jesus. We must also put greater stress on its eschatological character. Above all the Twelve are associated with the Master in the governing of the New Israel. Their properly apostolic activity is subordinate to it.

In tackling the so often neglected theme of the Church as the Bride of Christ in Pauline theology, Dom Andriessen has offered some rather new views concerning its connection with the theme of the Body of Christ thus contributed to putting both themes in better perspective within the totality of the Apostle's theology.

Examining the contributions of the fourth Gospel, Prof. Van den Bussche has shown how John was keenly concerned with the interior reality of the Church without being overly preoccupied with its structure. The death of Jesus assured the universality of the Church which took form through the glorified Christ and in the perspective of the ultimate accomplishment of his mission. It remained for Msgr. Cerfaux to outline the ecclesiology of the Book of Revelation. After situating the book's composition in the historical context of the latter part of the first century, he showed that the notion of the universal Church had remained fundamentally unchanged since St. Paul. With a quick examination of various themes, Msgr. Cerfaux underlined the importance of the Old

Testament roots and the spiritual emphasis of the Johannine amplifications.

One of the most important New Testament institutions contributing to the Church's birth is incontestably the Eucharist. It is at the Last Supper that Jesus instituted the New Covenant, and it is around the repetition of this Supper that the first Christians learned to come together and to form a "church." It was therefore quite natural that a section be reserved for the institution of the Eucharist. Msgr. Coppens, to whom we are indebted for several articles on the *mysterium fidei* and who once edited the remarkable monograph of the late Werner Goossens, invited us to rediscover the most ancient formulas of the eucharistic liturgy and to uncover their meaning both in a sacramental and a sacrificial sense.

After so many detailed studies an over-all view is necessary. M. Grelot offers it to us by studying systematically the question of the various ministries in the New Testament writings. He carefully distinguishes the ministry of an Apostle from the ecclesiastical ministries, and consequently he is able to show what is peculiar to each and to demonstrate the real continuity that exists between the two.

Two studies are devoted to aspects of second century theology: the idea of "church" was a normal thing, and it proved to be useful. Actually it is rather artificial to isolate the New Testament writings from the various milieus where the currents of thought and the structures they reflect continued to be alive and to grow.

Prof. van Unnik of the University of Utrecht speaks of a *gnosis* of "ideas and not of systems." On the whole we can say that the Gnostics scarcely made any room for the Church in their thought. Certainly they knew her, and the bonds between several groups and the Church herself were not entirely severed. But they looked upon themselves as an elite that was capable of attaining the hidden and mysterious meaning that escapes the mass of the *hylikoi*. All things considered, it was this profound individualism of theirs that prevented them from grasping the meaning of the people as God's assembly and the eventuality of a community-centered eschatology.

Finally, it is normal that the scope of this work be broadened to include certain problems of hermeneutics. We asked Fr. Marlé to present R. Bultmann's views on the Church. This study was carried out with a sympathy and a deep understanding that in no way impeded the lucidity and the keenness of his judgment. In retracing Bultmann's notion of the development of the Message over the history of the first century in the various original milieus and communities, he shows the stages in the Church's becoming aware of her own existence. This history passes from a purely eschatological notion to *Frühkatholizismus* and to the "institution of of salvation" (*Heilanstalt*). This outlook is the result of a rather special philosophy which in the last analysis is rather narrow, and also of a particular tradition within Lutheranism. Ultimately it seems incapable of taking account of many aspects of New Testament thought and particularly of the idea of the Church as the Body of Christ or the Bride of Christ, along with the true role of the hierarchical structure. It is quite striking to observe how many of Prof. van Unnik's remarks with regard to the Gnostics could also be relevant to the system of the theologian of Marburg.

Louvain

J. Giblet

I

Joseph Coppens

The Church, The New Covenant of God with His People

Among the titles given by New Testament writers to the Church we do not find that of "community of the new covenant," a title which the Qumrân sect took for itself, at least according to the Damascus document.[1] Yet this does not prevent the Church from having looked upon herself as having made this covenant a reality.[2]

That is indirectly evident from the fact that she believed herself and proclaimed herself to be the "people of God," the recipient of the power to forgive sins, the possessor of a gift of the Spirit that made the spiritual presence of the divine law a reality in the hearts of the faithful. Furthermore this is shown explicitly by the fact that the New Testament uses Jeremiah 31: 31-34 in describing the Christian economy.[3]

If we accept the date generally proposed for the composition of the Epistle to the Galatians, this letter offers us probably the most ancient New Testament text where two covenants are

---

1. CDC, VI, 19; VIII, 21 (text AI).

2. On the theology of the Church in the New Testament, see the important article of R. Schnackenburg, *Die Kirche im Neuen Testament*, in *Quaestiones Disputatae*, No. 14, Freiburg-am-Breisgau, 1961. We are somewhat surprised at the small importance given by the author to the concept of "new covenant." Bibliography on the subject will be found in a very recent booklet: *L'Eglise dans la Bible. Communications présentées à la XVIIᵉ Réunion annuelle de l'Acébac. Bibliographie*, in Studia. *Recherches de Philosophie et de Théologie publiées par les Facultés S.J. de Montréal*, Bruges, Desclée De Brouwer, 1963.

3. On this text, see our commentary: J. Coppens, *La nouvelle alliance en Jér., 31, 31-4*, in *Cath. Bibl. Quart.*, 1963, t. XXV, pp. 12-21.

mentioned, one covering the whole Old Testament and the other beginning with the coming of Christ.[4]

Through an allegorical exegesis Paul makes them go back to Abraham through the two wives of the patriarch. In this way he connects the New Testament with the father of the chosen people, following a theological theme which is dear to him and which bestows on the great patriarch the promise of the definitive salvation in Jesus Christ.[5]

Both Testaments are thus symbolized by Hagar-Sinai, the earthly Jerusalem on the one hand, and by Sarah and the heavenly City on the other. These figures are not without their element of surprise for us, but let us remember especially that in the light of the allegory there arises implicitly the idea of a new covenant. It is characterized by a birth not according to the flesh (whereby we enter into the realm of the spirit), and by the charism of freedom that is so dear to the Apostle of the Gentiles (*Rom.* 8: 21; 2 *Cor.* 3: 17; *Gal.* 5: 13; 4: 26, 31).[6]

It is in the great Pauline letters that we meet the first explicit allusions to the text of Jeremiah. In Romans 11: 27, Paul deduces from Jeremiah's prophecy that one day Israel will obtain forgiveness of its sins from God and that on that day the chosen people will return into the flock of the great family of those who were called to be saved in the messianic age. With the support of this thesis, Paul unites three prophetic texts: Isaiah 59: 20; Isaiah 27: 9 and Jeremiah 31: 31. In using the Jeremian passage Paul departs from the literal sense but not to the point of distorting it. For the Apostle it is not a question of a simple amnesty in the divine perspective. God truly forgives sins. Far from being exterminated by God, so formidable in his justice, sinners will be the object of his mercy and his benevolence in conformity with Christ's teaching.

The text of Jeremiah is particularly evident in the background of 2 Corinthians 3: 2-3, 5-11—a pericope where for the first time in St. Paul's own words we meet with the expression "new covenant." The Apostle declares that he is its minister, its *diakonos* (3: 6). Because of this mission he professes himself able, with the help of the Spirit of the living God (3: 4), to write an Epistle

(3: 3), one that is from Christ (3: 3), on the hearts of the Corinthians.[7] Paul enumerates some attributes of this new covenant. The new covenant (3: 6) is spiritual (3: 3, 6, 8), permanent (3: 3), filled with divine glory (3: 7-13). Those who commit themselves to it are assured of life (3: 6) as well as justification and righteousness (3: 9). The author of the covenant who transmits these supreme spiritual goods to the faithful is God (3: 3), the Spirit of God (3: 3, 17-18) and Christ (3: 14, 16).

In this entire pericope Paul makes abundant use of Old Testa-

---

4. W. K. W. Grossouw, *Die Entwicklung der paulinischen Theologie in ihren Hauptlinien,* in *Studiorum Paulinorum Congressus Internationalis Catholicus, 1961. Simul secundus congressus internationalis catholicus de re biblica,* t. I, Rome 1963, p. 86: "In bewegter Sorge reagiert Paulus sofort in Gal. Später kommt er . . . auf diese Fragen zurück in Röm."; p. 88: "Nach der landläufigen Auffassung sind 1 und 2 Kor in der Zeit zwischen Gal und Röm entstanden." Cf. also M. Goguel, *Introduction au Nouveau Testament,* t. IV, 2nd part: *Les épîtres pauliniennes,* in *Bibliothèque historique des Religions,* Paris, 1926. W. Michaelis, *Einleitung in das Neue Testament,* Bern, 1946. A. Wikenhauser, *Einleitung in das Neue Testament,* Freiburg-am-Breisgan, 1953. In *Saint Paul et ses lettres* (*Studia Neotestamentica, Subsidia 2,* Bruges, 1962), B. Rigaux does not concern himself with working out an absolute or relative chronology of the Pauline epistles.

5. On Paul and the Old Testament, read the pertinent reflections of Christian Dietzfelbinger, *Paulus und das Alte Testament,* in *Theologische Existenz Heute,* fasc. 95, Munich, 1961.

6. Cf. L. Cerfaux, *Condition chrétienne et liberté selon saint Paul,* in *Recueil Cerfaux,* t. III, Gembloux, 1962, pp. 287-296.

7. We do not see how A. Richardson (*An Introduction to the Theology of the New Testament,* London, 1958, p. 230) relies on the text to infer from it the general priesthood of the faithful: "The fulfillment of Jeremiah's prophecy was certainly in the mind of St. Paul when he wrote this chapter; and it underlies his description of the *Christian laity* (italics ours) as διάκονοι καινῆς διαΘήκης (II *Cor.* 3: 6), an expression suggestive of the NT conception of the priesthood of the laity, since the ministers of the old testament were, of course, the Jewish priesthood." If the author simply wishes to say that since the introduction of a new economy suppressing the Jewish priesthood laymen without distinction may be called to the priesthood, his remark is pertinent.

8. Cf. J. Coppens, *La nouvelle alliance en Jer. 31, 31-4,* in *Cath. Bibl. Quart.,* 1963, t. XXV, pp. 12-21.

ment texts. For our particular concern the chief texts are Jeremiah 31: 31; 36: 18; 38: 33 and Ezekiel 11: 19; 35: 26. The Apostle considers that he can therefore interpret the prediction of Jeremiah 31: 31 in the light of other prophetic passages which are all more or less parallel and refer to the eternal covenant whose coming the prophets had foreseen.[8] Then he judiciously connects the interior law predicted by Jeremiah with the gift of the spirit that Christians have been granted. This "spirit" is not merely a light which lights from within and a power which intimately transforms Christians. It is also—and here we have a new image and a different point of view—a force that takes away the veil covering the Scriptures and preventing the Jews from understanding their spiritual meaning. Paul concludes his thought by pointing once again to Christ as the author of the new economy, and asserts that Christ is not to be separated from the Spirit. As we know, the interpretation of this latter assertion is replete with multiple difficulties.[9]

A third mention of the new covenant is found in 1 Corinthians 11: 25, a verse that gives the words of the blessing of the eucharistic cup. Paul in this instance rejoins the synoptic tradition, at least that of Luke 22: 20 and even Matthew (26: 28) and Mark (14: 24), provided we are willing to look upon the variant that speaks of a "new" covenant as authentic and original.

For a number of authors such as J. Behm[10] there is no doubt that Jesus had the text of Jeremiah in mind at the time of the celebration of the Last Supper. Others hesitate to consider the reference here to Jeremiah as historical, the term "new" being not sufficiently guaranteed in Mark and Matthew.

Yet let us note that the presence of the word "new" is not strictly required for us to be able to attribute to the Evangelists and to Jesus a reference to the prophet's text. It is hardly likely that the Lord thought of substituting the shedding of his own blood for the blood of animals within one and the same covenant, that of the old law. With new blood and a new sacrifice it seems that there should be a corresponding new covenant. Furthermore if we accept as original and historical Matthew's reference to the foregiveness of sins, an allusion which may be justified by the presence of other allusions in the same context to the Songs of the Servant of Yahweh, it seems that we may exclude any serious doubt about the reference to the new covenant predicted by Jeremiah.

Let us add that it is more than likely that the sectarians of the Judean desert thought that they too were called to establish a "new covenant." The theme of Jeremiah 31: 31 was therefore the order of the day in certain pietistic circles of Jesus' time and the era of the birth of Christianity. From this we have no difficulty in understanding that for his part Jesus focused attention on this text envisioning the establishment of a new order in Israel. He himself was indeed conscious of being called to establish the new era.[11]

Until now we have met with merely fleeting—if explicit— references to the text of Jeremiah. In the Epistle to the Hebrews the text is appealed to more directly and in a more noteworthy fashion.[12] The writer of the letter refers to it twice. In the first instance (8: 8-12) he quotes it entirely in order to deduce from it the existence of a new economy of salvation. In the second case (10: 16-17) he is content to cite the positive part of the text and to insist on the forgiveness of sins in order to conclude that any new sacrificial offering for sins is superfluous. Once and for all Christ has made expiation for them. He has remitted them

---

9. I. Hermann, *Kyrios und Pneuma. Studien zur Christologie der paulinischen Hauptbriefe*, in *Stud. z. Alten und Neuen Testament*, t. II, Munich, 1961. Cf. *Eph. Theol. Lov.*, 1961, t. XXXVII, pp. 607-609.

10. J. Behm, *Der griechische Begriff diathèkè*, in *Theol. Wört.*, 1933, t. II, pp. 127-137, esp. pp. 136-137.

11. See the study of R. F. Collins, *The Berîth-Notion of the Cairo Damascus Covenant and its Comparison with the New Testament*, in *Eph. Theol. Lov.*, 1963, t. XXXIX, pp. 555-594.

12. See J. Coppens, *Les affinités qumrâniennes de l'Epître aux Hébreux*, in *Nouv. Rev. Théol.*, 1962, t. LXXXIV, pp. 128-141, 257-282, and in *Anal. Lovan. Biblica et Orientalia*, ser. IV, fasc. 1, Bruges, 1962, in-8o, 52 pp. — A. Vanhoye, *La structure littéraire de l'Epître aux Hébreux*, in *Studia Neotestamentica. Studia I, Bruges*, 1963.

by his blood, the blood of the new covenant of which he is the mediator.

Although the Epistle to the Hebrews underwent the influence of Alexandrian religious speculations[13] and combines, not without some ambiguity, the juridical Greek notion of *diathèkè*-testament with that of *diathèkè*-covenant-institution of salvation (a notion deriving obviously from the Old Testament),[14] the writer's primary emphasis is on this second meaning.[15]

The new covenant that the Epistle celebrates and justifies possesses a series of properties that set it off from the Mosaic covenant and present it as the fulfillment of the Jeremian prophecy. It is spotless (8: 7), eternal (13: 20; cf. *Jer.* 32: 40; 50: 5; *Is.* 55: 3; *Baruch* 2: 35), capable of taking away sins (9: 15), of sanctifying (9: 13; 10: 10, 14, 29; 13: 12) and of communicating the spirit (6: 4; 10: 29).

Consequently,—and this is the chief argument of the sacred writer—it is founded on the person, work and priesthood of Jesus, on a mediator and a work of mediation which overshadows all the institutions of the Old Covenant.[16] Because of these various qualifications the covenant established by Jesus deserves to be called νέα (12: 24) or καινή (9: 15) and to be looked upon as fulfilling Jeremiah's prediction.

Before leaving aside the analysis of the Epistle to the Hebrews, let us point out that its author develops his theology of the covenant from a clearly cultural point of view. This is undoubtedly the reason why among the pacts of the old Law he retains that of Sinai (8: 9; 9: 4, 15), a pact presented explicitly as the "first covenant of God with his people" (9: 15).

Here again are two general observations.

Everywhere, even in the Epistle to the Hebrews, faith in the presence of a covenant that can and must be looked upon as new, namely as the pre-eminent new covenant predicted by Jeremiah, is something that is already present in the background of the sacred writer's argumentation. In other words it is a basic principle received from tradition.

Then, two passages, Romans 11: 27; Hebrews 10: 17-18,

explicitly insist on the forgiveness of sins and the obtaining of salvation. Furthermore, Pauline theology connects these blessings with the saving death of Christ and consequently with the Eucharist which is its commemoration (I *Cor.* 11: 27). From this it seems that we may deduce that the eucharistic setting is the primitive and original *Sitz im Leben* of the notion, in consistency with 1 Corinthians 11: 25 and the Synoptic tradition about the blessing of the cup at the Last Supper. Moreover this eucharistic setting is bound up so intimately with the notion of covenant that in Hebrews 9: 20 the terms of the Old Covenant's conclusion (*Ex.* 24: 18) are conveyed in words that seem to have been influenced by the eucharistic words the Church pronounced over the cup of blessing. Actually τοῦ τὸ αἷμα (Heb. 9, 30) is substituted for the ἰδοῦ τὸ αἷμα of the Septuagint. It seems permissible for us to infer from this that we are in the presence of one of the most ancient apostolic traditions and that its origin goes back to the words Jesus himself pronounced at the Supper, words that his disciples remembered as his spiritual testament, to the point that the author of the Epistle to the Hebrews did not hesitate to couple the notions of covenant and testament in his interpretation of the sacrificial oblation of Jesus.

It is therefore sufficiently established that both the Savior and St. Paul as well as the Pauline disciple who composed the Epistle to the Hebrews, looked at the Church from the angle of a new covenant and believed in the fulfillment of the prophecy of Jeremiah 31: 31-34. We are left to ask what right they had to appeal to this pericope which traditional exegesis classes among the great messianic texts.

---

13. J. Coppens, *Les affinités qumrâniennes de l'Epître aux Hébreux*, in *Anal. Lovan. Biblica et Orientalia*, ser. IV, fasc. 1, Bruges-Louvain, 1962, pp. 39-43.

14. Cf. J. Schildenberger, *Bund*, in J. B. Bauer, *Bibeltheologisches Wörterbuch*, 2nd ed., Graz, 1962, pp. 151-158.

15. J. Coppens, *op. cit.*, pp. 12, 29.

16. *Ibid.*, pp. 14-16. Cf. A. Vanhoye, *op. cit.*, p. 153.

In a previous study[17] we attempted a close look at the exact meaning of the passage and should like to refer our readers to it. Let us be content here with taking up its chief conclusions.

We think that we have shown that while the Jeremian text possesses certain affinities with other passages from the same prophet or from Ezekiel, it contains so many peculiar traits that he has a special place and importance in prophetic literature. First of all Jeremiah is the only one to speak explicitly of a "new" covenant, and he gives a notion of this covenant that is revolutionary in several aspects. Finally he attributes to it a totality of effects that nowhere else are so forcefully assembled and brought to light.

The pact consists essentially in the substitution of a code of life for Sinai's stone tablets. The miracle will come about through the divine law being written on and in the hearts of Yahweh's faithful. The prophet acknowledges therefore that the external promulgation of the Torah was not successful in bringing about the essential note of religion, obedience to God: More implicitly he also acknowledges that even the preaching of the prophets has failed to achieve this end.[18] Yet he remains silent about the way that this mysterious writing on the heart will come about, although other passages of the same prophetic book are more specific.[19] In reading them we learn that God will put his fear in the hearts of the faithful (*Jer.* 32: 40), or that he will transform them through a new circumcision (*Jer.* 4: 4; 9: 25), or even that he will give new hearts to his servants (*Jer.* 24: 7; 32, 39). Later Ezekiel puts side by side the gift of a new heart and that of a new spirit (18: 31; 36: 26), namely the spirit of Yahweh himself (36: 27; 39: 29).

As effects of the covenant, the text of Jeremiah speaks of the communication of a universal and immediate knowledge of God. As a result of this divine knowledge which henceforth will be possessed by all without distinction, even the youngest, the true people of God will be born. It will be bound to the Lord by faithfulness in every trial, a faithfulness that the first covenant on Sinai was not able to effect.

Commentators have often included the forgiveness of sins among the effects of the new covenant.[20] But on closer examination we see that this benefit comes before the conclusion of the new pact. It is preliminary to it and an indispensable requisite. Moreover it seems that it consists above all of a decree of amnesty (*Jer.* 31: 34, cf. 5, 1: 7; 33: 8; 36: 4; 50: 20).[21]

As for the beneficiaries of the covenant, the prophet's idea is that they will be the whole people of Israel, although we ought not therefore conclude that his view was truly universalist. To say that this universalism is already potentially present,[22] *viz.* from the fact that whoever knows God, whether grown-up or child, belongs to the people of God, is to lose sight of the fact that the prophet explicitly limits this gift of knowledge to the members of the chosen nation alone.

It seems to us no less an exaggeration to assert that in view of the future covenant the prophet had a glimpse of the establishment of a universal priesthood which according to some is promised in Exodus 19: 6.[23]

Lastly, his view is not, strictly speaking, eschatological. Jeremiah places the fulfillment of the prophecy on the plane of history. He foresees it in an historical future,[24] namely in the days that will follow the return of the exiles and the organization in the land of Israel of a remnant which will be saved because of the goodness and omnipotence of God.

---

17. J. Coppens, *La nouvelle alliance en Jer. 31, 31-4 in Cath. Bibl. Quart.*, 1963, t. XXV, pp. 12-21.

18. P. Volz, *Prophetengestalten des Alten Testaments. Sendung und Botschaft der alttestamentlichen Gotteszeugen*, Stuttgart, 1949, p. 233.

19. J. Coppens, *La nouvelle alliance en Jer. 31: 31-4*, p. 18. — Cf. *Hos.* 2, 16, 20; *Ezk.* 34: 27, 30; 36: 27, 28; 37: 28-29; *Is.* 54: 10.

20. Cf. P. Volz, *op. cit.*, p. 234.

21. On the particular characteristics of the forgiveness of sins in *Jer.* 31: 31-34; cf. J. Coppens, *art. cit.*, p. 19.

22. P. Volz, *op. cit.*, p. 234.

23. P. Volz, *op. cit.*, p. 234.

24. *Jer.* 29, 11: "... reserving a future full of hope for you."

It does not seem therefore that from the point of view of the literal sense, Jeremiah envisioned the work of Christ directly and explicitly. The prophet's horizon is limited to Israel (*Jer.* 29: 11). The law to be written in the hearts of the faithful and the knowledge of God which is its essential object—a knowledge which will be manifested by the quest for God (*Jer.* 29: 12-14) and by obedience to his word (*Jer.* 7: 23),—are hardly differentiated from what the great prophets of earlier days, particularly Hosea, had already proposed and inculcated.

Moreover, we may assert that Jeremiah's prophecy found partial fulfillment in the Judaism that followed the Babylonian exile. Beginning with this captivity, Israel concentrated more and more on the study and practice of the law, and it succeeded in organizing itself into a *qahal,* i.e. a religious community, a premature "church" concerned with preaching faith in God and living his commandments. Similarly the deutero-Isaiah dared to proclaim that once the remnant of Israel had escaped the great catastrophe and was called to return to the holy land under God's crook, it bore the divine law inscribed upon its heart (*Is.* 51: 7).[25]

Yet when we are looking for the final and definitive accomplishment of our text, in other words its plenary fulfillment,[26] we cannot stop at an isolated passage from Old Testament scripture however important it may be (and this is true of the complete fulfillment of almost all the prophecies in the Old Testament). Above all we cannot deduce definitive conclusions from the Old Testament without taking into account the rereadings from which it has eventually benefited and the complementary material it may have received in other books where revealed doctrine is expounded at a more advanced stage of its evolution. This rule of hermeneutics, we must repeat, flows from a primordial fact, the continuous and progressive character of revelation in the Old Testament, a revelation which never ceased to be enriched and clarified over the course of time.

As far as the prophecy of Jeremiah 31: 31-34 is concerned, let us point out that it does not give us all of Jeremiah's thought on this future covenant. We must interpret it in the light of other

passages from the same prophetic book like Jeremiah 3: 10;
4: 4, 14; 9: 25; 18: 9; 24: 7; 32: 29, 39, 40; 36: 3.[27] Then there
is reason to tie it up with various texts of an almost contemporary
prophet, Ezekiel, who also has in sight the conclusion of a new
covenant (16: 60, 62; 34: 25; 37, 26). Finally, in regard to the
two most important spiritual boons that Jeremiah connects with
the new covenant (i.e. the forgiveness of sins and the immediate
knowledge of God) it is important to note that Old Testament
revelation went through a process of evolution. The first one has
benefited from the great prophetic rereading offered to us by the
fourth song of the Servant of Yahweh (*Is.* 53: 11-12). According
to this passage, God will not be content with granting an amnesty
to the children of Israel, i.e. the mere forgetting of their faults.
He will wipe them out because they have been expiated. This
expiation will come about chiefly as a result of the salvific passion
of the Righteous Servant, the Suffering Servant, the *Ebed Yahweh*.
As for the knowledge of God, other texts underline its universality

---

25. J. Coppens, *art. cit.*, p. 17.

26. P. Volz, *op. cit.*, p. 234: "Die Weissagung Jeremias ist nicht mit
einem Male und nicht in alsbaldiger Zukunft erfüllt worden.... In ihm
(Christus) allein ist die Weissagung Jeremias *volle Wahrheit* (italics ours)
geworden."

27. Cf. J. Coppens, *art. cit.*, pp. 18-20. — It is known that several
passages of the book of Jeremiah are "deutero-Jeremian." Cf. R. H.
Pfeiffer, *Introduction to the Old Testament,* New York, 1941, p. 505: "It
is hardly an accident that after Jeremiah dictated his oracles in 604-598, so
few of them have been preserved intact: only 10: 17-22; 13: 18-27; 23:
9-32 (and the words of consolation in 30-31 that Jeremiah himself dictated as a separate book) of all his utterances from 597 to 586 seem to
have escaped the revision of Baruch. All the others from this period have
come down to us couched in the pedestrian style of Baruch — a good
historian, but no poet." And then there are all the additions in prose
or verse with which, according to not a few critics, Baruch's Jeremiah was
augmented. This is not the place for a discussion of these problems of
authenticity. The additions, to the extent that they are essential, present
us with rereadings that illustrate the fluid and progressive character of Old
Testament revelation.

(*Hab.* 2: 14; *Is.* 11: 9) or they re-enforce its immediate character
(*Is.* 54: 13), or again they refer to the gift of the Spirit in order
to explain its miraculous character (*Is.* 59: 21).[28] In this matter
the prediction of Joel 3: 1-2 (2: 28-29) seems to constitute a final
rereading. It puts the gift of the Spirit eminently in relief and
insists particularly on its universality at least within the people of
God itself.

In short, in the light of the biblical pericopes that complete
the tenor of the Jeremian passage and in the light of the texts
which have deepened its content through successive rereadings,
it appears that Jeremiah 31: 31-34 did not find total fulfillment
under the Old Law. Just as the book of Joel notes explicitly with
regard to the gift of the Spirit, it also makes reference to an era
of a definitive spiritual salvation, in other words to eschatological
salvation. Consequently the Savior, St. Paul and the Epistle to the
Hebrews were not wrong in interpreting this passage in connection
with other texts relative to the coming of eschatological times, and
in applying it to this genuinely new economy which the Christian
era will inaugurate. In fact only this economy offers forgiveness
of sins to all peoples without distinction as a result of the vicarious
passion of the one who made the prophetic portrait of the *Ebed
Yahweh* fully come true. Moreover, it gives promise of and actually
effects a spiritual union with God that guarantees to its beneficiaries a knowledge of God that in a certain sense may be called
direct, a result of the ministry and the gift of the Spirit.

We may therefore correctly assert that the glorious promise
of Jeremiah 31: 31-34 finds real fulfillment in the economy
founded by Jesus. This fulfillment is in harmony with the literal
original sense of the Jeremian text, a harmony which becomes
increasingly evident as we read the passage in the light of later
prophecies that have deepened the import of the new, eternal,
spiritual economy predicted by Jeremiah, Ezekiel and the deutero-
Isaiah for the end of time. Certainly it was necessary to have the
New Testament fulfillment in order to get from the text all the
depth of its meaning—a result of a gradual evolution in conformity
with the dynamism of a divine intentionality. In other words,

once again we find ourselves in the presence of the fulfillment of a prophetic promise. It seems most fitting to us that it be called its "plenary sense" since it expresses its characteristic traits.[29]

3, place de l'Université

J. Coppens
Professor at the University
of Louvain

---

28. The gift of the spirit is foretold without being directly connected with the knowledge of God by *Ezk.* 18: 36; 36: 26-27; 39: 29.

29. On the plenary sense read J. Coppens, *Les Harmonies des deux Testaments. Essai sur les divers sens des Écritures et sur l'unité de la Révélation*, in *Cahiers de la Nouvelle Revue Thélogique*, t. VI, Tournai, 1949, and R. E. Brown, *The Sensus Plenior of Sacred Scripture*, in *Pont. Theol. Faculty of St. Mary's University*, Baltimore, 1955. — During recent years various authors have accepted (with certain particular shades of meaning in their explanation) the hypothesis of the existence of a plenary sense: cf. P. Benoit, *La plénitude de sens des Livres Saints*, in *Revue Biblique*, 1960, t. LXVII, pp. 161-196. — P. Grelot, *Sens chrétien de l'Ancien Testament*, in *Bibliothèque de Théologie*, ser. I., vol. II, Tournai, 1962. — Ed. Schillebeeckx, *Exegese, Dogmatik und Dogmenent-wicklung*, in *Exegese und Dogmatik*, publ. by Herbert Vorgrimler, pp. 91-114, Mainz, 1962. — C. Larcher (*L'Actualité chrétienne de l'Ancien Testament d'après le Nouveau Testament*, in *Lectio Divina*, t. XXXIV, Paris, 1962) also adopts it without stating explicitly his manner of understanding it. — See again Ph. J. Murnion, *Sensus plenior and the Progress of Revelation*, in *The Dunwoodie Review*, 1962, t. II, pp. 117-142 and F. E. Elmo, *Christ, the Fulfillment of the Old Testament*, ibid., 1963, t. III, pp. 6-38, as well as J. Coppens, *Comment mieux concevoir et énoncer l'inspiration et l'inerrance des saintes Écritures?* in *Nouv. Rev. Théol.*, 1964, t. LXXXVI, pp. 933-946 and *An. Lov. Bibl. Or.*, ser. IV, fasc. 14, Bruges, Desclée De Brouwer, 1964.

II

Albert Denis, O.P.

Structural Evolution in the Qumran Sect

The first 40 years of Christianity were the last 40 years of the Qumrân community. Archeology tells us that the buildings near the manuscript caves were destroyed in the year 68. This community was therefore a witness of the last preparation for the Christian Church and its first flowering.

Let us add that in both cases an organized religious movement was worked out. It was not a simple movement of ideas such as eschatology, the wisdom movement or the prophetic movement, a particularistic movement that existed on the fringe of ordinary religion. In addition both originated in Palestinian Judaism. The time, the place and the human and religious backgrounds were identical in both cases.

Yet the history of the Qumrân community extends over a period of 250 years. From its beginnings to its disappearance there was the same lapse of time as in the Church between the year 50 and the year 300. Of the four or five hundred writings that we have been able to salvage from the fragments at Qumrân and the surrounding area, five are more or less complete: the Damascus document, the *Sérek* (Manual of Discipline) and its supplements A and B, the *Pésher* (commentary) on Habakkuk, the *Hodayôt* (Hymns) and the *Milhamah* (War). These works themselves are made up of several documents that differ in the date of their composition, their ideas and the particular life setting they suggest. In accordance with good method, a synthesis of these documents will be precluded for a long time to come, and today we have to be content with presenting the facts and putting them

in some sort of order. Furthermore, only the Damascus Document
(Dam) and the *Sérek* (S), along with a small part of the *Pésher*
of Habakkuk (pHab), teach us directly about the community.
Because of their literary type, this study will by-pass the *Hodayôt*
(Hod) and the *Milhamah* (M).

Even a simple presentation of facts cannot avoid the ineluct-
able problem of at least the relative chronology of the works
available to us. The understanding of almost every partial development that we can see depends upon what solution is adopted,
or is at least related to it. In resolving this problem, the documents'
age is a questionable criterion since it cannot be used to date the
composition of the document and much less its various parts.[1]
The historical allusions are indecisive and undoubtedly polyvalent.
What remain are the internal criteria, although each author chooses
and interprets these somewhat at whim. Still a working hypothesis
seems legitimate if it is based on the following criteria: an eschatology of waning intensity; a concept of revelation which has an
evolution parallel to that of eschatology; certain preferences shown
to the name by which the community was known; perhaps the
intervention or absence of the Teacher of Righteousness; and
finally the oldest role of the priesthood. Following this, *Dam*
would be the oldest, with the exception of the codes, followed
by *pHab,* the *S, Sab,* and finally the *Milh*. The *Hod* are from
various periods.

The use of these criteria will take account of the conservative
and even archaizing trends in each document as well as the
progressive aspects. An evolution did take place, although it was
more or less accentuated depending upon the particular group and
the individual.

§ 1. *The Community of the Damascus Document.*

The Damascus document has been preserved for us in two
partial manuscripts. One, ms. A, is from the 10th century and
is by two hands: pages 1-8 and 9-16 (the great Code). Ms. B

is from the 12th century: pages 19-20 of the original edition of S. Schechter. Page 19 is parallel to pp. 7-8, whereafter ms. A remains suspended and is completed by p. 20 of the B document. [2] This work is composed of several parts, i.e., several documents.

I. The first part of *Dam* is made up of three admonitions which all begin in the same way: "And now, hear me ..." (1: 1; 2: 2; 2: 14), interpolations like those found in Wisdom,[3] or the prophets[4] or even with Moses: "And now, O Israel, give heed to the statutes and the ordinances which I teach you" (*Deut.* 4: 1). This discourse of a sapiential or prophetic type is colored in this first part of *Dam* by the revelations pronounced each time.[5] The section's unity is established then by its admonitory or revelatory literary type and from the textual point of view in 4: 6 by the poorly made transition to the following section. A list of the members of the community is announced but omitted, and the document that follows begins in the middle of a sentence and is of a different literary type.[6]

The first admonition (1: 1-2: 1) suggests that the community began in two stages. In the age of vengeance, God raised out of Israel and Aaron a plant-shoot, a small remnant of repentant

---

1. Cf. K. G. Kuhn, *Zum heutigen Stand der Qumrânforschung*, 3. *Paläographische Datierung und literarische Fragestellung*, in *Theol. Litztung*, 85, 1960, c. 651-653.

2. Cf. the description of the first study of the text in the *editio princeps* by S. Schechter, *Documents of Jewish Sectaries*, I *Fragments of a Zadokite Work*, Cambridge, 1910, pp. ix-xii; comparison of common passages: J. Carmignac, *Comparaison entre les manuscrits "A" et "B" du Document de Damas*, in *Revue de Qumrân*, 2, 1, 1959, pp. 53-67.

3. Cf. *Wis.* 6: 1: "Listen therefore, O Kings, and understand."

4. Cf. *Is.* 51: 7: "Hearken to me, you who know righteousness."

5. The verb *glh* is read three times. It is found again in 15: 13; to know what is revealed of the law, as a trust (this is the sense of the *Serek*), and 20: 20; revelation of salvation in the concrete sense of its accomplishment.

6. It is nonetheless possible to see here merely a gap, as is the case with other passages in *Dam*, cf. S. Schechter, *Fragments of a Zadokite Work*, pp. x-xi; Ch. Rabin, *The Zadokite Documents*, Oxford, 2nd ed., 1958, in 4, 6.

people. After half a generation,[7] he sent them the Teacher or *a*
teacher of righteousness, whose task it was to teach them virtuous
behavior in accordance with God's will and to make known to the
last generations what God will do to the final generation, the
generation of the great apostasy, of traitors (cf. *pHab* 2: 1,
3, 5), the unruly, the willfully wayward, the seekers of "flatteries" [8]
at the time of the breaking of the covenant and of persecution.
And the wrath of God will be aflame against them.

The second admonition (2: 2-13) is the revelation of the
eternal divine plans for the ungodly in revolt. God will deliver
them over to the flame of fire by means of the angels of destruction.
He will preserve a tiny remnant of converts (2: 5; or exiles),[9]
and he will know them and will call them by their names [10] in
order to populate the (holy) land. His revelations to them
will be through his prophets (his anointed ones), the holy spirit
and his faithful seers.[11]

The third admonition (2: 14-3, 18 ? with a possible repetition
as far as 4: 6) is a revelation about the divine works. It retraces
the history of apostasy from that of the angels, and in a parallel
way the history of the covenant's renewal up to the last definitive
covenant (2: 16-3: 12). Those who "stood fast" (3: 12; cf.
Dan. 11: 32) were established in this covenant for eternity through
the revelation of hidden things that God had not revealed (*Deut.*
29: 28) and from which Israel went astray at the time of Exodus.
They dug the well of the life-giving waters (3: 16) [12] and as a
result of the pardon God granted them through the wonderful
secrets of these waters (3: 18),[13] they were able to build an unshakable house in Israel. The "steadfast" are destined to a life
that will last forever.[14] In this way Ezekiel's prophecy was fulfilled (44: 15): the priests and the levites and (an addition to the
Ezekiel text) the sons of Sadoq who remained faithful to their
charge in the temple at the time of Israel's apostasy will continue
their service in my presence. And the author explains what he
means: priests are the exiles (the converts?) of Israel who have
come out of Judah; the levites (mutilated text) have joined them;[15]
the sons of Sadoq are the chosen of Israel, called by name, who

will rise up on the latter days. In all likelihood in the integral text the list of names followed at this point.

The group to whom the three admonitions are addressed does not form a sect or a community.[16] They are spoken of as members of the covenant (2: 2; 3:10), the "steadfast" (3: 12, 20), the chosen, the converted exiles, the tiny remnant raised up by God to receive the eschatological revelations and to constitute the Israel that will remain faithful until the latter days (2: 11-13). There is no organization and no allusion is made to any sort of

---

7. This is a possible recalling of Nehemiah 1: 1 and of the religious restoration attempted by Josiah before the Exile, cf. G. Jeremias, *Der Lehrer der Gerechtigkeit*, Göttingen, 1962, pp. 152-153.

8. *hlqwt*, see *Hodayot* 2, 15 and 32 and *Daniel* 11: 32: through flatteries, slippery (Cf. root *hlq*) doctrines, that are facile, Antiochus won to idolatry the violators of the covenant at the moment of the abomination of desolation, 11, 31. According to G. Jeremias, *l. c.*, pp. 130-131, it is a group of Hellenizers. The author makes no reference to Daniel, but only to *Isaiah* 30: 10, cf. *ib.*, p. 93.

9. The expression *šabê pesa* undoubtedly recalls first of all *Isaiah* 59: 20: go to the converts from Jacob's wickedness, cf. *Dam* 20: 17, but also perhaps, at a later period, the captives of Jerusalem, *šebi* of *Ezra* 3: 8; cf. *Num.* 31: 12; *Is.* 49: 24, cf. *Dam* 4: 2; 6: 5; 8: 16 and par. Through a word-play the tiny remnant of the true converts becomes the Remnant of the exile or of the desert, cf. 4Q *pPs.* 37, II, 1. Cf. A. van der Woude, *Die messianischen Vorstellungen der Gemeinde von Qumrân* (1957), p. 11. The theme of the exile is frequently recalled at Qumrân: cf. *Dam* 7, 15.

10. The expression comes from *Numbers* 1: 16; 16: 2, etc., to designate the people in the desert.

11. On this passage, cf. A. van der Woude, *l.c.*, pp. 16-20, rather than P. Wernberg-Möller, *The Manual of Discipline*, 1957, *in* 3, 7, note 21.

12. The image is developed further on, 6: 3-11.

13. *raz*, a term proper to Daniel in the Massoretic text.

14. Cf. Daniel 12: 2: eternal life.

15. This is a play on words: *lwym-nlwym*, upheld by the etymology of Levi: attach, from Genesis 29: 34.

16. The following terms are absent: *'êdah*-congregation, except that of the traitors, *'êsah*-counsel, *yakhad*-union, *sôd*-foundation, *rôb*-all together, *rabbîm*-totality, for in 2, 16 it does not have the sense it has in 13: 7, etc.

authoritative control.[17] Nothing is said that would give any indication that these men had separated themselves from the rest of the people.[18] The law is not named;[19] the temple is hardly mentioned.[20] The priests are nowhere in prominence; the priestly origin of the Teacher of Righteousness is not brought up;[21] God raises up a plant-shoot from Israel and then from Aaron (1: 7; cf. 6: 2; 19: 11; 20: 1; 10: 5 etc.). The "liturgical text of Ezekiel receives an interpretation that has nothing priestly about it. The lack of preciseness, the stress on the apocalyptic and the eschatological, and the description of a movement rather than a corporate group, all give evidence of a very ancient document in the history of Qumrân. It must go back to an age where an eschatological disturbance had just taken place and was still making itself felt.

II. The second part of our text (4: 6-7: 4) speaks at length of two opposite religious groups. Those who are perfect in holiness [22] observe justice in their relations with others, in accordance with Deuteronomy 25: 1;[23] they accurately fulfill the law's prescriptions [24] in the way that the ancients were instructed according to the covenant which God established at that time in order to grant them forgiveness (4: 6-10). Opposing them are those who allow themselves to be snared by Belial's nets (4: 13), as God had told Isaiah (24: 17). The *pésher* (4: 14) [25] of Isaiah is found in Levi the son of Jacob: [26] Belial's three nets are fornication, (ill-gotten) riches, and defilement of the sanctuary (4: 16-18). Fornication, it is explained, is bigamy (4: 20-5: 6); the sanctuary is defiled by the use of marriage when the wife is in a state of uncleanness (5: 6-7) and by marriages in the forbidden degrees (5: 8-11). In this way they became impure, blasphemers of the covenant, sowing havoc and the poison of error.

As in the desert, which becomes a reality now like a prophecy, God will visit them and his wrath will be aflame against them (5: 11-16). But as in the desert after sin and punishment, God remembered the covenant with the ancients and raised up discerning men out of Aaron (i.e., the priesthood) and wise men from Israel (the laity) (cf. *Deut.* 1: 13; 6: 2-3). He made a revelation to them ("he made them understand") and (cf. *Num.* 21: 18) in the desert they dug the well which is the law (6: 4). Those who dug are the convert exiles of Israel (cf. 2: 5), who came out of Judah in order to go to the land of Damascus. The divining rod (*mehhôqqêq*) is the seeker of the law and what the rod orders (also *mehhôqqêq*) [27] will show the patterns of behavior throughout the period of ungodliness (6: 4-11).[28]

As an ending to this second document or as an introduction

---

17. Except perhaps in the calendar 3: 14, but the passage is difficult.

18. Except 4: 3, which is identical with 6: 5, exiled-converts who "have come out of Judah."

19. G. Jeremias, *Der Lehrer der Gerechtigkeit*, p. 91, wishes to see an allusion to the law in the quote from Hosea 4: 16 in *Dam* 1: 13: Israel went astray like a stubborn heifer. A passage from the Mishna, *Aboth Rabbi Nathan* 23 (cf. Strack-Billerbeck, III, p. 665), interprets it as an apostasy from the law. Is the argument from the Mishna valid here?

20. Cf. 1: 3 to complete the curse, according to Ezekiel 39: 23, he hid his face from Israel and from his sanctuary (the allusion to the temple is possibly an addition, cf. G. Jeremias, *l.c.*, p. 151, note 3), and 4, 1, again quoting Ezekiel 44: 15 to enumerate the "steadfast" who guard the sanctuary: priests, levites and sons of Sadoq.

21. To the contrary: *pHab* 2: 8, and 4Q *pPs.* 37, II, 15.

22. The faulty text of 4: 6 is perhaps to be restored in this manner.

23. "These must declare the one who is right to be in the right, the one who is wrong to be in the wrong." The idea is expressed with other terms in *Dam* 2: 15 and S 1: 3, perhaps *Hodayot* 17: 24, a possible recalling of the entrance oath, cf. G. Jeremias, *Der Lehrer der Gerechtigkeit*, p. 95, note 3. One of the great faults of the adversaries is to act in an opposite way, cf. *Dam* 1, 19, according to Proverbs 17: 15. The references to different passages from the Bible permit us not to unify the *Dam* documents.

24. 4: 8, it is named here for the first time in *Dam*.

25. The term is found there in full.

26. Is this the Levi T of the Testaments of the 12 Patriarchs? Cf. P. Grelot, *Notes sur le texte araméen du Testament de Lévi*, in *Rev. Bibl.*, 63, 1956, pp. 391-404: the explanation to which *Dam* is referring here is not to be read in the present versions of the Patriarchs.

27. The wordplay is made on the two senses of the term.

28. Cf. the exegesis of this passage by A. van der Woude, *Die messianischen Vorstellungen*, pp. 67-74, along with the rabbinical parallel, G. Jeremias, *l.c.*, pp. 270-275.

to the third, a code of morality in twelve precepts is inserted here
(6: 15-7: 4). It is preceded by a temple prescription but the
condition of the texts makes any interpretation risky (6: 12-14).
It may be the prohibition of "offering vain sacrifices" as long
as the "exactness of the law" is not observed.

Section 4: 6-7: 4 is set off from the foregoing by its vocabulary:
law (six times), covenant at Damascus, temple, teaching (4: 8),
Belial, *pésher,* and also by the literary types used, the *pésher* of
Isaiah, the midrash of the well, and even the codes (4: 21 - 5:
11; 6: 15 - 7: 4).[29] Its content gives us a description of a religious
fellowship that is quite different from the eschatological movement of the admonitions of the first document. It is now the
righteous and holy men, the converts of Israel (their name?)
who have left Judah for the "country of Damascus," a new place
of exile or of Exodus. They represent the Israel that has been
renewed through the new covenant, the exact observer in this age
of ungodliness of the rediscovered law [30] in the new desert. From
now on this law is comprehended as a result of the revelations
God has made, particularly to the seeker of the law who is perhaps the Teacher of Righteousness.[31] This group does not have
a name for itself,[32] but it is set apart and separate from the rest
of the Jews. There are the beginnings of an organization, even
if the fragments of the code are inserted from elsewhere. The
eschatological revelations of the admonitions at the beginning
have found a specific object: the law. They make it possible for
it to be known and to be observed accurately.[33] A teaching
develops. Like their ancestors they study (4: 8), for intelligence
and understanding are necessary.[34] The latter days are still on
the horizon (6: 11) but they are no longer imminent for it is
stressed that the principles set down are valid for the *whole*
age of ungodliness (6: 10; cf. 4: 13). Questions of worship assume importance, especially in the codes;[35] the sons of Aaron
are henceforth mentioned before Israel (6: 2, God raised up
from Aaron and from Israel . . .).

In comparing it to the first document, the second reflects a
more advanced stage of evolution: eschatology is put off, an
organization is drawn up, contrasts with other Jews become fixed;

grievances become specific in law, worship and the rules of purity. The group may now be defined: it is the converted Israel, the Israel of the true law that has been discovered or rediscovered in the desert.

III. The third part of *Dam* begins at the point where the parallel text of the B manuscript will begin. This part is not homogeneous [36] and the pericopes are confused.

The first pericope (7: 4-13 and par. 19: 1-7 = 7: 5-10) speaks of the "perfect in holiness" whose conduct in the camps is in accordance with the admonitions, the ordinances, the rules of

---

29. The *Dam* fragments discovered in the 6th Qumrân cave are all four of them situated in our section, cf. *Discoveries Jud. Des.*, III, 1, pp. 128-131; the fragments, all from one and the same manuscript dated in the 1st century A.D., correspond to *Dam* 4: 19-21; 5: 13-15; 5: 18-6: 2; 6: 20-7: 1. A fifth fragment forbidding sodomy is lacking in our text of *Dam*. The editor proposes to place it in the B document, *Dam* 10-12. May we not prefer our own section, where faults of sexual impurity are also dealt with? Other fragments of *Dam*, from seven manuscripts, are mentioned in 4Q, and still unpublished. — The lexicology and the cut of 4: 6 allow us to place at this point the beginning of a document; the three nets of Belial, 4: 14, are commented on further on: 4: 15 — 5: 11.

30. The book was sealed and was reopened: 5:5.

31. Cf. A. van der Woude, *l.c.*, pp. 69-71.

32. Perhaps they are called the wise men, cf. 6:3, quoting Deuteronomy 1: 13, or the convert-exiles of Israel, cf. 6: 5, the nobles, cf. 6: 8, quoting Numbers 21: 18, a possible play on words with the term "consecrated-professed" of the *Serek*, unknown however in *Dam*. This distinction is not made by A. van der Woude, *l.c.*, p. 71.

33. The exegesis of *Dam*, however, is not (yet?) that of the *Pesharîm;* it tries to find in the past types of the community; the *Pesharîm* shed light on the ancient texts, cf. G. Jeremias, *Der Lehrer*, p. 270.

34. Cf. 5: 16; 6: 2, the perverse are without intelligence, cf. *Is.* 27: 11.

35. The temple is profaned by not observing the laws of purity in marriage, 5, 6; perhaps the abandonment of the sacrifices since they are thereby invalid, 6: 12-14.

36. Cf. J. Maier, *Die Texte vom Toten Meer*, Munich, 1960, II, p. 52, *in h. e.*

the country, the guidance of the law, the decision of the admonitions, the rules of the law. For them the covenant is assured. On the other hand, those who scorn (7: 9) the ordinances and statutes are punished at the time of God's visitation.

In the third pericope (8: 14-21 and par. 19: 26-34; 19: 35-20: 15) [37] the same people who scorn the ordinances reappear (8: 19) and the same men who are perfect in holiness (20: 2, 5, 7). These latter are the converted exiles of Israel (8: 16), they succeed (cf. 4: 7) the fathers whom God loved; they have left the people's way behind them and have entered into the new covenant in the Country of Damascus,[38] which for them is the covenant of the fathers. Those who scorn the ordinances (8: 19), the wall-builders (8: 18) [39] are despised by God; his wrath will flare up against them. Some entered the covenant and have *betrayed* (19: 34), withdrawing from the well of living waters (cf. 6: 4 in the second section). They will no longer be counted (cf. *S* 3: 1, 4; 5: 11, 8) in the foundation (cf. *S* 2: 25 etc.) of the people, and will no longer be inscribed in its register (cf. *S* 5: 23; 6: 10 etc.) and that is definitive until the time of the raising up of the messiah from Aaron and Israel (cf. the two messiahs, *S* 9: 11). The person who joined the congregation and then *grew sick and tired* (20: 2) of the orders of upright men (cf. *S* 3: 1; 4: 22) will be excluded from the congregation like one whose lot has not fallen (cf. *S,* fifteen times this expression) among God's enlightened. After a period of repentance involving the study of the Law (cf. *S* 8: 15) he will resume his post (cf. *S* 2: 22) among God's instructed, but while waiting he will have no share in the goods of the congregation nor in its work (cf. *S* 5: 14 and 8: 16-19). Finally, that the *scorner of the ancient and recent* (*precepts*?) has abominations in his heart (cf. *S* 2: 11, 17; 4: 5) and is a rebel. Those who have turned away (20: 10, cf. the traitors of 19: 34) together with lying men will be treated similarly. They have perverted the statutes of justice and scorned the security of the covenant established in the Land of Damascus, which is the new covenant (cf. 8: 21). They will have no part in the House of the Law.

The first and the third pericopes have more than one point that connects them: the appellation of the two groups, the juridical language and the concern for differentiating delicts and sanctions. Contacts with the *Sérek* are numerous, although in *Dam* it is always a question of married men (cf. 20: 13). There are also contacts with the second section of *Dam* (4: 6-7: 4): the sojourn and covenant at Damascus, the teaching, the well of living waters and the codes inserted in this section, in connection with the matrimonial questions of the first pericope, 7: 4-13. Yet the two pericopes 7: 4-13 and 8: 14-20; 15 have an even more juridical atmosphere than the second section of *Dam;* they develop and specify the law. The community is now minutely organized. It seems to have a name: the "perfect in holiness." It has its hierarchy, its peculiar rules and customs, like the study of the law which replaces the revelations (6: 3). The temple is no longer named, although it has perhaps been transposed into the House of the Law (20: 10, 13). The death of the Teacher of Righteousness serves as a beginning date for the whole of history up to the end when the messiahs (messiah?) will appear.[40] The explanation of these differences is understandably found less in the chronology of the composition of the texts than in an evolution of ideas which may be contemporary, but more or less late depending on the case. Yet they must correspond to a real evolution in the religious group and the succession of the documents in the text of *Dam* corresponds to the growth in ideas.

The second pericope (7: 13-18 and par. 19: 7-26 = 7: 21-8: 13) breaks off the regular succession of the various documents of *Dam*. It brings the "steadfast" [41] on to the stage, the survivors

---

37. Cf. the study and the particular explanation of this pericope by L. Rost in *Theol. Litztung,* 78, 1953, c. 143-148.

38. Cf. the second part, 6: 5, 19.

39. The expression, here stereotyped, is complete in 8: 12.

40. But is the "seeker of the law" in 6: 7 still alive?

41. 7: 13, cf. *Dan.* 11: 32, perhaps I Maccabees 1: 65 and the first part, *Dam* 3: 12, 20.

who emigrated to the North. According to a midrash, combining *Amos* 5: 26-27 and *Numbers* 24: 17, they are exiled people who are equipped to be the ideal Israel in expectation of the appearance of these eschatological personages. On the opposite side are the apostates (7: 13, 21), allied with the traitors (cf. 1: 12 in the first admonition, and *pHab*), the rebels, those who are unclean because of the vices of Belial, and they will be handed over to the sword (7: 13; 19: 10, 13; cf. 1: 17; 3: 11, in the first part), punished by the kings of Javan (cf. *Dan.* 8: 23 ff.), annihilated by Belial. They are the ones who "shift boundaries" (cf. 1: 16), wall-builders who smear their walls with plaster (cf. *Ezk.* 13: 10).

The words used, the names given to the two groups, the particular points of emphasis: vices (8: 5-7), not transgressions, depth of insight (8: 12: cf. 1: 1, 8; 2: 14), not study, an imminent and threatening eschatology, repeated contacts with the first part of *Dam* and with the Book of Daniel, the absence of juridicism and its corresponding vocabulary show a spirit that is different from the other pericopes and betray a more archaic frame of mind. The document's insertion at this particular point is perhaps explained by the double midrash of Amos-Numbers that is similar to the citation of Isaiah, son of Amos at the end of the foregoing pericope (7: 10-13).

The fourth pericope seems to be a composite. First (20: 15-27) the converts from the iniquity of Jacob (cf. 2nd pericope and 2, 5 keep the covenant and practice righteousness, according to a midrash of *Malachi* 3: 16-18: they follow God's way and receive the revelation of salvation and righteousness; they have separated themselves from the holy city (cf. 4: 3) for Israel has made the sanctuary unclean. As for those who entered the covenant but broke the limit of the law, they will each be judged according to their intentions (cf. *S* 4: 26) in the counsel of holiness (cf. *S* 2: 25) and cut off from the camp when the glory of God appears in Israel. The eschatology, the small amount of juridicism and the general morality, the still timely revelations, the midrash of *Malachi* are all common points with the second pericope (7: 13 - 8: 13) and the first part (1-4: 6). Nevertheless the concept of an organized community is beginning to be formed and juris-

prudence is being established. The lexicography is not that of
the second pericope and the evolution of its ideas does not reach
the level of the third. It is in the process of development.

In the continuation of the same pericope (20: 27-34), the
steadfast (cf. 2nd pericope) listen to the Teacher of Righteousness,
observe statutes, regulations, commandments, admonitions. They
confess their faults (cf. *S* 1: 24-26), do not raise their hands in
rebellion (cf. *S* 5: 12 etc.: four times), are instructed in the ancient resolutions which are the rules of judgment for the men
of the community (cf. *S passim*). The lexicographical contacts
with *S* are noteworthy. The organization is taking shape with an
official lawmaker. The community is stabilized, although it is
still not at the stage of *S* nor at that of the first and third pericopes.

IV. The great Code (9-16). Like all codes, it contains elements from several periods and moreover it is fragmentary.[42] Let
us point out the existence of property,[43] the custom of marriage [44]
and the importance of the priests (13: 2-6) who are always
present, preside and everywhere take precedence. Nevertheless
the executive office seems to be entrusted to the overseer-*mebaqqer*
(13: 7-9; 13: 16 etc.) who does not seem to be a priest. He
directs the admission of candidates, administers justice, controls
the common finances, the teaching and the general organization.
The temple worship seems to continue (9: 14; 11: 17-21; 16: 13)
— Is this only in theory? — Finally let us point out four groups
in the camps: priests, levites, Israel, foreigners (14: 3).

V. Conclusions. Three stages of evolution can be seen in
the way *Dam* speaks of the religious group.

A. The first stage is that of the three admonitions (1-4: 6)
and of the second pericope of the third part (7: 13-8: 13), with
the possible addition of section 20: 15-27. A religious movement

---

42. Cf. S. Schechter, *Fragments of a Zadokite Work*, 1910, p. x.

43. 9: 10-16; slaves: 11: 12; commerce: 12: 9, etc.; contributions to
the community: 14: 13-14.

44. 12: 1; the sons: 15: 5-6; the wife: 16: 10 and ff.

arose from the Jewish people among the pious who were contrite for their faults, who stood fast and resisted the attraction of the traitors' "flatteries." This plant-shoot of Israel and Aaron (1: 7), this tiny remnant (2: 11) receives from God a teacher who will guide them and reveal to them God's imminent threats against the apostates of the ultimate apostasy, the rebels, filled with vices and impurities, who are soon to be handed over to the sword of execution. At the same time the teacher will reveal God's will for his faithful, the members of the definitive covenant, the exiles of the new Exile (4: 3; 7: 14; 20: 22).

B. The second level is that of the second part (4: 6-7, 4) and perhaps also the end of the fourth pericope in the third part, 20: 27-34. The concern for holiness and the revelations have found a landmark in the law, the well of living waters in the new Desert (6: 4), but in a law that has been rediscovered through reading (5: 5) and research (6: 3-10: the well must be dug). This study was inaugurated by the seeker of the law (6: 7), the Teacher of Righteousness whose voice has been heeded (20: 28, 32), and by the wisdom-seekers of Aaron and the wise men of Israel (6: 2-3). The sense of the original covenant is thus rediscovered (4: 9; 20: 31) and its transgression takes precedence over moral fault, with the laws of purity (4: 20; 5: 8) and the laws of worship (6: 12-14; cf. 20: 33). The codes are perhaps later but they do not clash with the context (4: 21-5: 11; 6: 15-7: 4). The priesthood went unnoticed on the first level, but now there is mention of the polluted sanctuary (4: 18; 5: 6; 6: 13-20) and of enlightened priests (6, 2).

C. The third level is represented by the first and third pericopes of the third part (7: 4-13; 8: 13-20: 15). Those who are perfect in holiness (20: 2, 5, 7) henceforth scrupulously observe the law, along with its precepts, ordinances, prescriptions, rules and admonitions (7: 4-9). They are inscribed in the foundation (19: 35) and constitute a congregation (20: 2-3) where they have their function (20: 5) and are united (casting lots: 20: 4) in a community of goods and activity (20: 7). With these men who have become instructed about God (20: 4) the study of the

law creates jurisprudence (20: 6). All the others are doomed
to punishment, but not all in the same way. Those who merely
scorn the law (7: 9; 20: 8) will be punished at the time of God's
visitation and will have no part in the House of the Law (20: 10,
13). They may be likened to idolaters (20: 9). Those who have
left the covenant and betrayed will be excluded from the foundation until the rising up of the messiah of Aaron and Israel (19: 33;
20, 1). (Is there no hope left for them then?) Finally the person
who has revolted within the interior of the congregation will be
excluded temporarily until he sees the error of his ways through
checks and sanctions handed down by the "perfect in holiness"
(20: 2-8). The initial religious movement has changed into an
organized sect, with a hierarchical, juridical and administrative
apparatus. An institution has succeeded the eschatological fervor
of the beginnings.[45]

The composition of these documents was not necessarily made
at the different times when the ideas expressed were conceived or
officially admitted. If it was made in the same community — and
this is likely — it could represent currents of thought that were
either advanced or archaizing, depending on the individuals and
the particular tendencies involved. Archaism can be preserved
for a long time and new ideas sometimes exist for a long time
prior to the moment that they actually become accepted.

VI. The *pésher* of Habakkuk. It is in the course of this
evolutionary process that the *pHab* must be situated. As in *Dam*
1: 12 and 8: 5, the "traitors" have "profaned" (*Dam* 5: 6; 20:
23) the temple.[46] The Teacher of Righteousness makes revelations,
but now he centers them in the prophecies, a thing which is
required by the literary type of the *pésher* of a complete book.

---

45. The documents brought together or used by *Dam* are therefore
in a regular sequence in the present text, with only the second pericope,
7: 13-8: 13 of the third part to be attached to the first part, and the fourth
pericope to be shared between the first and the second part: 20: 15-27 and
27-34.

46. *pHab* 12: 8: the only uses of the terms traitors and desecrate in
1Q.

Its purpose is to see that the law is fulfilled. Eschatology is still present, but it has not come as soon as had been thought. The community of the *pHab* is situated after the "steadfast" of the first part of *Dam* to whom the eschatological admonitions were addressed and before the new covenant of the second part, which was concerned with the study of the law in the desert.[47]

§ 2. *The Community of the Manual of Discipline.*

The scroll of the Manual of Discipline or *Serek* was considered by the scribe as ending at column 11 for he leaves blank five or six lines. The beginning of column 1 is possibly the beginning of the work, but this is not completely certain. Before the final psalm, the eleven columns are divided rather easily into three parts by the insertion of two special sections: the treatise on the two spirits (3: 13-4: 26) and the disciplinary code (6: 24-7: 25). Three sections remain to be analyzed: col. 1-3: 12, where we read a sort of general prologue and an entrance ritual; columns 5-6 which may be called the rules of entry and organization; columns 8-9 which present pieces that are undoubtedly ancient or in any case special.[48]

I. The prologue (1: 1-15) makes known the general aim of the "Union" (*yakhad*). Men come to lead a virtuous life in community: to seek God (cf. 5: 11), avoid evil and wicked men, love the chosen ones, and do good in accordance with the prescriptions that God gave through Moses and the prophets (1: 1-3; cf. *Dam* 5: 21: the same terms). The "professed"[49] are committed to turn away from all rebellion, covetousness and perversity; to join with the other professed in fulfilling the statutes in the covenant in order to be one with God's counsel and to act in accordance with all the revelations made at the times of their manifestation (1: 4-9); to love the sons of light, each in his own rank, and hate the sons of darkness (handed over) to God's vengeance (1: 10-11). They commit themselves further to bringing to God's Union their knowledge in order to purify it with the truth of God's decrees, their activity (fortitude) to perfect it, and their goods (1: 11-13). Finally they must respect with exactness the words of God in accordance with (at?) the precise times, without making any change in them (1: 13-15).

The "union" is a religious community living apart. There a person vows to follow the religious perfection of Moses and the prophets in accordance with the revelations.[50] To this community body and soul are consecrated; its particular rulings are followed as well as possibly a calendar, a time-division. Its context then is well defined.

The entrance ritual into the covenant [51] (1: 16-3: 12) requires from its members constancy in every trial.[52] After recalling the justice, the great deeds and the mercies of God, and the waywardliness of Israel confessed by those taking part,[53] the ritual expresses the blessings formulated by the priests, following *Numbers* 6: 24-26. For the perfect, the members of God's party, they wish

---

47. Cf. K. Elliger, *Studien zum Habakuk-Kommentar vom Toten Meer*, Tübingen, 1953, pp. 275-276; the author underlines this partial evolution of eschatology, but must we deny any theological synthesis at this moment?

48. Cf. P. Guilbert, *La Règle de la Communauté* (The Qumrân texts translated and annotated), Paris, 1961, pp. 11-12; the author believes that it is the work of one author composed according to several literary types. On the other side, the following believe in several sources: P. Wernberg-Möller, *The Manual of Discipline*, p. 56, note 49; J. Maier, *Die Texte vom Toten Meer*, p. 9. In regard to paleographic arguments, cf. K. G. Kuhn, in *Theol. Litztung*, 85, 1960, c. 652.

49. *niddabîm*, cf. *Num.* 21: 18, quoted *Dam* 6: 4, 8, but in the S the appellation is regular and without reference to *Num.* cf. S 1: 7, 11; 5: 1, 6, 8,. 10, 21, 22; 6: 13, it is the *hithpael* form in columns 5 and 6. Cf. Ezra 7: 13 and Nehemiah 11: 2, they are the volunteers who return from Babylon. The verb in Nehemiah 11: 2 that the Septuagint translates (= *Ne.* 21: 2) by ἐχουσιάξεσθαι, designates in the Greek of I Maccabees 2: 42, the valiant who are "attached" to the law, but Ezra 7: 13 is translated by the Septuagint (= Ezra 8: 10) by βούλεσθαι.

50. These are the revelations of Moses and the prophets, but perhaps of others also.

51. The term has taken on a very limited sense, the Union.

52. The ritual is undoubtedly to have a yearly celebration, cf. 2, 19.

53. The custom of confession, cf. among others, *Dam* 20, 28.

every good thing: light, wisdom, eternal knowledge, peace. The levites call down on the sinners, the members of Belial's party, the terror of the vengers of vengeance, extermination and the fiery darkness,[54] the privation of mercy, forgiveness and peace (2: 5-9). Then especially on the false brother who is obstinate in his revolt they wish the wrath of God, all the curses of the covenant, expulsion from the sons of light and a destiny with the eternally damned (2: 11-17). This detail suggests an already ancient experience admitted by the Union. The very strict rules of precedence in accordance with which each person has his function and rank (2: 22) confirm it. In addition the pre-eminence of the priests and levites has become a fact, together with the fact that knowledge is a discriminatory factor (2: 19-23). To end the passage there is a description of the Union itself: the counsel of holiness, the eternal foundation; and an enumeration of the virtues practiced within it: humility, kindness, benevolence, right intention. The beginning of the prologue made similar statements.

A diptych then contrasts what a person who refuses to enter the Union is deprived of (2: 26-3: 6) and what the convert finds (3: 6-12). The obstinate scorner (cf. *Dam* 7: 9; 8; 20: 8-11) repudiates (cf. *Lv.* 26: 43) the "admonitions of the knowledge of right decisions" [55] (or "which make them known"?) He firmly refuses to be converted and to be counted among the upright, to dedicate himself totally — intellect, activity, goods — to the Union. Stubborn in his straying in darkness, he will not be justified nor counted at the fountain [56] of the perfect, nor purified and sanctified in the purification rites. He remains unclean as long as he scorns the practices approved by God and is deprived of access to the instruction of the Union's counsel. Let us point out a succession of elements: being accepted, conversion, vow, justification, instruction, purification. Primacy is given to what is interior: entrance into the Union follows conversion, and the rites themselves come after one's submission to the practices.

On the other hand, in the faithful counsel of the Union, the convert receives forgiveness of his sins and is enabled to contemplate the light of life. By the spirit of holiness of the faithful Union, he is purified from his faults. Having been forgiven through submitting himself to God's decrees, he will take part in the rites of purification and sanctification. He will correct his behavior so as to act in perfection and with exactness in accordance with the ordinances uttered at the times when (God) proclaimed them (3: 10). Then he will be the object of the divine benevolence as a sacrifice accepted by God and the covenant of the eternal Union will become a reality for him.[57] The covenant is named here for the first time in passage 2: 25-3: 12 and is the high point. The concrete situation in the Union is not forgotten — entrance, instruction, practices — but it is returned to in a deeply religious sense which brings the essential realities of the law and the covenant alive. In the community (and in the community alone, we might say) can they become authentically real by holiness and virtue as lived within the fellowship. Outside of the Union there is only darkness, revolt, impurity and sin.

This whole first part of the *Serek* is a complete unit. Each element is completed by the others and where there is repetition there is no contradiction.[58]

II. The entrance regulations and the rules of organization (5-6). The treatise of the two spirits (3: 13-4; 26) is perhaps a commentary on what has previously been said about the distinction between the good and the wicked, but it goes beyond the horizon of the community and points at the whole of mankind. Columns 5 and 6 may form a whole,[59] but they are subdivided into several sections. After a prologue (5: 1-7) in three instances there is mention of the candidates' entrance into the community

---

54. This darkness of fire is perhaps a slight eschatological reminder.

55. *mshptym*: sanctioned practices, "constitutions" according to P. Guilbert, *in h.l.* This whole phrase, partly faulty, is obscure.

56. Or ought the text be corrected?

57. Cf. *Num.* 25: 13, but the priesthood is here replaced by the Union.

58. This does not prevent the hypothesis of prior sources, particularly for the blessings and curses.

59. Cf. P. Guilbert, *Le plan de la Règle de la Communauté,* in *Rev. Qum.,* 1: 3, 1959, pp. 330-333.

(5: 7-13; 5: 20-23; 6: 13-23). The series of rules on this subject is interrupted for the first time by the law of the ungodly person from which it must be separated (5: 13-20),[60] and the second time by questions of internal organization (5: 23-6: 13). These are inserted on the occasion of the entrance examination, the second point of the regulations. Strict logic cannot be expected in such a work, and we may speak rather of digressions than insertions. Only a very pains-taking literary analysis will be able to discover a possible diversity of sources.

A. The prologue (5: 1-7) recalls things already known about the community, and first of all its purpose: the professed have been converted from evil, hold fast to God's commands, and set themselves apart from the congregation of the men of iniquity. The authority of the union in law and in financial matters is exerted in compliance with the counsel (interpretation?) of the sons of Sadoq, the priests, who are guardians of the covenant, and following the advice of the totality (*rabbîm*) of the men of the Union, those who are "holding fast" (5: 3) [61] to God's covenant. Every decision on the law, goods, recognized practices, is made (by "lot," a vote?) by both groups. There follows a sort of theological presentation of the community: through a virtuous life, faithfulness, humility, justice, regularity ("toward the practices"), and mutual love without the stubbornness of a wayward heart, or of the eyes (fornication? cf. *Dam* 2: 16) or the instinct, the circumcision of the heart and of the "stiff neck" becomes a reality in the Union. The Union of the eternal covenant is thereby an assured foundation (cf. *Is.* 28: 16) in Israel. The forgiveness granted to the professed makes it a temple [62] in Aaron, a faithful House in Israel. Twice in this passage the priests are named as a special group with the right of precedence. The conclusion adds to the customary description of the community a note of spiritualized worship: Israel is a temple [63] of which Aaron perhaps is the Holy of Holies.

B. The regulation of admittance into the heart of the Union of God's covenant (5: 7-13; 5: 20-23; 6: 13-23) treats of the entrance oath in its first paragraph.

a) The entrance oath is a public oath to convert one's self to the Law of Moses in accordance with all that has been ordained in regard to the law. It had been hidden before but is now revealed to the sons of Sadoq, the priest guardians of the covenant and the seekers after (God's) good pleasure, and (revealed also) to the totality of the men of the covenant, dedicated in the Union to acting as God wills (5: 9-10). The naming of the two groups, let us note, is here complete.

The general prologue of the Manual (1: 9) mentioned the revelations in passing. They are now fully in focus and certainly constitute an essential motivation for the *S* community. It observes the law, but it does so in accordance with the revelations made to the members of the Union.

By the oath, the text continues, one sets one's self apart from the men of wickedness. This is understandable for they are not counted in the covenant since they are not concerned with searching (studying, cf. *Zeph.* 1: 6) God's decrees in order to know those hidden things. Instead they are wayward and sinful (cf. *Dam* 3: 14). They scorn what has been revealed and call down upon themselves the wrath of the judgment, the vengeance as described in the course of the covenant (cf. *Deut.* 29: 20) and annihilation (5: 11-13, cf. *Ezra* 9: 14). Research, i.e., study (*drsh*) and the revelations are correlative, as are also the knowledge of things hidden and things revealed. It is by studied research that revelation comes about. Further on, the workings of these "revelations" will be made more specific (cf. 6: 3-8).

b) The second point of this rule of entry for one who wishes to join the holy congregation and apply the statutes (5: 20-23) is an examination of his mind in regard to the others in the Union, of his intelligence (*śhkl*) and his religious behavior ("in accordance with the law"). This examination will be made under

---

60. Cf. P. Wernberg-Möller, *in* 5: 13, note 51, and J. Maier, *in h.l.*
61. Cf. *Is.* 56: 4, sole instance in *S*, cf. *Dam* 3: 12, 20; *Dan.* 11: 32.
62. *qôdêsh*, cf. P. Wernberg-Möller, *in h.l.*, note 27.
63. At least if we must translate in this way according to J. Maier; cf. 8, 5.

the authority of the sons of Aaron, dedicated in the Union to upholding the covenant and to the scrutiny of God's statutes, and by the totality of Israel, *viz.,* those dedicated to be converted to God's covenant within the Union. The titles given to the priests shed light on their functions. Research (5: 9) is explained by the responsibility of upholding the covenant.[64]

c) The third paragraph of the regulation (6: 13-23) gives in detail the formation of the Israelite who dedicates himself to the Union.[65] This formation seems to have been entrusted to an "officer" (*paqîd*) selected by the whole group (?). After the examination of the intelligence, the docility and the behavior of the candidate, the officer introduced him to the covenant in order for him to make his conversion. He then instructs him, explains (*bîn*) the practices of the Union, and then presents him to the assembly. After the questioning and the vote, he is introduced into the heart of the Union and undergoes one year of probation. At this point he still takes no part in the rites nor does he share in the common goods. Upon a second examination on what he has learned and on his behavior before the law, a second vote of the priests and the men of their covenant admits him into the foundation of the Union, although he still remains excluded from community meals. At the end of the second year of probation, if a third vote is favorable to him, he is introduced into the Union and becomes a full-fledged member with his place among his friends in accordance with the order of precedence and with the right to take part in the meetings.

This section has furnished an opportunity of penetrating further into the Qumrân community. According to the general prologue, one joins in order to be converted, to dedicate one's self, to be instructed and purified. Here we learn that agreement by the members of the community is required for the candidates' admission and that they are thoroughly examined at the time of their entrance, take an oath to convert themselves and undergo a long period of probation. Within the community, which is a spiritual temple (*the* Temple?), the priesthood decidedly has the first rank, but it exercises its authority only together with the other members; the law is observed, but in accordance with an interpretation proper to the community, revealed to its members; intelligence and study are therefore of great importance, for they are directly related to the revelations.

C. Inserted after the first paragraph of the rules of entrance, the law of the ungodly person (5: 13-20) shows him concretely excluded from the community. The oath — which is the subject of this paragraph — obliges one to keep apart from the men of iniquity. The present ordinance regulates its application and merely repeats what is already known: the ungodly person may not take part in the purification rites, he is unclean since he has not been converted. No one may have anything to do with him: in activity, property of goods, interpretation (?) of the law, meals or any kind of fellowship. He is but vanity and is unworthy of trust for he does not know the covenant and scorns the word of God. God will make him disappear together with his works, just as one wipes away a stain.

Situated before the account of the formation of candidates and after the entry examination of 5: 20-23,[66] the rule of internal organization (5: 23-6: 13) supplies interesting details. Each year an examination on the spirit and the religious mores fixed, as it were, the order of precedence in accordance with one's degree of knowledge and one's behavior, so that each one would obey the superior and exhort his neighbor in humility and benevolence (5: 23-26; cf. the codes of *Dam* 7: 2; 9: 2). This is followed by other rules on fraternal charity and on discipline. In every group of ten persons (6: 3-6) a priest will be found who will have precedence in every discussion and will bless the meals as the individual of highest rank. Day and night, there will also be a person who takes his shift in studying (*drsh*) the law (6: 6-7).

---

64. Cf. also in *Sb* 3, 22-25.
65. Cf. P. Wernberg-Möller, *in* 6: 13, note 39.

66. A digression can be noted here in regard to the entrance examination, before it is returned to in 6: 13, just as it was returned to in 5: 20 after the description of the perverse person in 5: 13-20. Even so, the digression 5: 23-6: 13 is a complete ruling.

The whole group will be on watch a third of the night and will use the time to read the Book (undoubtedly the Bible), to study (*drsh*) lawful custom, and to prayer (blessing) (6: 7-8): The session takes place in orderly fashion; there is an order of precedence, of subjects treated and of discussion, and the privilege of intervention [67] or direction of debate [68] is reserved to the me-baqqer-supervisor (6: 8-13). Further on it is the same supervisor who administers the goods (6: 20); in the great code of *Dam* he often appears and enjoys great authority (*Dam* col. 9; 13; 14; 15). Did he lose this function in *S* or did he not yet have it?

This chapter on the internal organization gives an explanation why there is so much emphasis on the intelligence. Each person must continually study the law and the practices. In some way this is the organizing principle of the community, which is regularly connected with virtuous conduct. If the precedence of the priests is confirmed, on the other hand it seems to be honorific.

D. The penitential code (6: 24-7: 25) completes the regulations. It insists upon the social virtues: kindness, understanding, obedience, on the correction of one's actions and words, and like *Dam* 20: 3-13, it especially punishes insubordination (?). It is sanctioned by the obligation of beginning all over again the time of trial of the entrance into the community, except that it excludes the guilty person definitively if he has betrayed the Union and left it (7: 16-25).[69]

The regulations of this community reveal a rigid organization. Precautions are taken in regard to new members. They commit themselves under oath and are submitted to manifold examinations on their intelligence and their moral tone. There is a strongly established hierarchy, although it is undoubtedly modified each year. The primacy of the priesthood is incontestable, although it is not absolute since a lay officer is charged with the executive office (*paqîd, mebaqqer*). Parallel to the revelations and to the instructions, a very important place is given to study. Nor are the community virtues forgotten, and the rites retain their importance as well as the community of goods. The whole community is balanced and seems to be tried and solid.

III. The charter of the community and the regulations for the Maśkîl (8-9). Columns 8 and 9, after the code, may be divided into two parts.[70] A special regulation directed toward a person called the Maśkîl (9: 12-26) makes up the second part. The first part stresses a formula that recurs three times and is peculiar to this passage of the Qumrân writings [71]: "when these things happen (these men appear?) in Israel" (8: 4; 8: 12; 9: 3). On the other hand it could be said that the law of the secret in 8: 10b-12 is an insertion [72] as is most certainly the code of 8: 16-19 [73] and perhaps also the legislative summary of 9: 7-11. Four sections remain to be treated as a whole, the first one at the beginning and the three others that are introduced by the aforementioned formula: 8: 1-4; 8: 4-10; 8: 12-16; 9: 3-6.[74]

A. The first passage (8: 1-4) speaks of twelve men and three priests who have a special function in the Union. They will be (or all the members of the Union will be [75]) perfect in accordance with all the revelations made with regard to the law. They will

---

67. P. Guilbert, *in h.l.*

68. P. Wernberg-Möller, *in h.l.*, note 32.

69. The text is somewhat mutilated and uncertain at this point, as it is frequently at the end of a column in S.

70. On the state of the text and its explanation, cf. P. Guilbert, *Deux écritures dans les colonnes VII et VIII de la Règle de Communauté*, in *Revue de Qumrân*, 1, 2, 1958, pp. 199-212; the author remarks that the difficult text and the somewhat unexpected expressions confused the scribe. Shall we not conclude that the document was different from the rest?

71. This expression is not found in the Massoretic Text of the Bible.

72. Line 10b indicates the condition under which the secret is handed over: if a person's behavior is perfect for two years, it will not be hidden from him (line 12). J. Maier, *in* 8: 11, also thinks that 11 is an insertion but not 10b.

73. In 4Q Sc (cf. *Rev. Bibl.*, 1960, p. 413) begins directly in 8, 16 the regulation of the *Maśkîl* of 9: 12-26; the code undoubtedly continues as far as 9: 2.

74. J. Maier, *in* 8: 1, p. 30 notes the composite and reworked character of the pericope.

75. According to P. Wernberg-Möller, *in h.l.*, note 2.

practice all the virtues of the community as well as private virtues, keep faithfulness in the Country, make expiation for the aberration of sin by observing the practices and supporting persecution,[76] and finally they will behave towards each other in accordance with the dictates of truth and the exactness of the time. Here in their usual presentation we have the community's objectives, restricted to what may be a symbolic group representing the twelve tribes and the three priestly families.[77]

The second passage (8: 4-10) describes the Counsel (the closed circle?) of the Union for us. It is assured its own fidelity, an eternal plantation (?: cf. *Dam* 1: 7), the temple of Israel, the foundation of the holy of holies of Aaron, the faithful witness of the judgment (of sanctioned custom?); it is chosen out of benevolence [78] in order to purify the Country and punish the ungodly. It is the tried rampart, the cornerstone of price, the fortified and unshakable foundation, the foundation of the holy of holies for Aaron because of (all?) knowledge. It is all of these things for the covenant of righteousness so that it might offer a sacrifice of pleasing odor. It is the house (temple) of perfection and faithfulness for Israel so that it may keep (establish?) the covenant in the light of the eternal statutes. Object of (or faithful to) the divine benevolence, the Counsel will purify the Country in order to determine the judgment of ungodliness and to wipe out iniquity.[79] This accumulation of metaphors to describe the community is exceptional in *S* as are the references made to the Bible for this purpose. The second passage is a figurative, religious, and even theological description of the community. Is the pair Israel-Aaron on line 5 a sign of archaism? [80] The spiritualized worship of the community is mentioned and eschatology is recalled but without being stressed.

The third repetition of the same formula (8: 12-16) announces that "then" the community [81] will cut itself off from the abode of men of iniquity in order to go out into the desert to prepare the way of faithfulness [82] in accordance with the prophecy (*Is.* 40: 3): to prepare the way (of God) in the desert. This is the study of the law ordained through the intermediary of Moses. Through it men will learn to behave in accordance with all the revelations made in their time, in accordance with what the prophets have revealed through the holy spirit of God. The essential task of the community is to cut itself off from the ungodly and to dwell in the desert, for the fulfillment of the prophecy does not seem metaphorical in studying the law [83] and the revelation received through the inspired prophets (cf. *Dam* 6: 1).

The last occasion that the formula is used (9: 3-6) introduces the statement that "then," through these dispositions, the foundation [84] comes about in the faithful and definitive holy spirit, so that every kind of fault will be expiated as a result of the (divine) benevolence toward the Country. This is fufilled by the flesh [85] (by more than the flesh?) of the holocausts and the fat of the sacrifices, which (become a reality through the) [86] praise of the lips in accordance with sanctioned custom, an exact (just) sacrifice of pleasing odor, and also by perfect behavior, a pleasing and accepted offering. At that time the men of the Union will set themselves apart (cf. 5: 1). They are the temple of Aaron, coming together in one (or: in the Union of) holy of holies, and

---

76. Cf. this term 1, 17, in an enumeration.

77. Cf. P. Wernberg-Möller, *in* 8: 1, note 1; J. Maier, *in* 8: 1c.

78. Or else: who chose benevolence according to the scribe's correction; cf. *Dam* 2: 15.

79. This whole last sentence of 10a is an addition of the correcting scribe. It goes back to the ideas and to several terms of lines 6-7. Cf. P. Guilbert, *Deux écritures, Rev. Qum.,* 1, 2, 1958, p. 209.

80. Cf. *Dam* 1: 7. This is perhaps a stereotyped expression.

81. "... in accordance with these decisions," the correcting scribe adds.

82. Cf. 4Q, manuscript 5. The text of 1Q has: the way of (God).

83. Cf. *Dam* 20: 6 and the midrash of Numbers 21: 18 in *Dam* 6: 6-7.

84. The ms of 4Q, literally: Union.

85. Cf. J. T. Milik, *Rev. Bibl.,* 1960, p. 414; in the *Sd* ms, from the Herodian age, all the complements are governed by the one preposition contained in *mbsr.*

86. Cf. P. Wernberg-Möller, *in* 9: 5, note 9.

the house of the Union in Israel;[87] their behavior is perfect. The community of the saints, set apart as it is, is a spiritual realization of temple and worship.

These four paragraphs [88] describe the community to us. Its longing is to be the virtuous and faithful Israel. It fulfills the ancient prophecies and does so by being established in the desert and by the study and integral enforcement of the law. Theologically it is the spiritual temple and its entire life is the legitimate worship of expiation and praise. The words used, the metaphorical style, even the ideas like persecution (8: 4), the prophetic fulfillments asserted repeatedly (8: 4-10), the spiritual worship (9: 4-5) all contrast sharply with the rest of *S*. These passages seem more polished and older than the rest, rather like an antiquated charter of the community. This is at least a possible hypothesis.

B. Among the insertions, the first one (8: 10b-12),[89] following the "biblical" description of the community, is remarkable: any matter that had been hidden from Israel and was discovered by a seeker, out of fear of the spirit of apostasy [90] will not be concealed from the members of the Union who have lived two years of a holy life. The discoveries made by those who study the law (cf. ruling, 6: 6), belong to all. Each person performs his research in the name of all and there are no secrets within the interior of the community.[91] The *S* returns later (9: 13, 20) to these discoveries.

A small code [92] has been inserted (8: 16-9: 2) after the third paragraph on the obligation of living apart in the desert and enforcing the whole law. It treats of grave cases. Arrogant disobedience to a *mswh*-ordinance [93] excludes a person from the rites of purity of the counsel until his behavior is purified and sanctioned by the members' vote and reinscription (8: 16-19). The arrogant or negligent but voluntary transgression of an article of the law of Moses entails definitive exclusion from the counsel. Any community of goods and of deliberations is forbidden (8: 20-24). If the transgression is involuntary, it is punished by exclusion from the rites and from the counsel and a two year probation period, followed by a vote of the members and reinscription (8: 24-9: 2). If the text 8: 16-9: 3 is from one single source, there is a distinction made in it between a formal fault against the law and the involuntary material fault to which a formal fault against an ordinance is likened.

One passage, after the fourth paragraph (9: 7-11) resumes the great lines of legislation: the sons of Aaron have the executive power over the ordinances and property, and they resolve all questions of precedence.[94] Fraudulent and wicked men must be totally cut off from the community goods, for they are unclean and have not separated themselves from wickedness in order to live in perfection.[95] The practices of the community which have

---

87. The passage is destroyed in the ms. The *Sd* ms has: they will separate themselves, the house of Aaron, as a temple for a Union of the holy of holies.

88. P. Wernberg-Möller, *in* 8: 4, note 12, suggests the hypothesis of a hymn. J. Maier arranges 8: 2-10 in poetic stichs, and sees in the pericope a summary of what the community thinks about itself, cf. *in* 8: 1.

89. The sentence breaks the continuity of the context and the vocabulary is that of the codes, cf. 6: 12-23; foundation of the Union: 6: 19; in the midst of the men of the Union: 6, 18, 21; cf. 8: 16-9: 3: the perfect in the way of holiness: 8: 18, 20, 21; cf. J. Maier, *in* 8: 11.

90. The verb *swg* is read only in 2: 12, 16, in the curses of the entrance ceremony. Cf. *Dam* 7: 13; 8: 1, a document which is possibly archaic in this section (cf. *supra*). Here the term, which is a rare one, is found in this fragment that may be an insertion into the regulation of entrance.

91. Is it also a question, out of esotericism, of concealing secrets from strangers to the community? Cf. P. Guilbert, *in h.l.* Further on, in 9: 17, the same interpretation can be defended, but here the interpretation of the passage does not oblige us to make this conclusion. Cf. P. Wernberg-Möller, *in h.l.*; J. Maier, *ib.*

92. Or else two fragments of the code: 8: 16-19; 8: 20-9: 2. A comparison will be made with the third part, the third pericope of *Dam* 8: 14-21 and 19: 26-20: 15.

93. The only use of the term *mswh* in *S*, while it is frequent in *Dam*. Is this an oral law? Cf. Rabin, *The Zadokite Documents*, 2nd ed., 1958, *in* 10: 3.

94. P. Wernberg-Möller, *in h.l.*, note 19.

95. The following sentence seems to have gaps in it, or else it has been inserted clumsily. Perhaps it means that every transgression of the law is equivalent to apostasy.

been accepted from the beginning, are of definitive value until
the coming of the prophet and the messiahs of Aaron and Israel.

C. The ruling for the *Maśkîl* (9: 12-26; ?-10: 8) introduce us
to a personage on whose behalf the treatise of the two spirits was
incorporated above: "To the *Maśkîl,* to make the sons of light
understand and to teach them" (3: 13). He appears in the great
code of *Dam,* in regard to the sessions held in the camps (12: 21;
13: 22) with the same title as here: "Here are the statutes for
the *Maśkîl* relaying to his behavior toward every living thing."
In *Sb* the introductions to the blessings add: "to the *Maśkîl"* [96]
(*Sb* 1: 1; 3: 22; 5: 22; 5: 20) but this is perhaps in imitation of
the massoretic text [97] — a simple annotation, musical or otherwise.
The *hiphil* form (to cause to understand) suggests a function,
at least an activity, and also the description of his occupations.
This is the case in *Daniel,* 11: 33 and 12: 3, where the *maśkîlim*
are teaching the people.

"Statutes for the *Maśkîl* in order that he will behave toward
every person in accordance with the dispositions of each time
and the importance of each man" (9: 12); "Do the will of God
in accordance with everything that has been revealed at each
time" (9: 13); "Teach all the understanding that has been
discovered (cf. 6: 2; 8: 11) in accordance with the times" (9:
13); "Set aside (single out) the statute of the time" (9: 14);
"Evaluate (weigh) the sense of righteousness in accordance with
their spirit and make the chosen ones of the time stand fast in
accordance with God's will" (9: 14). The time dimension is
fundamental in this pericope. It is again brought up further on:
the *Maśkîl* will deal with the person who has chosen the way
in accordance with his spirit and the disposition of the (present?)
time (9: 8); "Now is the time to clear the way in the desert" (9:
19); he will explain everything which has been found (the discoveries!) to be done at this time (9: 20) [98] and will cut himself
off from every man of wickedness; these are the patterns of behavior for the *Maśkîl* at these times to be loving, or to hate the
men of the pit with a spirit of discretion (9: 21-22); he will be
zealous for the statute and its time [99] until the day of vengeance

(9: 23); in all things he will do God's will (9: 23-26). A hymn at the beginning of column 10: 1-8 insists at length that at all times (*qes*) he must praise God. The term '*êt* is found fifteen times in the *S,* three of which are in the community charter (8: 4-15; 9: 5) [100] and ten are in the 11 lines of 9: 12-23.[101] This particular emphasis sets this passage apart just as it also does to a lesser extent with the community charter.[102] This is a particular theology, or at least a special theological trend, which may possibly be quite ancient or outmoded in the community, a theology of time.[103]

The *Maśkîl* is to teach the community (cf. *Dam* 13: 8) the entire knowledge of the law that has been acquired by study and assembled as a trust (9: 13), particularly (?) the time statute. He evaluates the "righteous" in accordance with their spirit and strengthens the chosen of the time in accordance with God's commandments. He decides upon each person's advancement(precedence?) and his gradual progress towards the full

---

96. Cf. *Ps.* 32: 1; 42: 1; 44: 1, etc. Two manuscripts of 4Q S have the same indication in S 5: 1, in the prologue of the entrance regulations (cf. *Rev. Bibl.,* 63, 1956, p. 61).

97. Cf. 5, 1, 3, and the terminology of *Dam* 3: 12, 20; 7: 13; 20: 27.

98. This whole formula is read in *Dam* 15: 10.

99. Should the translation be the statute *of the* time? But this would be a correction of the present text.

100. In the prologue: once; in the final psalm, once. In *Dam* 1: 13, with the formula of S 9: 19: now is the time; also in *Dam,* five times in the great Code: two of these, 12: 21 and 16: 3 quote S 9: 12 and the *Book of the Division of Time,* respectively.

101. *qes* is used in the treatise on the two spirits: 8 times; in the hymn of the times: twice; in the final psalm: once, and in the general prologue: once. In *Dam* it is found 17 times throughout.

102. In 8: 4, the community acts in proportion to the truth and the disposition of the time-moment; in 8: 15, the revelations came about at their time; in 9: 5, the community will separate itself at that time.

103. In several places we may understand that the *Maśkîl* has to conform to a juridically fixed series of acts, e.g., 9: 12, and even 9: 14, 18, 23; but some expressions are in special relief like the discoveries in accordance with the time (9: 13); the chosen ones of that time, 9: 14; the time of the way in the desert, 9: 19, and the accumulation of the uses of the same term. The passages of *Dam* 12: 21; 16: 3, confirm it.

right of association with the community. He sees that everything
is done when and as it should be, but he does not engage in
polemics with the men of wickedness. He conceals from them
the counsel of the law. With faithful knowledge and correct custom he governs the chosen ones of the way in accordance with
each individual and the circumstances (the time?) (9: 14-18).
He directs them and instructs them in the wonderful and faithful
(trustworthy) secrets, (kept) within the community so that
everyone will behave in concert and in accordance with what
has been revealed to them for this is the moment to clear the
way in the desert (cf. *Is.* 40: 3; *supra* 8: 13-14) (9: 18-20). He
causes people to grasp what has been found to be observed at
this time and cuts himself off from wicked men (9: 20-21). He
himself must practice every virtue in conformity with the revelations, accomplish God's good pleasure, hate the men who are
cursed in their furtive spirit, obey God in everything, praise him
always (9: 21-26).

A model of the virtues extolled in the community, the *Maśkil*
is charged with teaching the knowledge of the law kept in trust
and the secrets of the community, the revelations and discoveries
(is there a difference?) in connection with the time. He is also
charged with overseeing and governing, although possibly only
those whom he teaches, but he does not have any control outside
this group.[104] The esotericism of the community is rarely evi-
denced in *S*.[105] This passage (9: 17) seems to recommend it [106]
and if the fact is demonstrated, it confirms the presence of the
doctrine here proposed in the community, although it was not
widespread.

D. The *S* does not speak of family — marriage, wife or
children. It makes no clear allusion to historical events, to the
Teacher of Righteousness and his revelations, or to persecutions,[107]
any more than it does to the new covenant, the exile, an establishment in the Country of Damascus, nor, quite clearly, to an imminent eschatology. Yet the sojourn in the desert is no mere metaphor. Except in one passage of the charter it looks upon the temple
and the worship of Jerusalem as things of the past, save in claim-

ing that they are spiritually realized in the Union (5: 6; 8: 5, 8; 9: 6-7).

In the Union of *S* a person dedicates himself through an oath to be converted, i.e., to lead in complete community of goods and activity the virtuous life as set down by the law of Moses, but a law that has been explicitated by the revelations of the prophets and by the revelations resulting from an institutional study. Study requires appropriate intelligence and formation. Alone in possessing the complete law and authentic "righteousness," the Union claims that it is the faithful Israel which alone realizes the covenant perfectly and alone possesses perfect purity and the valid purification rites, the true spiritual worship and the priesthood chosen by God. The community must keep itself carefully apart from all who refuse to admit the law as known and practiced in this way, and within the community itself, it must separate itself from those who rebel against God's will conceived in this way. Finally, one passage suggests that all of

---

104. Strictly speaking, the whole passage could be interpreted of any member of the community who has the right, in common deliberation (cf. col. 8), to decide on the admission of the candidates and the general government, who devotes himself to study and communicates his findings to the others. Nevertheless this interpretation does not arise immediately from the present passage itself, but from a synthesis with other pericopes. Another question is that of the connections between, or the identification of the *Maśkîl* and the *Paqîd* of 6, 14 and the *Mebaqqer* of 6: 12, 20, who is certainly an individual authority. The *Mebaqqer* of *Dam* 13: 7-19; 14: 8-12 has functions that are very similar to those of the *Maśkîl* of S.

105. In 8: 12, it is a question of the common sharing of the revelations: to tell something that has been hidden without fear of apostasy; in 10: 24, the passage is poetic and seems to have been corrected: "I shall conceal knowledge."

106. In 9: 17, the text enumerates the duties of the *Maśkîl*: he must have no polemics with the ungodly, he hides from them the counsel of the law. The verb *str* does have the sense of concealment and of secret, but it connotes an overtone of refuge and protection, as well as the noun: *Is.* 16: 4; 28: 18, etc. Must the *Maśkîl* conceal or protect the counsel of the law?

107. With the exception of passage 8: 4 in the charter. On celibacy in S, cf. the remarks of J. Maier, *in* S 1: 1.

this has come about at this time, a time of special grace. The organization of the Union, chiefly in the admission and formation of new members, is rigid and often punctilious. It relies upon a ritual of purifications and prayers, recognized practices and a tradition of teaching whose esotericism is perhaps affirmed by one sentence in the document. The hierarchy is not only priestly, and the authority is exercised conjointly by the community as a body and by certain individuals who are responsible.

If we are to situate *Sa,* it will be put on the level of evolution of *S* [108] among the Qumrân documents, or slightly after. The words in the title, "at the last days," ought not to be misconstrued; there is nothing eschatological in this document. This is merely a stylistic turn. Moreover we are perhaps dealing with a theoretical ruling. Study is an important point of the ruling of *Sa* and it is no longer likened to a revelation. The community is at the institutional stage and to a degree that is even more advanced than in *S.* But here we have an institution where the family has its place, and particularly the education of children. The two institutions are parallel. They are not identical.

§ 3. *Conclusions.*

The Qumrân documents have given us a sketch of a religious community. Less perhaps from the date of their composition than as a result of the more or less pronounced archaism of their concepts, the community spoken of in these documents is multiform both by virtue of the doctrinal evolution it underwent and the progressive stages of its internal organization. By reading each particular document and comparing it with the others we do obtain a few results.

"At the time of wrath" (*Dam* 1: 5) a serious happening has provoked a profound religious emotion in the Jewish people. The attitude of the Jews was either mass apostasy (*Dam* 1: 13-21) or a resolute reaction (*Dam* 1: 7-10). The faithful who "stood fast" (*Dam* 3: 12-20; cf. *Dan.* 11: 32) soon grouped themselves "after twenty years" (*Dam* 1: 10) about a more stirring teacher.

He "taught righteousness" (*Dam* 1: 11) by revealing the "secrets" (cf. Daniel) of God, imminent divine punishments for apostates, seekers of the "easy life" (cf. Daniel). At the same time he preached the moral attitude that was to be taken at this time of destitution and expectation of the end (*Dam* 1: 11-12). This is what is behind the three admonitions at the beginning of *Dam* 1-4: 6, the third part, second pericope (*Dam* 7: 13-8: 13) and perhaps section 20: 15-27.[109]

Subsequently this emotional movement must have lasted for some time at first, and withstood the passage of time and the adversaries who opposed it. This is the community of *pHab*. It was then also to find a meeting place and, interiorly, gradually to specify its objectives, justify itself as to the past of the chosen people, and organize itself. The idea of a similar organization was not a new thing in the world of the time. Rather than being reminded of somewhat outdated Rechabites (cf. 2 *Kg*. 10: 15 ff.; *Jer.* 35), let us not forget the Hellenistic religious associations had been known and widespread in Palestine for 150 years.[110] This is what the new covenant in the Country of Damascus was in the second and third parts and the end of the fourth pericope (4: 6-7: 4; 20: 27-34), with the progression of priesthood, study and legalistic morality. Israel, renewed and strengthened with the promises of the covenant and the lawful priesthood, separated from the ungodly "in the desert," seeks there the living waters of the law of Moses, rediscovered through *midrashîm* and *pesharîm,* and henceforth directed towards perfection (6: 4-11; 7: 13-20). What is this Desert? Where is it? Is it a desert in the proper sense of the term, or does it refer simply to groups living by themselves

---

108. Cf. L. Rost, in *Theol. Litztung,* 82, 1957, col. 667.

109. The archeological findings of the excavations of kh. Qumrân (cf. R. de Vaux, *Rev. Bibl.,* 63, 1956, p. 538) authorize the hypothesis of an installation under John Hyrcanus, 135-105 B.C. The literary and doctrinal clues of these sections of *Dam* connects them with the Book of Daniel. The occasion of this movement must have been a contemporary event, and probably Antiochus IV's attempt at hellenization.

110. Cf. H. Bardtke, in *Theol. Litztung,* 86, 1961, col. 93-103.

but in the midst of the people in the spirit of the Desert of Exodus? Undoubtedly it is both, but this part of *Dam* does not yet permit us to settle the debate. Whatever the answer, the "institution" assumes an increasingly more prominent place and it ends up by completely absorbing the emotion of the beginning. The vibrant reaction of the faithful to the apostasy survives in a "Jewish worship association."

This evolution will continue and will reach the point of *S* together with *Sa* on the one hand, and *Dam,* part 3, pericopes 1 and 3 on the other (*Dam* 7: 4-13; 8: 13-20: 15). The *S* group is set up far away from the people and separated from everything. It is no longer a religious movement, even an institutionalized one, but a cenobitic group, the "Union," the Union of God (*S* 1: 12), the Holy Union (*S* 9: 2). Undoubtedly it too underwent an evolution (cf. the ancient parts: *S* 8-9), but one that was peculiar to its cenobitical life. This cenobiticism preserves the first idea of the movement as expressed in *Dam,* part 2. It claims to possess the law, perfectly known and accurately practiced in accordance with God's will. But this idea is lived in a separate community, with its laws, customs and its severe discipline, its hierarchy and its authorities, its meeting place, its prayers and its rites in common, its community study of the law leading to new revelations. The life of the "professed" of the Union (for the terms "steadfast" — once in 5: 3 —, the converted or the exiled are no longer used), as described in *S* and not contradicted by the archeological findings of kh. Qumrân, is the one that will be lived much later by Christian solitaries in their desert *laurae.*

Parallel to this, there live in the camps (*Dam* 7: 6) those who are perfect in holiness. Along with their family, it seems, (7: 7; 20: 13) they observe all the prescriptions of the law in one congregation where their children are also brought up (*Sa*). The spirit is identical with that of *S,* but the concrete setting is different. What are these camps? And what is the congregation, set up in a hierarchical form like a permanently billeted Roman legion (*Sa* 1: 25-2: 2)? Again, we may think of an organized life of a religious sect, but lived in the midst of the people. The Hellenistic world was used to this situation. Parallel to the cenobitic community there were devout Jews who endeavored to imitate "in the world" the retired life of the Qumrân solitaries. The discipline here was just as rigorous and they shared privileges in common: the new covenant in the new exile and the authentic Israel of the true and complete law. It will be out of their midst that the messiah of Israel will come (*Sa* 2: 11).

The term "Qumrân community" then covers two realities that are not strangers to each other although they are distinct.[111] Both live their own lives, akin to each other because of the same starting point, and undoubtedly in mutual contact.[112] *Dam* III a, c is related to *S* as to perhaps an ideal fulfillment, but *Dam* (with *pHab* and *Sa*) cannot be reduced to the pattern of *S*. The grave event that is at the beginning of an historical movement gave birth in Judaism to a twofold or at least two-sided reality: a religious association and a cenobitical religious order.

La Sarte-Huy   Albert-Marie Denis, O.P.
Belgium   Professor at the Dominican
               Studium Theologicum of La Sarte (Huy)

---

111. Cf. K. G. Kuhn, *Zum heutigen Stand der Qumrânforschung*, in *Theol. Litztung*, 85, 1960, c. 653.

112. The buildings of kh. Qumrân are not large, cf. the plans drawn up by R. de Vaux, *Rev. Bibl.*, 63, 1956, p. 576. If they served as a meeting place, the community could not have been numerous. The adjacent cemetery has some 1,100 tombs, a number which certainly considerably surpasses the number of dead in a small community, even over the course of two and a half centuries. More than one person who did not belong to the community must have been buried there.

III

Jean Giblet

The Twelve, History and Theology

I. STATE OF THE QUESTION

We are going through a change in perspective in the study of the primitive Christian apostleship. Undoubtedly, there was agreement in acknowledging that Jesus chose and sent forth apostles, but questions have arisen concerning the exact meaning of this mission. A kind of dilemma was trumped up between spirit and authority, between the charismatic and the institutional. We need only refer to the controversy started by Sohm and Harnack in Germany and the works of Sabatier and Battifol in France.[1] In the opinion of some men, and R. Bultmann in particular, this debate is still open.[2] But modern thought tends to recognize the complementarity of these aspects, and E. Käsemann wrote recently that the old views of the liberals are definitively outmoded.[3]

Today, study is directed rather towards a more basic historical problem: did Jesus actually originate the apostleship? If the answer is to be in the affirmative, then what meaning did he give it? But if by chance the answer should be negative, where

---

1. R. Sohm, *Kirchenrecht*, I, Munich-Leipzig, 1892, cf. S. Grundmann, art. Sohm, RGG, 3rd ed., t. VI, col. 116s; A. von Harnack, *Entstehung und Entwicklung der Kirchenverfassung und des Kirchenrechts in den ersten drei Jahrhunderten*, Leipzig, 1910.

2. R. Bultmann, *Theologie des Neuen Testaments* (*Neue Theologische Grundrisse*), Tübingen, 1953, p. 447.

3. E. Käsemann, *Sätze heiligen Rechtes im NT*, in *New Testament Studies*, t. I, 1954/55, pp. 248-260: "In der frühesten Christenheit sind Geist und Recht nicht geschieden" (p. 259).

must we situate the origin and development of this notion, so incontestably important for the later Church? Some hold that Jesus himself is the founder of the institution of the Twelve and that it is he who made them apostles. Others say that it is Paul who was the first to work out this notion of apostle, and only subsequently did it come to be applied to the group of twelve privileged disciples that the Jerusalem community speaks of. Still others, most recently, claim that Jesus did not even set up a group of disciples, and that the origin of this concept should be sought in the primitive community, possibly in St. Luke.

1. The majority of the authors agree in acknowledging that the first current is very well presented by Rengstorf in his article ἀπόστολὸς published in the *Theologisches Wörterbuch zum Neuen Testament*.[4] After stating (as does everyone else) that the Greek uses of the word hardly prepared it for playing a religious role, Rengstorf goes back to and bolsters up a suggestion of J. B. Lightfoot, connecting our word apostle with the Jewish juridical institution of the *Shaliah*. Actually this was hardly a question of an institution, but it is a fact that the Judaism of the first centuries of our era knew of envoys who received the right from religious people who sent them out to act in their name. It should be translated by the terms legate, agent, representative. While admitting serious differences,[5] Rengstorf believes that he can demonstrate important points of similarity, and that it is legitimate to speak of a relationship between the two concepts. And what is more important, the parallelism would have been maintained up to the end of the New Testament period, although we can observe the appearance of various modifications. Rengstorf divides his article into three points: Jesus and the first circle of apostles, the primitive Christian apostleship as a gift of the Risen Jesus, and the classical expression of the apostleship in the person of Paul.

a) Jesus was not content merely with surrounding himself with disciples as the Rabbis did. At a given moment, he commissioned several among them to act in his name; and in order to do this, he conferred on them a power and an authority which made them his authorized representatives. Their number is hardly easy to determine and it is likely that the figure twelve has a symbolic value more than anything else. They are essentially his delegates, his *sheluhim,* his *apostoloi,* and everything seems to indicate that Jesus himself use this title. But at the same time Rengstorf, faithful to the data of the old controversy, strives to show the relative disappearance of the juridical aspects. It was a question of tasks to be performed, rather than of a function.

b) The Easter events brought a new basis to this mission, but there is such a continuity that we must speak of a renewal of the first task. There are certainly some modifications. First of all the content of the teaching is now organized in the light of the Easter event; then, the apostleship takes on a per-manent character which contrasts it to the essentially transitory Jewish legateship; finally, the functional or institutional tone tends to be accentuated. The number of the first apostles remains un-certain, but it ought hardly be increased. It goes without saying that it encompassed the Twelve, joined by a few witnesses of the resurrection. The Twelve themselves seem indeed to have had a certain activity of a missionary nature. If a few of them are known to us, like Peter and James, the majority have disappeared without leaving a trace.

c) But it is Paul who was to develop this notion of apostle in the most noteworthy way. He places it in the framework intro-duced by the great prophets of the past.

These views have received approval by a great number of critics. Rengstorf has been reproached for being too attached to the antithesis: charism-institution, since his hypothesis itself ought to have brought him to stretch it to the utmost.[6] It was also a pity that he limited himself only to the major New Testament

---

4. K. H. Ringstorf, *art. cit.,* t. I, pp. 406-444; id., *Apostolat und Predigtamt,* 1934.

5. *Art. cit.,* p. 414, n. 1.

6. J. Brosch, *Charismen und Ämter in der Urkirche,* 1951.

writings.[7] But on the whole he has gained credence. We might add that the too rare and too hasty contributions of Catholic critics take this direction.[8]

2. Still, for some years, reactions have appeared that go in quite different directions, and we must carefully sort them out.

a) First of all the existence of this *Shaliah-Institute* that Rengstorf speaks of has been questioned. A. Ehrhardt has systematized a certain number of facts and has shown that the importance of the information on this institution has been overestimated.[9] Certainly Judaism did know delegations of power for a time, with a definite task in view, but this was strictly in the juridical order. No real delegation in properly religious matters is found before a much later age than that of the New Testament. The word *Shaliah,* according to Ehrhardt, is not met with before 140 A.D.[10] The criticism was taken up again in the recent work of Schmithals, and it seems so relevant that several of Rengstorf's partisans have abandoned this presupposition.[11]

b) But at the same time, it might be asked whether Jesus himself used the word *apostolos* or its Aramaic equivalent. At the end of a painstaking study, Fr. Dupont observes that this is possible, but that "nothing in the Gospel allows us to assert that he really did so." [12]

c) From this point, paths diverge depending on whether one acknowledges or not that Jesus founded a restricted group of disciples who were associated with the Master's activity. For some, this goes without saying, and it is glossed over since it seems so obvious: "The first point, on which we have not delayed," writes Fr. Dupont, "but which is important is that we must consider as beyond all doubt the fact that Jesus set up the college of the Twelve." [13] It is for this reason that A. Fridrichsen, J. Munck, H. Mosbech and E. Lohse acknowledge the fact itself, a certain missionary type activity in Galilee and an indeterminable paschal activity as well.[14] But it is Paul who was the real initiator of the word *apostolos* and of the properly Christian notion of apostleship. In this way he would have expressed his own missionary awareness. It is only later that the title would have been given to Peter and by him to the Twelve.

Another infinitely more radical trend has just been stated in two large works dedicated to this problem. They bluntly deny even the existence of the college of the Twelve during Jesus' public life. The Twelve would be hardly more than the first (an ephemeral) attempt at organizing the paschal community.

Certainly this position is not totally new. To acknowledge that the college of the Twelve was a reality is at the same time to admit a desire for organization, and because of that, a desire for a lasting quality of the group which does not correspond to the image of Jesus as a prophet of the imminent end of time — an image which several scholars have accepted. With his *imperatoria brevitas,* R. Bultmann wrote at the beginning of his theology of the New Testament that as unlikely as it is that Jesus called the Twelve, so the Twelve are as characteristic of the eschatological

---

7. E. M. Kredel, *Der Apostelbegriff in der neuere Exegese,* in ZKTh, 1956, t. LXXVIII, pp. 288 ff.

8. H. Stirnimann, *Apostelamt und apostolische Überlieferung,* in *Freib. Zeit. f. Phil. u. Theol.,* 1957, t. IV, pp. 129-147; K. Schelkle, *Jüngerschaft und Apostelamt,* Freiburg-am-Breisgau, 1957; J. Colson, *Les fonctions ecclésiales aux deux premiers siècles,* Bruges, 1956.

9. A. Ehrhardt, *The Apostolic Succession in the First two Centuries of the Church,* 1953.

10. *Op. cit.,* p. 17.

11. W. Schmithals, *Das kirchliche Apostelamt. Eine historische Untersuchung* (*FRLANT,* t. lxxix), Göttingen, 1961, pp. 87-99; L. Cerfaux, *Pour l'histoire du mot ἀπόστολος dans le Nouveau Testament,* in *RSR,* 1960, t. XLVIII, pp. 76-92, reprinted in *Recueil L. Cerfaux,* t. III, Gembloux, 1962, pp. 185-200.

12. J. Dupont, *Le nom d'apôtre a-t-il été donné aux Douze par Jésus?,* in *L'Orient chrétien,* 1956, t. I, p. 445.

13. *Art. cit.,* p. 443.

14. A. Fridrichsen, *The Apostle and his Message,* in *UUA,* 3, Uppsala, 1947; H. Mosbech, *Apostolos in the NT,* in *St. Th.,* 1949/50, t. II, pp. 166-200; J. Munck, *Paul, the Apostles and the Twelve,* in *St. Th.,* 1950/51, t. III, pp. 96-110; E. Lohse, *Die Ordination im Spätjudentum und im NT,* Göttingen, 1951; id., *Ursprung und Prägung des christlichen Apostolates,* in *Th.Z.,* 1953, t. IX, pp. 259-275.

awareness of the Community; they are not the Twelve because they are apostles, but because they are eschatological regents.[15]

The argumentation has been presented, rather hastily I am afraid, by P. Vielhauer, G. Klein and G. Schmithals.[16] They isolate and discuss the classic arguments about the existence of the group of the Twelve before Easter. In their opinion, the Twelve are hardly more than a restricted community that would have been organized on the day after Easter. They go so far as to deny it any missionary activity outside of Jerusalem. The group which, after all, is barely mentioned in Acts, and which Paul practically never mentions, had hardly any influence and rapidly disappeared. It would be giving them too much importance to suppose, with Fridrichsen and Munck, that the name apostle would have come to them from Paul. In their opinion it is only much later, at the end of an evolutionary process of which Paul is undoubtedly not the primary source, that the Title would have been given to the Twelve by Luke and a Hellenistic current that Schmithals calls synoptic, to contrast it with the Pauline Hellenistic current. The Twelve would thereby have become the guarantors of the gospel facts. Recourse to them permits victorious opposition to the Gnostics.

3. Such being the present state of the question, we must now return to examining the question of the existence and the original significance of the group of the Twelve disciples. We may certainly admit that the college itself was the object of later theological reflection and that we can observe in the second century an emphasis on its role as a witness. On this point Schmithals' work has some elements worthy of our attention. But it is important to ask whether this theological reflection simply created its object, or whether on the other hand, given special circumstances, it emphasized certain aspects of the original fact. Developed to a certain extent to counter Gnosticism, is the theology of the Twelve merely a theory or is it rooted in fact?

Our task then will be to investigate the question historically, although this path may be frought with difficulties. In another context, Fr. Teilhard de Chardin spoke of the disappearance of peduncles, i.e., of the great difficulty experienced by those study-ing the evolution of the species in rediscovering the moment of transition and the first stages of development. For his part, Mr. Guitton observed that every living being begins twice: in a first implicit moment which is its origin, and in a second explicit moment which is its emergence.[17] The Christian communities seem to us to have been relatively structured from the outset, but is it possible to reconstruct the first stages of this organization process? The question is an important one and we well see that it is con-nected with the more general problem of Christian origins.

But we must point out at the start that there is a capital differ-ence between this law that governs the evolution of biological groups and ordinary living beings, and the question of the appear-ance of Christianity. In our case, the point of departure is con-stituted by an eminent personality. It is actually impossible to attribute to a community of anonymous persons the appearance of such a reality as Christianity.[18] That this personality, Jesus, intended to set up a new center of religious life and that he then laid the groundwork for a certain organized society is completely normal. To reduce Jesus to the obscure personage that Bultmannian criticism wishes to do, is to go counter to a certain number of laws of human history.

Yet we must still examine whether present-day documentation supplies us with enough material for us to be able to sketch

---

15. *Op. cit.*, p. 38.

16. Ph. Vielhauer, *Gottesreich und Menschensohn in der Verkündigung Jesu*, in *Festschrift G. Dehn*, Neukirchen, 1957, pp. 62 ff.; G. Klein, *Die zwölf Apostel, Ursprung und Gehalt einer Idee*, in *FRLANT*, t. LXXVII, Göttingen, 1961, pp. 34 ff.; G. Schmithals, *op. cit.*, p. 56 ff.

17. J. Guitton, *L'homme a commencé*, in *Qu'est-ce que l'homme?* (Semaine des Intellectuels catholiques 1954), Paris, 1955, p. 64.

18. Cf. H. Dumery, *Philosophie de la religion. Essai sur la signification du christianisme*, t. II, Paris, 1957, pp. 44-49.

what the first structuring process actually was.[19] We are therefore
brought to a study of the Gospel documents themselves. But we
must first tackle a Pauline text that is of inestimable importance.

II. THE TWELVE IN THE SETTING OF JESUS' ACTIVITY

1. *The evidence from Paul (I Cor. 15: 5) and the paschal position of the Twelve.*

Only one Pauline text speaks of the Twelve. It deals with
the confession of faith about which he solemnly reminds the Christians of Corinth at the beginning of his statement on the resurrection of the dead. We are familiar with its content:

*"Well then, in the first place, I taught you what I had been
taught myself, namely that Christ died for our sins, in accordance
with the scriptures; that he was buried; and that he was raised
to life on the third day, in accordance with the scriptures; that he
appeared first to Cephas and secondly to the Twelve. Next he
appeared to more than five hundred of the brothers at the same
time, most of whom are still alive, though some have died; then
he appeared to James, and then to all the apostles; and last of
all he appeared to me too . . . ."*

The unique importance of this text has been often stressed.
Paul declares that he is speaking of a tradition that he himself
received and that he proclaims together with the other witnesses
(I *Cor.* 15: 3, 11); the literary characteristics allow us to
add that we are dealing with a tradition of Palestinian origin;
the plural ὑπὲρ τῶν ἁμαρτιῶν the expression κατὰ τὰς γραφάς, the
word ὤφθη, the construction ἐγήγερται and finally οἱ δώδεκα, do
not belong to the current language of the apostle. In fact the text
that Paul has repeated with such care reflects essential aspects
of the original gospel — the major facts to which the preaching
of the primitive community is added. Paul who taught this confession of faith to Corinth in the year 51 must have received it
at the time of his stay in Jerusalem, no later than the year 49.

The text places Cephas at the head of the witnesses, and in connection with him, the *dôdeka*. It is because, as M. Schmitt showed, they are the privileged witnesses of the Easter events.[20] Moreover, there are other witnesses: James and all the apostles. We may argue at this point about what is part of the most ancient tradition since there are literary indications of some retouching, but we may leave this question aside. At all events, what must be stressed is that the group of the Twelve to which Cephas belonged in all likelihood has been very well known since the first decade; they appear jointly to be privileged witnesses of the risen Lord. Peter, whatever his special importance may be, does not suffice. It is a group acknowledged as such and not a sum of individuals.[21] Let us further point out that at this time the group of the Twelve was clearly distinguished from the *apostoloi* mentioned in verse 7. We may then conclude that the primitive Palestinian Church, in the most ancient confession of faith known, attributes an unequalled place to Peter and the group of the Twelve. By priority they are the witnesses of Christ's resurrection, but this alone does not suffice to characterize them since there are other qualified witnesses. This text does not permit us to be more specific about their special status. In any case we have a glimpse here of the first paschal community and we may be permitted to suppose that Cephas and the Twelve played a dominant role in it. To some extent they must govern it.

---

19. Cf. B. Rigaux, *Die "Zwölf" in Geschichte und Kerygma*, in H. Ristow-K. Matthiae, *Der historische Jesus und der kerygmatische Christus. Beiträge zum Christusverständnis in Forschung und Verkündigung*, Berlin, 1961, pp. 468-486; L. Cerfaux, *La mission apostolique des Douze et sa portée eschatologieque*, in *Mélanges E. Tisserant*, t. I, Rome, 1964, pp. 43-66; B. Gerhardson, *Die Boten Gottes und die Apostel Christi*, in *Svensk Exegetisk Aarsbok*, 1962, t. XXVII, pp. 89-131.

20. J. Schmitt, *Jésus ressuscité dans la prédication apostolique*, Paris, 1949; J. Giblet, *La résurrection de Jésus et les études récentes*, in *Collect. Mechl.*, 1954, t. XXXIX, pp. 437 ff. Here we should also like to recommend the very important work of P. Ladeuze, *La résurrection du Christ devant la critique contemporaine*, Brussels, 1909.

21 .J. Schmitt recalls the Jewish juridical adage: "Let every case be judged on the deposition of two or three witnesses." *Op. cit.*, p. 137.

2. *Mark*

Is it possible to go back beyond the Easter event? Certainly, the synoptic Gospels do speak in many instances of the Twelve, but we must look very carefully and critically at what they say. Before examining the details supplied for us by Mark, it seems fitting to give a rapid analysis of the vocabulary used in the Gospels.

a) Most often Mark uses the simple expression *the Twelve* (3: 14, 16; 4: 10; 6: 7; 9: 35; 10: 32; 11: 11; 14: 10, 17, 20, 43); in one case he replaces it by the formula *his disciples* (6: 35). In looking at the parallels in Matthew and Luke, certain rather meaningful differences can be observed in Matthew we meet a longer formula, *the twelve disciples,* in four instances (10: 1; 11: 1; 20: 17; 26: 20) and the term *disciples* is used many times (*Mt.* 13: 10; *Mk.* 4: 10 and *Lk.* 8: 1; *Mt.* 14: 15; *Mk.* 9: 35); finally we see the formula *the twelve apostles* appearing once (10, 2). In Luke we most often meet with the short formula, *the Twelve* (*Lk.* 6: 13; 8: 1; 9: 1, 12; 18: 31; 22: 3; 22: 47) but in one important case the Twelve are replaced by the formula *the apostles* (*Lk.* 22: 14).

From this we may conclude that among the disciples we must single out a very specific group normally called the Twelve. Although in Matthew and Luke the term is specified, we may say that from the point of view of the composition, the formula *the Twelve* is most ancient. Surely we must add that all these passages dealing with the Twelve are redactional, but we can conclude that the formula belongs to the most ancient layer of the synoptic tradition. It therefore reflects an important piece of information which in the light of I Corinthians 15: 5 confirms the existence at the beginning of a group of twelve privileged disciples who not only exert a certain authority in the Palestinian community but present themselves as chosen by Jesus and constituted as a group from the time of his earthly ministry.

b) But would we not be dealing with a theology created by Mark himself? In the majority of cases we could maintain this view on first sight. But B. Rigaux has shown that in the passage — a very complicated one from the redactional standpoint —

of Mark 3: 13-19, the formula ἐποίησεν τούς δώδεκα is clearly Semitic and can only with difficulty be attributed to Mark himself.[22] The use of the verb "make" with the name of a person as its direct object is in itself rather surprising. We should have to refer to an Old Testament use in regard to the instituting of priests (I *Kg.* 13: 33; II *Chr.* 2: 18); it may be said also that the Lord "made" Moses and Aaron (I *Sam.* 12: 6). This use is found again in the New Testament (*Heb.* 3: 2; *Ac.* 2: 36). We must therefore conclude that the fact of the Twelve is not looked upon as something accidental; we are dealing with an entity, recognized as such, which must enjoy special capacities and a particular power in bringing about the transformation of the world inaugurated by Jesus. Mark did not create this notion. He received it from more primitive tradition. But then where do we find the *Sitz im Leben* that will account for the appearance not only of this formula but of the reality expressed by it? Can we remain within the setting of the paschal community or must we go back still further?[23] What we know to be most certain about Jesus' activity ought to help us here.

c) From the outset we must underline a turn of phrase that occurs many times in the language of the synoptic tradition and allows us to go back with genuine assurance to the events of pre-paschal origins. Judas is often designated as one of the Twelve (*Mk.* 14: 10, 20; *Mt.* 26: 14, 17; *Lk.* 22: 47; *Jn.* 6: 71). While emphasizing what is painful and scandalous in the fact that one of the privileged disciples betrayed the Master, the formula attests at the same time to the existence of the group of the Twelve before the Passion.

The adversaries of the college's historicity are rather embarrassed by this fact, but they are quick to have recourse to certain expedients. Schmithals seems to say that the betrayal by Judas — who indeed was one of the Twelve after Easter — is for us of

---

22. *Op. cit.,* pp. 472-475.

23. H. Schürmann, *Die vorösterlichen Anfänge der Logientradition. Versuch eines formgeschichtlichen Zugangs zum Leben Jesus,* in H. Ristow K. Matthiae, *Der historische Jesus und der kerygmatische Christus,* Berlin, 1961, pp. 342-370.

unknown nature, and it was only after that this betrayal would have been inserted in the Passion account.[24] But it is only too clear that this thesis is demanded by the desire to deny at all costs any indication about the historicity of the college before Easter.

Surely we may admit, with Fr. Benoit, that recollections about Judas' death were subject to certain theological reflections: "They are not accounts of a purely historical type, but within the bounds of their particular literary genus they still supply us with a solid tradition since it is the result of genuine recollections." [25] That a disciple called Judas betrayed Jesus and in some way set the process of the Passion in motion is a fact that cannot be seriously questioned.

As for the well-attested fact that he was one of the Twelve, it is difficult to see how the primitive Palestinian community could have affirmed it. Would they have attributed to one of the members of the college of the Twelve an act which by its very nature would have disparaged the authority of the whole group? We must certainly admit that they would not. Therefore we can hold as certain that there is continuity between the group of the Twelve in the tradition with regard to the first Palestinian community, and that which goes back to the activity of Jesus himself. But what was the meaning of the college for Jesus at that time?

d) We must now return to the passage where Mark relates the institution of this group of disciples by Jesus.

"He now went up into the hills and summoned those he wanted. So they came to him and he appointed twelve; they were to be his companions and to be sent out to preach with power to cast out devils. And so he appointed the Twelve . . . ."

Let us note first of all that the various versions offer somewhat different readings of these verses. In verse 14, an important series of manuscripts and versions add to the assertion that "Jesus appointed Twelve" the phrase "and they were called apostles" (A C 2 D Lᵖ fam. 1, 33, 565, 579, 700, 892, 1071; and the it., vg., syrˢ ᵖᵉˢʰ, geo.2 and arm. versions). But we have the right to prefer the shorter reading which is attested to by A B C Δ Θ W, fam. 13, 28, 238, 543; and the sy ʰˡ (in margine) sa. bo. aeth. geo. versions. It is likely that it is a repetition of the formulation of Luke 6: 13

since otherwise it would be hard to explain its suppression by so many witnesses. This is the opinion of the majority of witnesses (among the most recent; Lagrange, Taylor, Lohmeyer, W. Grundmann). We shall have the opportunity to confirm this interpretation further on. Similarly, certain texts add to verse 15 Θεραπεύειν τὰς νόσους καὶ (A C ² D W ² al. min.; the it., vg., sy.[s] [pe] [hl], arm. bo. and aeth. versions). The text has therefore been subject to developments in the course of the manuscript tradition.

But what is much more to the point is that its rather coarse literary construction seems to indicate that the original text itself fixed the final stage of an evolution. But what is most primitive in all likelihood is the beginning: "he appointed twelve; they were to be his companions . . . ." The second final proposition actually offers only an apparent symmetry; while the first verb is in the third person plural and has the twelve as subject, the second has Jesus as subject.

From this we can elucidate the first significance of the group of privileged disciples. The scene is a mountain and it is possible that the Evangelist wished to recall the constituting of the first Israel on Sinai. In any case, the Twelve are the objects of an absolutely free election and of a calling by Jesus, a call to which they responded. It is the group of the Twelve which is the object of a real institution of a religious nature. We have already pointed out that this Semitic turn of phrase (where the verb "to make" is followed by a noun designating already existent persons) recalls the institution of the priests and also Moses and Aaron. We are dealing with a sort of creation by Jesus conferring special powers on the members of the group. It must be immediately added — and this seems to us to be the essential and most ancient aspect — that they are established "to be his companions." In other words from now on they are to be closely associated with Jesus' activity and power. They will share his lot and will be

24. *Op. cit.*, p. 59.
25. P. Benoit, *La mort de Judas*, in *Synoptische Studien Alfred Wikenhause zum siebzigsten Geburtstag dargebracht*, Munich, 1954, pp. 1-9; reprinted in *Exégèse et Théologie*, t. I, Paris, 1961, pp. 340-359 (text cited, p. 359).

associated with the power that is being proclaimed. This close
association of the Twelve as such with Jesus is then explicitated
by the second final proposition where preaching and the power to
cast out demons are awkwardly coupled, although we may well
think that the first proposition is not restricted to these aspects.
This will be confirmed by the examination of an important logion.

3. *A logion preserved in Matthew and Luke.*

Matthew and Luke, each in his own way, preserve words of
Jesus than can further clarify the significance of this group of
the Twelve. In Matthew it is the answer to Peter's question about
the reward awaiting those who have left everything to follow
Jesus: "I tell you solemnly, when all is made new (lit: at the time
of regeneration) and the Son of Man sits on his throne of glory,
you will yourselves sit on twelve thrones to judge the twelve
tribes of Israel" (*Mt.* 19: 28). In Luke (22: 28-30) the sentence
is inserted in the course of the last declarations of the Master
at the Last Supper. After stressing humility, Jesus continues: "You
are the men who have stood by me faithfully in my trials; and
now I confer a kingdom on you, just as my Father conferred one
on me: you will eat and drink at my table in my kingdom, and
you will sit on thrones to judge the twelve tribes of Israel."

It can be seen immediately that the contexts are different and
that the sentence has been retouched in part, but we can also
rediscover the common kernel of thought. The group of the
Twelve will be closely associated with the kingly power of the
Son of Man and they will govern in fellowship with him the new
Israel.

But are we really dealing with the words of Jesus? Opinions
differ. One group of critics rejects the authenticity for reasons
of general order.

Some, like Goguel, think that such an assertion would be
in contradiction with Jesus' words underlining the fact that he
cannot promise the sons of Zebedee that they will sit at his
right hand and at his left.[26] But we may reply that this phrase

on the contrary already implies the promise made to the Twelve. It is because they wanted to have a place that is superior to the others that the sons of Zebedee were refused.

For Bultmann, the attribution of this phrase to the risen Christ, i.e., in the last analysis to the paschal community, causes no problem (*Auch hier spricht fraglos der Auferstandene . . .*).[27] For it is only at this point that the community would consider itself to be an eschatological reality. But this is precisely what is not so simple to assert.

Finally, Dalmain and several critics with him, have stressed that the word παλιγγενεσία (i.e., regeneration, "when all is made new") has no corresponding word in Hebrew or Aramaic, and that it necessarily presupposes the theological formation of the Hellenistic community.[28] But this remark, however exact it may be, does not automatically entail the rejection of the logion's authenticity. For no one would argue with the fact that it received certain retouches. Lohmeyer, for example, can see three modifications, and thinks that he can reconstitute the original sentence in this way: "You shall sit upon twelve thrones in order to judge the twelve tribes of Israel." In any case the phrase is in concord with the eschatological climate of Jesus' preaching. What could be more normal than his proclaiming that his closest companions would share in his triumph and in his messianic power? Finally, the judgment as to the authenticity of this logion depends on the acknowledgment of Jesus' messianic consciousness.[29]

The restoration of the twelve tribes actually belongs to the

---

26. M. Goguel, in *Rev. Hist. Rel.*, 1941, p. CXXIII, p. 32 ff.

27. R. Bultmann, *Die Geschichte der synoptischen Tradition*, 2nd ed., Göttingen, 1931, p. 170 ff., which recalls, following Bousset, the text of *Rv.* 3: 21.

28. G. Dalman, *Die Worte Jesu mit Berücksichtigung des Nachkanonischen Jüdischen Schriftums und der Aramäischen Sprache*, t. I, Leipzig, 1898, p. 145.

29. E. Sjöberg, *Der verborgene Menschensohn in den Evangelien*, Lund, 1955; B. Rigauz, *La seconde venue de Jésus*, in *La venue du Messie. Messianisme et Eschatologie*, Bruges, 1962, pp. 173-216.

Jewish hopes of the time. In fact, this situation had practically disappeared for many years, and the question is disputed as to whether there were two and a half or three tribes remaining.[30] But the fact is that the organization of the twelve tribes assembled by David belongs to the glorious time of the beginnings. At this stage eschatology is frequently expressed in terms that refer to the beginnings, if we think only of the exaltation of Abraham, Moses and David who are to return. It is in this light that a strong current looks upon the restoration of Israel as a return to the time of the twelve Patriarchs. The *Testament of the Twelve Patriarchs* proves it. Let us add that not only were many fragments of this collection rediscovered at Qumrân, but the Rule of the Community, which is undoubtedly very late, speaks of a government by twelve men and three priests.[31] Surely the tenor is different since the rule does not suppose an eschatological climate but rather the detailed organization of a community of virtuous and pious men. But it still remains in all likelihood that there was a desire to reproduce something of the Israel of the early days.

Jesus' words are indeed directed to the Twelve as a well defined group and not to the totality of those who have left everything and have the promise of fulfillment in the Kingdom that is to come.[32] It is here that the connection with Mark 3: 14 ff. is very important. It is in the perspective of the new Israel that Jesus associated a group of twelve disciples with himself. In a certain way they proclaim the nearness of the true eschatological Israel.[33]

4. *The Mission.*

Jesus' activity in Galilee to a certain extent inaugurated his eschatological kingship. There is nothing surprising about the fact that he wished to associate disciples, and particularly the Twelve, with his work. The strictest partisans of the eschatological interpretation admit this. They say that Jesus wished to provoke the supreme crisis by the penance of the people or by persecution.[34] The matter is still clearer for those who no longer adopt the radical eschatological thesis and who acknowledge a continuity between Jesus' activity in Galilee and the paschal community. Furthermore we retain some important indications about the Galilean mission.[35] On the day after Easter the Twelve will remain in this perspective and it will become broader. They will become more and more aware of the importance of the notion of mission and it will become an essential characteristic of the Twelve. But it is not without interest to have shown that this idea is not the most basic one. The Twelve have this mission because they were first of all established to rule the new Israel. The nature of their authority is eschatological.

Avenue de Croy, 7,   J. Giblet
Herverlée   Professor at the University of Louvain

---

30. J. Jeremias, *Jésus et les Païens*, in *Actualité protestante*, Neuchâtel-Paris, 1956, p. 16, n. 7.

31. "In the Counsel of the Community (there will be) twelve men and three priests, perfect in all that is revealed of the whole Law . . . ." (1Q VIII, 1-4). A certain ambiguity will be noted: is it a question of twelve men of whom three are priests, or of twelve men *and* three priests? This latter hypothesis seems more likely. Cf. A. Dupont-Sommer, *Les écrits esséniens découverts près de la Mer morte*, Paris, 1959, p. 105, n. 4; E. F. Sutcliffe, *The First Fifteen Members of the Qumran Community, Note on 1Q VIII, 1 ff.*, in *Journal of Semitic Studies*, IV, no. 2, pp. 134-138.

32. Against W. G. Kümmel, *Verheissung und Erfüllung. Untersuchungen zur eschatologischen Verkündigung Jesu*, in *Ab.Th.A.NT*, Zurich, 1953, p. 41.

33. The mention of the 120 believers in Acts 1: 15 undoubtedly has the same sense.

34. M. Goguel, *Jean-Baptiste*, Paris, 1928, p. 253. Cf. A. Descamps, *Les Justes et la Justice dans les Évangiles et le christianisme primitif*, Louvain-Gembloux, pp. 209 ff.

35. L. Cerfaux, *La mission de Galilée dans la tradition synoptique*, in *Recueil L. Cerfaux*, t. I, Gembloux, 1954, pp. 425-469; N. van Bohemen, *L'institution des Douze. Contribution à l'étude des relations entre l'Évangile de Matthieu et celui de Marc*, in *La Formation des Évangiles*, Paris, 1957, pp 116-151.

IV

Henri Van den Bussche

The Church in the Fourth Gospel

The fourth Gospel does not give us any precise information on the Church's canonical organization, functions or hierarchical structure. Nor does it formulate any definition of the Church or any Denzinger-Bannwart type phrase that could be used as a scriptural argument in a classical treatise on ecclesiology. Finally, it never uses the term *ekklesia* or equivalent notions or expressions found in New Testament tradition, such as people of God, the saints, the saints of the assembly (of Yahweh) or the assembly of the saints (κλητοὶ ἅγιοι), the sons of the Kingdom, the chosen, the called, Israel (the authentic Israel according to the Spirit), the Israel of God, the heirs (of the Promise of Abraham and of the testament-covenant), the heavenly Jerusalem, the body of Christ. Certainly the ecclesiological terminology of Old Testament origin as used in the New Testament is not totally absent from the fourth Gospel, but it is not immediately evident, and is used in a deliberately negative way.

There is nothing surprising then that the exegetical literature on the subject is not only sparse but also recent.[1] Actually, despite

---

1. E. Gaugler, *Die Bedeutung der Kirche in den johannesischen Schriften*, in *Internationale Kirchliche Zeitschrift* 14 (1924), pp. 97-117; pp. 181-219; 15 (1925), pp. 27-42. D. Faulhaber, *Das Johannes-Evangelium und die Kirche* (*Kirche im Aufbau* 7), Heidelberger Dissertation 1935, Kassel-Wilhelmshöhe, 1935. A. Corell, *Consummatum est. Eschatology and Church in the Gospel of St. John*, London, 1958. E. Schweizer, *Der Kirchenbegriff im Evangelium und den Briefen des Johannes*, in *Studia Evangelica* (*Texte und Untersuchungen* 73), Berlin, 1959, pp. 363-381. R. Schnackenburg, *Die Kirche im Neuen Testament*, in *Quaestiones disputatae*, 14,

the absence of an established terminology and a systematic ecclesial concern in John's Gospel, we must take the evolution of
the Johannine problematic into account. For more than a century
this problematic has focused on historical and literary question
and only in recent decades has it turned to a Johannine theology.
Yet this has been undertaken in order to study its antecedents
and its origins with the result that under the name Johannine
theology its prehistory was actually meant, and the Johannine
thought was not deeply studied for itself.[2] Let us add finally
that John's theology was correctly defined as Christology, and
that the exegetes had difficulty in tracing its chief themes and in
analyzing its central ideas.

Yet must we therefore exclude ecclesiology from the fourth
Gospel or minimize it? We think not. On the contrary, we feel
that Johannine ecclesiology — by which we understand the ecclesiology of the fourth Gospel — is rich and thought-provoking.
In accordance with good exegesis, however, we must approach
our task in a perspective that is the author's own, and not according to a preconceived system. Actually we can hardly deny
that the history of Johannine exegesis is generally presented in
regard to ecclesiology as well as the interaction of these and
antitheses. Even a quick review of the various opinions would
go beyond the scope of this article. Consequently we must limit
ourselves to indicating what the extreme positions are in order
to forge a positive and valid synthesis.

On the one hand, exegesis of the fourth Gospel stresses its
community and even ecclesial origin, its cultual *Sitz im Leben,*
its concern both for Jewish worship and Christian sacraments, and
the hieratical and liturgical literary form of the whole or of important parts of the work. Since the *parousia* is expected, eschatology seems to be realized first of all in the incarnate Word (theology of the incarnation) and then in the Church, which is governed
by the unique law of fraternal charity and which is concerned with
her mission either in the Hellenistic world or in the Jewish world.[3]

On the other hand it is claimed that this realized eschatology
is connected above all with the individual believer who has a
personal relationship with the glorified Christ through the one

thing necessary: faith in the Revealer. This faith would be a mystic and contemplative individual gnosis, inspired more by Hellenism than anything else. It is true that glorification or the Hour of the Death-Glorification dominates the whole Gospel,

---

Freiburg-Basel-Vienna (1961), pp. 93-106. A. Feuillet, *Le Temps l'Église selon saint Jean,* in *La Maison-Dieu,* no. 65, first quarter 1961 and *Études johanniques,* in *Museum Lessianum. Section biblique,* Bruges-Paris, 1962, pp. 152-174. J.-L. D'Aragon, *Le caractère distinctif de l'Église johannique,* in *L'Église dans la Bible (Studia . . . de Montréal,* 13), Bruges, 1962, pp. 53-66.

---

2. Some idea can be got of the evolution of the Johannine problematic and solutions proposed in the following publications: Ph. H. Menoud, *L'Évangile de Jean d'après les recherches récentes,* in *Cahiers théologiques de l'actualité protestante,* 3, 2nd ed., Neuchâtel-Paris, 1947; *idem, Les études johanniques de Bultmann à Barrett,* in *L'Évangile de Jean. Études et problèmes (Recherches bibliques publiées sous le patronage du Colloquium biblicum Lovaniense, III),* Bruges-Paris, 1958, pp. 11-40. W. F. Howard-C. K. Barrett, *The Fourth Gospel in Recent Criticism and Interpretation,* 4th ed., London, 1955.; X. Léon-Dufour, *Actualité du quatrième évangile,* in *Nouvelle Revue Théologique,* 1954, t. LXXXVI, pp. 449-468.; E. Haenchen, *Aus der Literatur zum Johannesevangelium, 1929-1956,* in *Theologische Rundschau,* 1955, t. XXIII, pp. 295-335.; R. Schnackenburg, *Neuere englische Literatur zum Johannes-evangelium,* in *Biblische Zeitschrift,* 1958, t. II, pp. 144-154.; J. A. T. Robinson, *The New Look on the Fourth Gospel,* in *Studia Evangelica (Texte und Untersuchungen, 73),* Berlin, 1959, pp. 338-350.; A. M. Hunter, *Recent Trends in Johannine Studies,* in *Expository Times,* 1960, t. LXXI, pp. 219-222. – On the various methods used along with the presentation of his "themageschichtliche Methode," a condensed outline will be found in the first part of S. Schulz, *Untersuchungen zur Menschensohn-Christologie im Johannes-evangelium. Zugleich ein Beitrag zur Methodengeschichte der Auslegung des 4. Evangeliums,* Göttingen, 1957.

3. Personally we are convinced, in agreement with several authors, that the Gospel is addressed to Christians whose faith the author wishes to deepen. C. H. Dodd (*The Interpretation of the Fourth Gospel,* Cambridge, 1954) thinks it is rather to a non-Christian public belonging to the varied and cosmopolitan population of a large Hellenistic city such as Ephesus. Others have looked upon the Evangelist as an apologist who is defending the Christian Messiah against the attacks of the Jews, a sort of precursor of Justin in his Dialogue with Trypho. W. Wrede follows this opinion in *Charakter und Tendenz des Johannesvangeliums,* 2nd ed., in *Sammlung*

although this culminating point is already anticipated in the incarnation. In any case the references to the last judgment and to the final resurrection should be looked upon as redactional retouches.

When all is said and done, even if agreement on the realized eschatology is reached by the exegetes, confusion still remains on certain essential points: the evaluation of the texts that express the expectation of a futuristic eschatology, the community (Church) or individualistic (i.e., the individual believer) concern of the evangelist, and finally, his Hellenistic or Jewish inspiration. This confusion is not limited to the works of different authors but is sometimes found in the same publication or in the publications of the same author. This means that we must make a few considerations of methodology, which we shall do very concisely. Its basic principle is this: all the data of the text must be respected and subsequently explained with their exact import in the context.

1. The notion of the consciousness of the Church cannot simply be deduced from qualifications which can designate a group of individuals just as well as a genuine community. Certainly these qualifications will have greater weight once it is proved from elsewhere that ecclesial consciousness is basic to the fourth Gospel. In this case they can enrich the very notion of the Church. First of all, however, we must establish that the Church is a reality in the consciouness of the evangelist. Strictly speaking, expressions such as the "believers," "born of God," or "from on high" (*Jn.* 1: 12-13; 3: 3-8; I *Jn.* 2: 29; 3: 9; 5: 1-4), "Children of God" (*Jn.* 1: 12; I *Jn.* 3: 1, 10), the plural "(to be or not to be) one of us" (I *Jn.* 2: 19-20), the assertions of the presence of the Father, Son and Holy Spirit (e.g., *Jn.* 14: 16-26), ideas such as fraternal fellowship through "union" with the Father and the Son (I *Jn.* 1: 3, 6) opposition to the world, the name "brothers" (*Jn.* 20: 17), the law of brotherly love — all of these things do not bring us necessarily further than a group of individuals who have the same convictions or live a common lot.[4] If we may not start (as we shall soon see) with a minimal definition of the Church, we must nevertheless begin from texts which imply some-

thing other than a group of believers. The believers do not constitute the Church, but God makes the believers into the Church.
How, under what conditions, and with what consequences? Perhaps the evangelist will tell us.

---

gemeinvreständlicher Vorträge 37, Tübingen, 1933 (1st ed., 1903), p. 66.
The same opinion has been defended by W. Heitmüller, *Die Schriften des
Neuen Testaments neu übersetzt und für die Gegenwart erklärt*, Göttingen,
1920, p. 16, by A. Jülicher--E. Fascher, *Einleitung in das Neue Testament*,
Tübingen, 1931, p. 418. K. Bornhauser, *Das Johannesvangelium eine Mis-
sionsschrift für Israel*, Gütersloh, 1928, goes still further: he claims that
the Gospel of John was destined to convert the Jews. His arguments are
unconvincing, but two recent publications have furnished other arguments
to bolster and specify the thesis: W. C. van Unnik (*The Purpose of St.
John's Gospel* in *Studia Evangelica*, pp. 382-411, reprinted in *The Gospels
Reconsidered. A Selection of Papers read at the Conference on the Four
Gospels at Oxford 1957*, Oxford, 1960, pp. 167-196) thinks that the Gospel
of John was written to convince the Jews of the diaspora that Jesus was the
Messiah; and J. A. T. Robinson (*The Destination and Purpose of St. John's
Gospel*, in *New Testament Studies*, VI, Cambridge, 1959-60, pp. 117-131)
believes that the Gospel is addressed to Jews outside of Palestine. L. Van
Hartingsveld (*Die Eschatologie des Johannes-evangeliums. Eine Auseinan-
dersetzung mit Rudolf Bultmann*, Assen, 1962, p. 3) shares the opinion of
these two authors. Still there is a great deal of truth in the phrase that
Robinson, p. 117, n. 2 quotes from C. K. Barrett, *The Gospel According to
St. John*, London, 1955, p. 115: "It is easy, when we read the Gospel, to
believe that John, though doubtless aware of the necessity of strengthening
Christians and converting the heathen, wrote primarily to satisfy himself.
His gospel must be written: it was no concern of his whether it was also
read." The fourth Gospel, as we have written elsewhere (*Het vierde
Evangelie*, t. I, Tielt-The Hague, pp. 56-57) certainly answers a need of
the Evangelist to convince himself that as a convert he is not a renegade
but that in giving himself to Christ he found the perfect realization of his
Jewish religious aspirations. This does not prevent his Gospel from being
presented as a witness and from being addressed to readers (*Jn.* 20: 30-31).
It certainly seems that these readers must be sought in the immediate
entourage of the Evangelist, in the Christian community to which he
belonged, over which he probably presided, and where the pagan or
Jewish origin is no longer of any importance.

---

4. This is, for example, the departure point of the article cited of
R. Schnackenburg.

2. However convinced we may be that the Gospel, the Epistles and the Book of Revelation are all by the same author, it is preferable not to take all the elements coming from the same author as if they were from the same culture medium. For, depending on circumstances, the author could be brought to reflect on the spiritual realities of his faith simply as a Christian, or establish his authority with one or several Churches, either as a witness to the faith or as a prophet, or finally as a parenetic preacher and disciplinary leader. In accordance with the views at the basic of each of the writings, the data coming from them will be colored by them and we ought not to overlook these shades of meaning by mixing the texts of distinct writings. As for the Gospel of John, we shall have to take precise account of its own perspective and its own structure.

3. Nor may we define Johannine ecclesiology in terms of an evolution that might seem to be normal following the synoptic and Pauline traditions. In the very heart of these two traditions the evolution is already complex enough. But above all we must not postulate a Johannine Church that would complete the previous evolution.[5]

4. A minimal definition of the Church that includes everything that is considered essential to the Church serves as a starting point for the examination of Johannine ecclesiology.[6] Everyone is drawn to make such a definition from his own knowledge, without saying, however, that this definition is actually present in the fourth Gospel. Verification easily follows: everything essential to the Church and even more is to be found in the Gospel. Yet for there to be a Johannine ecclesiology it is not necessary that the author of the Gospel mention all the elements, nor even those which are essential in his eyes. His Gospel is not of necessity an ecclesiological treatise. It is sufficient that he clearly stresses even only one element of his message that cannot be understood outside of a genuine ecclesial consciousness. As for other ecclesiological elements that we might hope to find here, the author had

full freedom to note them in passing, merely to hint at them or even to pass over them in silence. In addition John's ecclesial concern does not necessarily imply that it extends to the ministry, the confession of faith, the functions (e.g., of apostle or deacon), or to the worship and liturgy of the Christian Church.[7]

5. Similarly the evangelist's concern with certain aspects of the Jewish liturgy does not necessarily imply a transition to Christian worship. Certainly the evangelist remembers Judaism as an antithesis, but is it so obvious that the second element of the antithesis is the Church? On the contrary, it is very typical in John that all things are measured against Jesus, who for that reason is always the chief element of comparison. If the evangelist looks upon Jesus as present in the Church, the texts themselves must prove it. Just as it is the context that must prove to us the allusion to the ministries in the Church, rather than the material use of terms such as ἀπόστολοι, ἀποστέλλειν, πέμπειν, διακονεῖν, διάκονος.

Upon examination it seems to us that the ecclesiological data of the fourth Gospel are best explained in three stages, not because a classical paper might have three different sections, but because John's thought seems to take three different directions.

First of all, it is strongly rooted in the memory of the past: the Church replaces Israel. Then it contemplates the present: the Church is the presence of Jesus. Finally, it remains drawn toward the eschatological future: the Church of Christ present lives always in the expectation of the *parousia*.[8]

---

5. E. Schweizer (art. cit.) speaks in an already very brief summary of the primitive community, of Paul, of the Gospel of John, of the Johannine epistles.

6. Cf. A. Corell, *op. cit.*, pp. 3-5.

7. Cf. A. Corell, *op. cit.*, pp. 33-53.

8. A. Feuillet (*op. cit.*, pp. 152-155) was right in approaching the Johannine Church by situating it in salvation history. The title, *Le temps de l'Église selon saint Jean* is well chosen.

1. *The Church replaces Israel.*

A. Corell [9] claims that if the fourth Gospel does not contain an elaborated ecclesiology, it is due to the fact that for the evangelist and the Christians of his time the Church was an incontested reality that posed no problem. It is true that the fact of the Church posed no problem, nor did the assertion of faith that the Church to which the author belongs, i.e., the Christian Church, is the one authentic Church, founded by God. But beneath this assertion of faith, which is beyond doubt, there lies hidden a painful problem. The author has perfectly resolved it through faith, but its psychological lesions do not seem to be healed since they continue to urge the author to theological reflection. The author was not the first one to pose this problem, since is *the* problem, σκάνδαλον, of the whole primitive Church of Jewish background. How can it be explained that Israel, the religious and national community, did not in great majority make the transition into the Church of Christ? Without any doubt the Church is Israel's successor, and makes its vocation a reality. But it does so by transcending it (πληροῦν) and this transcendence is the result of a divine judgment (κρίσις). Depending upon whether the stress is on the "realization" or the "transcendence," Israel's transformance into the Chrisitan Church is considered in the New Testament in a twofold perspective. In the first this realization is a superlative one in regard to the provisional regime of Israel, the continuity between the two regimes is emphasized and the hope of Israel's conversion is not completely abandoned. In the second the realization comes about through a radical break with the past and by a completely new creation of a regime that surpasses the preceding one just as reality surpasses hope or shadow. The two perspectives are found side by side in the New Testament and at times are even intertwined since they differ only in the emphasis given to the break. Still let us point out that the break itself is also a kind of continuity, of bond. Actually the two regimes come from the same plan of God which remains in the second stage, or more exactly becomes realized there in an eschatological way.

The divine judgment (κρίσις) furthermore radically discriminates among the pagans.[10]

John stresses the break with Judaism and the new realized fulfillment of God's plan which is eschatological and definitive. There is no hope any more for those whom he calls "the Jews" —

---

9. A. Corell, *op. cit.*, p. 12.

10. The publications already mentioned of W. C. van Unnik and J. A. T. Robinson please us by their concern shown for the Old Testament inspiration of the fourth Gospel, but they do not at all convince us of the intention of the Evangelist to convert the Jews of the Greek diaspora. A detailed discussion of the argumentation would require a special study, but we must nevertheless point out here the major objections. First of all the authors reason from a postulate: the Gospel would be destined to convert, it would be "Missionsschrift." Nevertheless it is not proved from reading the Gospel that its author wishes to be a Jew among the Jews. There is nothing against his expressing his Christian conviction in a Jewish schema, without desiring to polemicize or proselytize. Must the Gospel be interpreted from the readers' point of view or from the author's? Must it be admitted that the Evangelist has perfectly adapted himself to the understanding of his readers? John seems to be expressing a personal meditation rather than attempting a controversy with those who contradict him. The Jews moreover are condemned in such an absolute and general fashion that it would be difficult to suppose that a partial conversion, i.e., of the Jews of the diaspora, is aimed at. Certainly the Evangelist is judging only the Jews of Palestine who were responsible for Jesus' death, but this is one further reason for not setting their condemnation at the time of the Gospel's composition. The Jews of the Gospel are contemporaries of Jesus and it is because they had the opportunity of seeing Jesus and denied him that John definitively rejects them as candidates for the faith. From the death of Jesus Judaism has belonged to the past. The judgment of the Jews is definitive and eschatological, with the result that the Jews at the end of the first century belong either to the world or to the Church. When Robinson writes (*art. cit.*, p. 119): "If Judaism is condemned, it is always from within and not from without," he is right in the sense that Judaism is condemned by someone who in the past, more than fifty years before, had belonged to that religion. At the time of the composition of his Gospel, the author no longer makes a distinction among Jews, Christians and pagans, but between believers and "the world." If there is dialogue and controversy in his Gospel, it is with the Jew that he was once himself. The confrontation is situated at the time of Jesus' manifestation. The authors mentioned are wrong in interpreting John in the light of Paul, who was

between the two (κρίμα 9: 39). The first recipients, ethnic Israel, the Israel which is necessarily to remain the Israel according to the flesh, is degraded in Judaism. It has missed its vocation and God has made a new creation in founding a new people of God a name practically implying a denial to them of the inherent value in the name "Israel." For John, although Israel never was the chosen people in the real sense of the term, i.e., eschatologically, it was nevertheless the prime candidate for that dignity. At the moment of eschatological election, few candidates came forward. At the end of chapter 6, John clearly gives the impression that the number of candidates chosen practically boils down to the Twelve (*Jn.* 6: 67-71). By this very fact, the *Israelitica dignitas* is lost for "the Jews," lost for that Israel that denied itself by denying Christ.

The divine judgment serves as a wailing wall against which the evangelist expresses his disillusionment with the renegades, but it also serves to encompass definitively the zone of incredulity and darkness, a ghetto of damnation without hope. The Johannine Church is the only true Church, not so much because it should be preferred to other churches (which in John's eyes would never merit the name Church), but rather because it replaces, by surpassing it through its eschatological character, what was thought to have been the people of God and which has lamentably proved itself to be the sons of the devil (*Jn.* 8: 37-38, 44-47). The attack John makes against this false Israel, "the Jews," shows that he continues to think in "chosen people" categories. Even if the antithesis only directly contrasts Israel with Jesus, it also implies from time to time the antithesis Israel-Church, since, for example, Jesus could not be the Shepherd if he did not have sheep.

But let us look at the texts systematically. Nathanael, the authentic and guileless Israelite, by that very reason is prepared to accept Jesus, and once his contact with Jesus is a reality he gives himself to him. From a candidate he becomes a member of the eschatological people of God: one day he will see the "greater" events, i.e., the eschatological ones (*Jn.* 1: 47-51; cf. 5: 20; 14: 12). All of the vital importance about which Israel had boasted was merely a preparation for the total eschatological import that was realized by God in Jesus. If before we spoke of the word of God or his light or the life that he gives, now since the coming of Jesus it is he who is the Word, the Light and the Life fully and exclusively (*Jn.* 1: 1-18). In the transition from shadow to reality, John (the Baptist) was present to point it out to Israel (1: 31). Israel then actually was the first candidate. Nicodemus (ch. 3) comes before the Samaritan woman and the royal official.[11] The Jew, if he had remained a true Israelite, ought to have known God better than any pre-Christian non-Jew. By this very fact he ought to have been able to render to God a worship that better befitted him, since salvation was to have come from the Jews (*Jn.* 4: 22). But even this "teacher of Israel" (*Jn.* 3: 10) defends himself against a re-birth from on high, against the fundamental break that the coming of the Kingdom of God was to have meant for the history of salvation. The Jew is no longer even a candidate because he has become stationary in his candidature, since he thinks he has already arrived. Moreover the Nicodemus chapter ends on a determinate judgment: "the anger of God (ἡ ὀργή) stays (μένει) on him" (3, 36), a judgment which anticipates the conclusion of chapter 9: "your guilt remains (μένει)" (9: 41).

This word μένειν looks both to the past and to the future. By

---

engaged in a real dispute almost half a century before. By what right is the quarrel with the Judaizers prolonged? There is another thing that we must point out: the authors reduce John's theme to qualifying Jesus as the Messiah and do not take sufficiently into account the titles Son of Man, Son of God, Son. Furthermore they singularly limit their argumentation to the conclusion of the Gospel (*Jn.* 20: 30-31) without taking the structure of the whole Gospel into account, and chapter 5 to 10 in particular, where precisely the accusation against Judaism is made. If a door remained open for the diaspora of the Hellenistic world, the Evangelist would have had to restrict his indictment. In the context the "Greeks" or the "diaspora" cannot be exceptional or late-coming Jews, but the first fruits of the Church of the nation (cf. J. Jeremias, *Jesu Verheissung für die Völker*, 2nd ed., Stuttgart, 1959, pp. 32 and 55).

---

11. The opposition of the enthusiasm of his compatriots (*Jn.* 4: 44) to the simple and sincere faith of the official, suggests that he is not a fellow-countryman of Jesus, but a pagan. Moreover he follows the Jewish prototype Nicodemus and the Samaritan woman who represents heresy.

refusing to accept Jesus, the Jews brought definitive condemnation on themselves, which at the very moment of their rejection implies a judgment on the whole past of Israel. For if Israel, called as it was to become the chosen people, has degenerated into Judaism, this means that the Israelite vocation had never captured the deep conviction and life of ethnic Israel. Since for centuries it was the first candidate for the Light and was prepared to receive it like no other nation, its first chance is also its last. This is why the stage of Revelation, which the Gospel of John calls the stage of Light or the Day of Jesus (his public life among the Jews), is charged with eschatological significance for the Jews: for them the Light has the meaning of eternal life or eternal condemnation. For as long as the Light shines, as long as the Day of Jesus lasts, Judaism can reevaluate its *Israelitica dignitas* and become the eschatological chosen people, although the evangelist as a good observer suggests from the very beginning and more than once that this last chance too will be lost. Little by little the self-styled chosen people is degenerating into the "world," becoming the epicenter of a world opposed to God. Once the Light disappears, the "world" falls into darkness and the believers can contemplate the Glory. We could not believe that it is only accidental that the texts speak of the Light only during the public life, and from the moment of the Hour of Death the Glory is revealed to the whole world.

If Israel becomes the "world," the whole world falls heir to Israel's lost vocation. Just as the evangelist likes to anticipate the events of the Death-Glorification of Jesus — which is precisely the judgment against the unbelieving Jews and the call to the Gentiles — so also he does not miss an opportunity to tell us from the beginning that the candidates with real chances are not so much the Jews but the Gentiles. The person whom the Jews will help to become the figure of the Servant-Lamb of God will take away the sin of the *world* (1: 29). God so loved the *world* that he gave his only son that *every man* who believes in him might have eternal life. It is not those who put the Son of Man upon a cross who will be saved but those who look upon him (3: 14-16; cf. 19: 37). The disciples may well wonder at the conversation with the Samaritan woman and think that four months are still necessary before the coming of the harvest, but the eschatological harvest is at its high point (4: 36) and if it is more or less disappointing in the land of Israel, it is rich in Samaria and the whole world (4: 42), because of the suffering of Jesus in his death (4: 38). If the *non*-Jews acknowledge him as the *Savior of the world* (4: 42), then surely the Jews can receive him, but Jesus knows only too well that a prophet is without honor in his own country (4: 44).

It is especially in chapters 5-10 that Jesus the Son of Man puts the Jews on trial eschatologically, as we have shown elsewhere.[12] Although, because of the Father's commission, Jesus is to remain Light for the Jews as long as his day lasts, he asserts his function as Son of Man and lays the groundwork for the last judgment (5: 29-30). For every trial witnesses are needed. Brought before this tribunal, the witnesses in Jesus' favor are witnesses who make a charge against the Jews. They are John the Baptist (5: 33-35), God himself who accomplishes his work through Jesus (5: 32, 36), and finally the God of the Old Testament. Since Sinai, he has revealed himself through theophanies and his essential testimony can be found in scrutinizing the Scriptures (5: 37-47). But all of God's teaching to the Jews from Sinai up to now has been unsuccessful with them. As a body the witnesses in Jesus' favor make a change against Israel and the Jews' own advocate, Moses, becomes their accuser (5: 45-47). The sign of the loaves brings us back to the desert, and the whole climate seems to invite us to believe that a stage of the new Exodus has been inaugurated. But the setting of a messianic community in the desert serves only to emphasize all the more the break between the Jewish messianic community and the eschatological community that Jesus soon will save, that is when he assumes his role as Son of Man. It is high time that we

---

12. *Het vierde Evangelie.* II. *Het Boek der Werken,* 2nd ed., Tielt-The Hague, 1960, esp. pp. 35-66. Without being in full agreement with his method and his conclusions we must mention the second part of the book already cited of S. Schulz, esp. pp. 96-123.

stop thinking of the signs of old. Now we see the works (ἔργα) of the judiciary activity of the Son of Man for he is already marked with the sign of the Father (6: 28) because of his function. This is why we should no longer work for a perishable food that allows those who eat it to perish. Rather we must prepare ourselves for the moment when the Son of Man will give a food that endures and makes us endure "to eternal life" (6: 26-27). The illusion of a heavenly bread is no more, because the one thing that can be called heavenly is he who comes down from heaven on the clouds as the Son of Man, and who consequently can give eternal life (6: 33). This is not far off since we are approaching the death of the one who through his death will assume his function as Son of Man (6: 51). At that time positions will become definitively fixed; the Jews who will not believe (6: 36) will be condemned, while those who believe will not be cast out (6: 37). However we understand "all that the Father gives" (6: 37), "power over all flesh" (17: 2a), or the "gift" of those who are willing to believe (17: 2b-6; 10: 28; 6: 65), those who believe owe their belief to a gift of the Father who at the precise moment makes the eschatological choice (cf. 6: 44: ἕλκειν: draw in the net) which is to be effected by the Son of Man. This choice is not an arbitrary predestination either to grace or glory. God's choice is based on Israel's past and on the history of salvation. Actually, if the Jews do not come to believe it is because even in the past they did not take the Old Testament revelation seriously. Whoever was willing in the past to listen to the Father and to be instructed by him comes to Jesus who shows him the eschatological teaching foretold by the prophets: "They will all be taught by God" (6: 45; cf. I *Th.* 4, 9). The almost total defection at the chapter's conclusion shows that the Jews in question were never open to the faith, and obviously were unable to adapt themselves to Jesus' words (6: 64-65). John wants to be as clear as possible about the Jews' situation: only Twelve are to be promoted to election, and the Evangelist does not hesitate even to question the number twelve itself by eliminating Judas who is of their number but does not belong to the Twelve by the same election (6: 67-71).

The twelve tribes of Israel have been greatly decimated. Even in the context of the Feast of Tabernacles — a liturgical cycle commemorating the formation of the people of God in the desert — Jesus denies one chief privilege of Israel after another. It is no longer their writings that merit the name divine teaching but Jesus himself (7: 14-18). Neither the water that gushed forth from the rock in the desert nor the other waters which were symbols of divine protection in the Old Testament up to the time of the Feast of Tents, can be compared to the rivers of living water that will gush forth from the dying Jesus' body (7: 37-39; cf. 19: 33-37). Instead of joyfully welcoming the day of Jesus as Abraham had desired, they reject the Light with the result that Yahweh, the I-Am of Israel and the very basis of its existence, who is actually present in Jesus' person, has left them behind forever (8: 28-29; 8: 58). Thus everything that had made Israel a privileged people — Yahweh's protective presence in the midst of his people, the teaching and the light that he furnished them, and the water of life he gave them, all of which had become incarnate eschatologically in the person of Jesus — is offered to them as their greatest but also their last chance. Yet, by refusing Jesus, they lose it all forever.

At the same time, the author does not fail to suggest from time to time that these eschatological privileges will be transferred to the *diaspora* of the Gentiles (8: 35) as a result of Jesus' voluntary death (8: 21-22: 28-29: 36). In the fourth Gospel every mission outside of Israel draws its vitality from Jesus' death. It is by his death that he will become the Light *of the world* (8: 12; 9: 5). Those who are willing to acknowledge their need for the Light will receive it (9: 41).

At the end of this lengthy diatribe against the Jews there is found the basic character of God's new flock, the allegory of the sheep-fold, of the gate and of the good (true) shepherd (*Jn.* 10). We belong to God's flock only if we enter through the unique gate, Jesus, only if we acknowledge Jesus as the true Shepherd who has known (i.e., who chose beforehand) his own sheep and gave his life for them (cf. 15: 13-16). For it is by his death that Jesus founds the new flock of the Father and gives it the mission and the strength to go out and recruit all nations without distinction (10: 7-16). One flock, one shepherd: the unity of the flock is guaranteed by the presence of a unique and true shepherd. This is a presence that is more real, more close, more penetrating than Yahweh's presence previously in the midst of his people ever was; in the Old Testament prophecy, Yahweh had said that he was going to re-assume his care over his flock; now Yahweh is humanly present in the Person of Jesus. It is a presence on which believers live, just as Jesus lives continually on the presence of the Father. It is an effective presence assuring the safety and the life of the flock (10: 9-10), and a dynamic presence for the Shepherd gives his life so that his sheep who do not belong to Israel may be brought to the Father's fold (10: 15-16). All those before Jesus who wanted to play at being the shepherd (i.e., to govern in any way) were thieves and pilferers. Jesus, on the other hand, has come only for life, a life in abundance, an eternal life (10: 10-28). The Shepherd and his Father, who are one (10: 30), will do everything so that no one can be snatched from their hands (10: 27-29).

After Jesus set out on his way toward death, two sentences uttered by the Jews ought to help us grasp the ecclesiological import of this death. First the unwitting prophecy of Caiaphas, explicitated by the Evangelist: Jesus' death will be a death for (*huper*) the nation and its purpose will also be to unite the dispersed children of God, i.e., the Gentiles (11: 49-52). Then the Pharisees, holding war counsel, state that everybody is flocking to him (11: 29). The import of this phrase is illustrated by the account of the arrival of the "Greeks," the first fruits of the Church of the Gentiles. They are the fruit which will grow plentifully from the grain of wheat fallen onto the ground which is Jesus. They ask to see Jesus, but there is no need for them to see the Light. They will soon contemplate his Glory (12: 19-24). Thus, the Day of Jesus is reaching its term. It is now, in his death, the judgment is brought definitively against the unbelieving world, in the center of which are found the Jews and their father, Satan. They think that they can extinguish the Light, but it shall shine in glory in order to attract all men to itself with eschatological force (12: 31-32). Many years before the prophet Isaiah was able to assert that every anticipation of glory blinded the Jews (12: 40-41).

To sum up, Israel is the first candidate for the eschatological light of Jesus. They had long been prepared for it. Their expected refusal shows that the age-long teaching of God which they had received has remained useless. Their condemnation will be crystallized in Jesus' murder. On the other hand, the pagans will see the eschatological light in all its brightness under the form of Glory. Jesus' death will give missionary vitality to the new flock which it has just formed.[13]

2. *The Church and Jesus' Presence.*

On Passover eve a page was turned. Jesus addresses himself to "his own" (13: 1). There is no doubt that there is no identification with the "own" of the prologue (1: 11). Here we are dealing with the same "elect" as at the end of chapter 4. The persons (the Twelve with special mention of Judas and Peter) are the same, as are the situation (defection, betrayal) and the surroundings (eucharistic discourse, the Supper). In speaking to the Twelve, the kernel of the new people of God, Jesus is addressing the Church. No distinction is made between their state of being believers and any particular function they may have; their circle is not closed. It is quite the contrary, and no time limit is envisioned. We must not think that his own are only his circle of friends. Certainly he loved them from the beginning (13: 1), but they are chosen and established in friendship only

---

13. The question of Johannine anti-semitism is evidently a false problem. John does not hate the Jewish people: on the contrary, he loves them, disillusioned as he is because Israel has not come to Christ. He does not attack the empirical people, but he denies the divine privileges of the "race of Abraham," of the self-styled chosen people, E. Grässer, *Die antijüdische Polemik im Johannesevangelium*, in *New Testament Studies*, 1964, t. XI, pp. 74-90, was wrong in not situating his study within the perspective of salvation history.

through an act (6: 70; 13: 18; 15: 16) which seems indeed to
be closely connected with Jesus' death (13: 13; 15: 13). Furthermore this is confirmed by what we have said above about Jesus'
death being a condemnation of Judaism, as the foundation of the
Church, and as the power of recruiting among the pagan world.
Everything therefore leads us to believe that the farewell discources
are ecclesial.

Before treating them, let us go back a bit. If we are to connect
"his own" of chapter 13: 1 with the Twelve at the end of chapter
4, then the denial of the privileges of the Jews (ch. 7-10) can
already be an indication for us of the privilege of a Christian in
the Church. *A priori* every Christian privilege must be some type
of presence of Christ since Jesus contrasted himself as a person
to every Jewish privilege. Furthermore, what formed the people
of Israel was Yahweh's protective presence, and consequently
we may likewise expect that the Church was basically constituted
by a presence of Jesus. Finally, the privileges mentioned all boil
down to one form or another of divine presence shaping a community. To the doctrine of the Jews (7: 16), which in the last
analysis was to go back to the teaching of the theophanies and
the prophets, Jesus contrasts his teaching; it does not come from
himself, but without intermediary from his Father (6: 45). In Jesus
God speaks directly to the person who wishes to believe. For the
symbolism of the water, signifying the protective presence of
Yahweh in Israel, and the symbolism of the temple whence flow
the waters in the Old Testament prophecy and the Jewish liturgy,
Jesus substitutes himself (7: 37-38) as the new temple. It is
from his body (death) that the living waters will flow. Let us recall that in John the identification of Jesus with the temple of
divine presence is frequent (1: 14: ἐσκήνωσεν; 2: 21-22; 4: 20-
26). Let us also note that this new divine presence is realized in
the Death-Glorification of Jesus (7: 39; 2: 17, 22; 4: 21, 23).
The Old Testament light is replaced by Jesus the Light (8: 12)
who at his death will become Jesus-Glory. Finally, the name
I-Am which in the Old Testament expressed all of Israel's trust
in God's protective presence is transferred by Jesus to himself,

and he adds that it is at the instant of his being raised upon the cross and to glory that its import can be grasped (8: 28).

This brief glimpse is enough to show that what is important for John is precisely Jesus and Jesus as a person. It is he who renders Israel's privileges superfluous, and he too who will shape Christian existence in the new flock of God. The Church of God's children (1: 12-13) becomes a reality to the extent that the divine self-revelation becomes a real presence among men, dwells among them and allows them to see his glory and the fullness of his condescendence which has become a perfect reality (1: 14).

We are tempted to restrict this presence to the moment of the Incarnation. But verse 14 of the prologue discloses a broader view; it englobes the entire coming of Jesus. For there are different "comings." The hour is coming and it has come (4: 23); the time has come insofar as Jesus has come, but it is still to come since the presence of Jesus remains veiled during his public life. The true coming, the total coming, happens at the moment of his departure, when the Glory of God is manifested in his Death, at the moment of his Hour. The divine Spirit remains upon him during his earthly life (1: 32-33) and yet the Spirit (which will be communicated to the faithful) is not yet present as long as Jesus is not glorified (7: 39). The ancient temple of the divine presence in Israel disappears with Jesus' death (2: 17) and the new temple will be the resurrected body of Jesus (2: 21-23). The true worship supposes the revelation and the presence of God, accomplished by ($\dot{\alpha}\lambda\dot{\eta}\Theta\epsilon\iota\alpha$) and contained within the Spirit, with the result that the worshipper can reach God as he is, namely as the Father (4: 23-24). Jesus communicates God's teaching (6: 45; 7: 16), but this teaching does not sink in (7: 28; 8: 19) until the divine presence becomes a reality at the moment of the "lifting up" of the Son of Man (8: 28). For if at this moment he seems totally alone, in reality his Father is with him more than ever (8: 29; 16: 33). The heavenly food is Jesus himself, but he will give himself as food only when the Son of Man acts (6: 27), when he will have given his flesh (= himself) for the life of the world (in his death, 6: 51), when the flesh and blood of the

Son of Man will be eaten and drunk in the Eucharist, the permanent memorial of the dying Lord (6: 53-58). The luminous presence of God in Jesus remains as long as his Day lasts, but for the time being it is veiled and limited to Israel. Once night falls (11: 9; 12: 35-36; 13: 30), the Glory of God will shine in him for the whole world (13: 31).

This presence of Jesus creates a spiritual space. On Passover eve it is only the Twelve, the same ones (6: 67-71) who received the eucharistic instruction (6: 53-58). Jesus addresses this farewell discourse to them, but not to them alone. The eve of Passover and the Hour will last throughout the time of the Church. The washing of the feet is the introductory sign of the assembling of the Church: first it is the symbol of Jesus' "charity" on the cross which founds this Church, and then the fundamental character for the conduct of the members of the Church. Besides insisting on this law of charity, the first discourse seems exclusively preoccupied with making those who remain in the world (13: 1) understand that Jesus is not taking away his presence by leaving. His own might think that their lot is no different from that of the Jews and Jesus confirms this, but adds *arti,* for a while (13: 33), which is not the case for the Jews who will never arrive at where Jesus is going (cf. 13: 36-37). While waiting for him to return to fetch them, the believers are not left orphans (14: 18); another Paraclete, the Spirit, will come (14: 15), Jesus himself will return (14: 19-20: 28) with his Father (14: 22-25) in order to abide in the believer. At this moment all he offers them is the promise that he will see them again soon (14: 29; cf. 16: 16), the promise of a presence which begins through the resurrection and includes the Spirit, Jesus and the Father.

The second farewell discourse is still more ecclesial because it is more positive. He does not treat so much of his non-absence as of the communion of life (15: 1-10), and of friendship (15: 11-17) in contrast to the world's hatred (15: 18-16: 4), and of the mission (to bear much fruit, to witness). It is introduced by the allegory of the true vine, which like the allegory of the true shepherd clearly sets it off from the hybrid vine that Israel was. All this must be read in the context of the Eucharist where the community again finds itself in the presence of its Lord, communicates with him, to renew the bonds of friendship, which are not the result of the chance of a prolonged encounter, but the result of a selection and an institution that depends uniquely on Jesus (15: 16). The prolonged stress on the inevitable hatred of the world (15: 15-16: 4) re-enforces the idea of community and even of communion with Christ, since it is because it bears his name that it will be persecuted.

The third discourse, the priestly prayer (ch. 17) is a truly ecclesial hymn. Jesus prays for those whom the Father gave him (17: 2) and whom he has taken from the world (17: 6). They belonged to the Father who gave them to him with the result that they became "his own" through a special divine act (17: 2, 6, 9-10). Like Jesus, they bear the name of the Father (17, 11-12), they are committed to the person of the Father who dwells in the person of Jesus. They are no longer of this world (17: 16). Finally the Lord prays also for those who over the centuries will receive the divine word, Jesus, in the word of the Church, so that all generations will be in immediate union with Jesus and the Father (v. 21: that they may be one in us as you are one in me and I am in you), that this unity will engender the unity of the believers among themselves (vv. 21-22: that they may be one) and that all will be integrated in perfect unity: Father-Son-Faithful. The prayer ends (17: 24-26) with a proclamation that seems to be a last judgment proclamation in order that all doubt about the Church's continuance to the last day may be excluded.

The data of the farewell discourse bring us right back into this spiritual space created by the presence of Jesus who knows no boundaries or limits of time.

This awareness of a real and active presence that surpasses time is related by John to the appearances of the Risen Christ. He recounts three of these precisely to illustrate the characteristics we have just mentioned in determining the presence of Jesus. It is of no use to see simply an external presence in an appearance. It must be understood in accordance with the Scriptures under the influence of the Spirit (20: 1-9; cf. 14: 17-21).

Mary Magdalene thought she had gone through a curious

nightmare that was dispelled with Jesus' return. But Jesus did not "return." He comes now in his true dimension. She must not try to keep him in a human context which he has now left behind. He must go to his Father who from that moment is also their Father, to God who from this instant is truly their God. The Old Testament dream of God-with-us is realized in an unexpected way. Jesus' return to the Father is therefore his real coming. He was never so close to them as now that he has the intention of leaving them. Now he is there with his Father who from now on is also their Father, and he therefore has reason to call them brothers. The divine presence is perfect (20: 17-18).

The second appearance illustrates the efficaciousness of the presence. Jesus breathes the Spirit on them so that as mere humans they become *spiritual,* born of the Spirit of God (3: 5-8; cf. 1: 12-13; 4: 24) and bearers of this Spirit for the world's renewal (cf. 14: 12).

The third appearance, the one to Thomas, is concerned less with Thomas than with those who will believe without seeing (20: 29). It illustrates the continuousness of Jesus' presence. Whatever generation he belongs to, the believer will be in immediate contact with the Savior, and no less so than those of the first hour, who saw him with their own eyes (cf. 17: 20-21). Jesus' presence will last till the end of time without lessening either in reality or in intensity.

There are no limitations in time or boundaries in space. It is useless to repeat the texts already amply cited. The believer, from the Twelve on down to the simple believer of all ages, if he wishes to be a "disciple" must "bear much fruit" (15: 8). The formula is always applied in the fourth Gospel to missionary effort and not to the individual moral life. As we recall, John always connects the missionary duty with Jesus' death, which gives vitality and success to the Church's missionary work. It is the Lamb of God who takes away the sins of the world (1: 29), it is the anguish of Jesus' death that accelerates the eschatological harvest (4: 37-38). The Jews do not know the whole truth of what they are saying when in answer to Jesus' words about "going away" they wonder whether he intends to go abroad into the *diaspora* to instruct them (7: 35). Nor does Caiaphas when he proclaims that only one man is to die for the people; John does not hesitate to explain this: Jesus was to die for the nation, and not only for the nation but also in order to reunite the dispersed children of God, i.e., the Gentiles (11: 49-52). Does the Shepherd not give his life for his sheep which were not only to be sought in Israel (10, 16)? Like a grain of wheat in the earth, he dies in order to bring forth much fruit, and the Greeks will be the first fruits (12: 19-24). Like the branches of the vine, the disciples in their turn are to bring forth much fruit, for in giving them the most perfect proof of his friendship, Jesus as a consequence of this friendship has destined them to go forth and bear fruit (15: 14-16). Only with difficulty can we avoid comparing the Twelve of Passover eve with the 144,000 from the tribes of Israel and the uncountable multitude coming from all nations that the Book of Revelation speaks of in chapter 7.

3. *The Church and Jesus' Return.*

No one will dispute the eschatological character of the fourth Gospel, but everything depends on what is understood by eschatological.[14] At this point we need not review all the texts. It is enough to point out the stages in Johannine eschatology.[15] For although every coming of Jesus is eschatological, it is not always destined for the same public nor does it manifest the same intensity. John knows these distinctions as well as the other New Testament writers.

Jesus' first coming during his public life is practically limited to the Jews. For them it is eschatological in the sense that it is the final minute before the definitive judgment. Prepared through an age-old teaching, they had to decide for or against Jesus. De-

---

14. For literature on this subject see L. Van Hartingsveld, *op. cit.*, which contains a good deal of material, but is lacking in order and exegetical logic.

15. A. Feuillet, *art. cit.*, pp. 152-154, underlines the importance of the perspective of stages.

pending upon what choice they made, they will be admitted into the chosen people or definitively condemned. The judgment which depends on their present reaction is retroactive in the sense that it implies a judgment on Israel's entire past. The person who has kept to his role of true Israelite, his vocation, is entrusted to Jesus by the Father, comes to Jesus and is saved (6: 37; 10: 29; 17: 2-19). John judges from the result: the Christian of Jewish origin seems to have been a true Israelite, just as the Christian who becomes unfaithful to Jesus proves that he never was a true Christian (I *Jn.* 2: 19-20). The divine judgment, after all, is manifested in history. Jesus did not come to pass judgment but to offer the whole world the certainty of salvation. Yet the fact that the majority of the first ones to whom his message was destined answered with a refusal gives Jesus' saving coming the character of judgment (3: 17-21, 36; 5-10). The author as a Christian prophet interprets the sense of history. The thought process here is not novel to the New Testament, but it is further extended (cf. I *Th.* 2: 15; *Mt.* 5: 12; 23: 30-39). Not to have understood the view of the past in 6: 37-40 results in a false way of interpreting it in the sole perspective of the future. The Father gives a particular person to Jesus, he comes to him and will be saved. The modern quarrel over predestination either to grace or glory neglects the background of salvation history. Those whom the Father gives belong to the Jewish people, and God gives them according to whether they are Israelites worthy of entering the Kingdom or not. Once he has come to Jesus the particular believer is sure of salvation at least as far as God's plan is concerned. God's own faithfulness is so strongly supposed or asserted that it resembles an automatic succession of events such as we find in Romans 8: 29-30. In like texts the sacred authors do not refer to man's instability but rather uniquely underline the stability and faithfulness of God.

The eschatology of Jesus' first coming is limited to the Jews and concerns their admission into the eschatological people of God, their participation in the Kingdom (3: 3, 5). The transferral comes about through a trial: Jesus must be acknowledged as the one sent from God, the Son of Man. Since the Jewish people had been prepared for this choice, their eventual refusal will be without appeal once Jesus is put to death. From this moment there will no longer be Jew or pagan, there will only be people who want to see and those who do not (9: 39-41): the believers and "the world." Once the Jews as a body renounced Jesus to the point of putting him to death, they became the first kernel of a world of darkness, and in the regime that will follow, the regime of the Church, it is Jesus' death that will be the touchstone in judging whether a person is a believer or not (16: 8-11). Those who understand Jesus' death as a triumphal return to the Father, as glorification, will be saved. But those who follow the Jews in believing that Jesus failed and that the victory is to be found elsewhere, will be swallowed up by the "world" to their eternal loss.

Jesus' second coming is found at the end of his life, at the moment of his Hour which encompasses all the events from his death to the pouring out of the Spirit. Raised upon a cross and in glory the Son of Man puts an end to the regime of Israel by condemning the Jews who in great part were unbelieving.

The Day of Jesus ends and the Hour begins the end of time: it is at this capital moment (cf. the "now" of 12, 31 and 13, 31) when the Jewish messianic future is closed and the gates of the Church are open. Reigning on the cross, the Son of Man attracts (with his eschatological net, ἕλκειν, 12: 32; cf. 6: 44) all men. There is nothing more astonishing than the Passion account's insistence on the proclamation of Jesus as King. The Kingdom of God for which the Jews had longed is inaugurated there on the cross by the very one whom they put to death. It is the Kingdom of God "come with power," efficaciously, of Mark 9: 1; it is also the setting up of the Son of God in power of Romans 1: 4. Jesus is King, Son of Man, Son of God, who has returned to his Father but who is more than ever present to his own, his flock, his friends; he is the conquering life-source just as the vine is for the branches.

The final coming is still to be awaited by the Church of John. If it is true that a man is saved depending on whether or not he believed, whether or not he abides in the word and the love of Jesus, whether or not he remains on the vine, it is no less true that there will be a last day. The eschatological net that worked among the Jews (6: 44) will continue to work through the judgment of the cross (12: 31) until the general summoning of all mankind. The voice that the Jews refused to heed, even though it had been already charged with eschatological efficacy for them, they must hear again at the general resurrection. Those who had heeded it before will live, while the others will hear it as the confirmation of their damnation (5: 25-29). Those whom the Father gave to Jesus will be raised by him on the last day in accordance with the Father's will (6: 39, 40, 44, 54). Since Jesus did not come into the world to judge his word will soar above the world and above time to condemn on the last day (12: 48). Jesus' promise to return and to take his own unto himself (14: 3) leaves the moment of this return indefinite. Must we think of an individual death or of the *parousia?* Both interpretations seem possible, and I should prefer to combine them. On the one hand Jesus is speaking to the Twelve and to the Church in such a way that the background of his thought envisions the global entry of his own into his Father's house (14: 2; 17: 24). On the other hand, the author is writing at the end of the first century at a time when the Church was frequently to pose to herself the problem of death. In John's thought — almost without his realizing it — is this individual departure of believers not part of the global return which supposes a general resurrection? We have to realize that in this discourse (14: 3, 18-19: 22, 28) the "return" of Jesus is looked upon as something close in time, and refers particularly to the day of his resurrection. If the author had intended to insist here only on the *parousia,* he ought to have expressed himself more clearly. On the other hand, it is a question of a formal promise that Jesus will come to fetch them, without the manner or the time being specified. But, granting that this discourse does not have a distant future in view, it seems preferable to think of a series of "goings up" to the Father at the moment of individual death, assumed in a general gathering together. Those who believe have already received the glory (17: 22), but they are still in expectation of seeing the glory of their Lord when they will be received by him (17: 24) "where he is." The conclusion of the priestly prayer is the anticipation of the proclamation of the judgment on the last day: believers already have the glory, the glorified One is already among them, but they are not yet in his house and they see the glory only by faith. Between the Hour of the farewell discourse and the last day there flows the time of the Church, in which Jesus is present in the word handed down from generation to generation (17: 20; cf. 20: 29). If the Evangelist no longer stresses the last day, and seems no longer preoccupied with its proximity, he still is convinced that it will come and he is able to wait for it without fear.

To conclude, a few words on chapter 21 which was added by a disciple of the author's. If up to this point there have been no allusions to function or to ecclesiastical hierarchy, the disciple, in publishing his teacher's work, felt obliged to add an account which reads like an ecclesiastical bibliographical note: the eminent place occupied by the author in the group of the Twelve. Actually, Peter seems to be looked upon as the head of the Twelve but to his great surprise since he himself had rather thought of the beloved disciple in this role. Therefore the author of the Gospel came second after Peter with the result that his witness had exceptional value for the Church. However this concern about the various functions in the Church seems foreign to the Gospel itself. One thing is important: the presence of Christ which gives the Church all assurance, vitality and dynamism.

40, rue de Namur   Henri Van den Bussche,
Louvain   Professor at the University of Louvain

V

Paulus Andriessen, O.S.B.

The New Eve, Body of the New Adam

The many publications since 1943 devoted to discovering precisely what Paul understood by describing the Church as the body of Christ clearly prove that the encyclical *Mystici Corporis* did not conclude the debate but instead was the cause leading to a more profound investigation.

We do not intend to write up a balance sheet of the results obtained over the last twenty years. Others have already done that in great part for us.[1] The aim of our study is much more restrictive: we should like to examine the extent that the bride image is contained in σῶμα Χριστοῦ, in all of the instances that the Apostle uses this idea to express the union of the faithful with the Lord and among themselves. The influence of this image is undeniable in Ephesians 5: 22-23 where we observe a real osmosis of the notions body and bride. Is this an isolated instance or must we admit that elsewhere too the bride image underlies the expression body of Christ? If the answer is yes, then armed with this fact we shall be able to plumb more deeply into the sense of the "mystical genitive" (Deissmann) of Χριστοῦ. And this is not without importance for, as F. Dupont has very rightly pointed

---

1. To be consulted: S. Jáki, O.S.B., *Les tendances nouvelles de l'ecclésiologie*, Rome, 1957; J. Meuzelaar, *Der Leib des Messias*, Assen, 1961; R. Schnackenburg, *Wesenszüge und Geheimnis der Kirche nach dem neuen Testament*, in *Mysterium Kirche*, Salzburg, 1962, pp. 89-199, further developed in *Die Kirche im N.T.*, in *Quaestiones disputatae*, XIV, Freiburg-im-Breisgau, 1961; P. Neuenzeit, *Das Herrenmal*, Munich, 1960, p. 201 ff.

out, "the real difficulty is not so much in the notion of *sôma* as in
the relationship of this *sôma* with Christ." [2]

We know that this relationship is not a purely moral one, nor
is it properly physical. Between these two extremes — rejected
with good reason by the encyclical [3] — there is a whole range of
solutions each of which tries its best to discover the real thought
of the Apostle on this point. Some will understand the genitive
in the expression σῶμα Χριστοῦ rather in an explicative sense: the
body which is the Church is actually Christ himself, his individual
body with which the Christians identify themselves. [4] Others will
wish to emphasize that it is above all a question of a possessive
genitive, of author or of origin: the Church is the body of Christ
because, since it issued from his side, it resembles him, or because
the organism that it makes up belongs to the Lord. He, as the
Victor over sin and death personified, changed the ownership
of our bodies: from *body of sin* and *body of death,* we have become *body of Christ* (*Rm.* 6: 6; 7: 24; cf. 6: 13; 8: 10). Consequently we should understand the genitive in the same sense
as the genitive of the expression which is found six or seven times
in St. Paul: "You are *of Christ.*" [5]

Some will see in the Church the "Ego" of Christ: "In this
mystical person," declares Wikenhauser, "it is Christ who is the
'I' (there is no 'collective I')"; [6] others will prefer to say that
the Church is the "alter Ego" of the Lord. It seems to me that
O. Casel, [7] J. González Ruiz, [8] G. Martelet [9] are among the latter.
According to them the Church is the body of Christ as the wife
is the body of her husband. It is in so far as she is the bride
of Christ that the Church is truly his body. This bodily identity,
since it is of a conjugal order, also implies a distinction of the
bodies themselves.

Until now this interpretation has not received a favorable
welcome [10] and we would be tempted to overlook it, based as it is
on too scanty a foundation, if a venerable author of Christian
antiquity had not already held it. Actually, in the second Letter
to the Corinthians, attributed to St. Clement of Rome, we read:
"You are not unaware, I think, that the living Church is the

body of Christ, for Scripture says God made man male and female. The male is Christ, the female the Church" (14: 1-2).

Jean Daniélou in quoting this text adds: "Our passage makes no allusion to Christ as the head. The Church is the body, not in contradistinction to Christ who would be the head, but insofar as she is the feminine element which is contrasted to the

---

2. *Gnosis, la connaissance religieuse dans les épîtres de saint Paul*, Paris, 1949, p. 440.

3. *Les enseignements pontificaux: l'Église*, vol. II, Tournai, 1959, p. 695 (no. 1061), 711 (no. 1087). The false mysticism against which "Mystici Corporis" puts us on our guard was again condemned by "Mediator Dei" in these terms: "(It has been wrongly taught) that the human nature of the glorious Christ really dwells and with a permanent presence in the justified or that a unique and identical grace would unite Christ with the members of his mystical body" (*ibid.*, p. 808, no. 1239).

4. Lucien Cerfaux, followed by a number of authors, maintains this in *La théologie de l'Église suivant saint Paul* 1st ed., 1942; 2nd ed., 1948. It is to this second edition that we refer. We were unable to consult A. Gutierrez, *Realismus incorporationis fidelium corpori Christi ressuscitati secundum s. Paulum. Studium theologiae biblicae.* Diss., Fribourg, 1961.

5. *Rm.* 8: 9; I *Cor.* 3: 23; 15: 23; II *Cor.* 10: 7; *Gal.* 3: 29; 5: 24. Cf. I *Cor.* 1: 12; 6: 19. Instead of the classical possessive genitive Paul uses the dative in Romans 7, 4: Blass-Debrunner, *Grammatik des neutest. Griechisch*, par. 188, 2*; 189, 2. The terms "slave of Christ," "minister of Christ," "Christian" explain the same appurtenance: A. Deissmann, *Licht vom Osten*, 1908, p. 232 ff., 275 ff.

6. *Die Kirche als der mystische Leib Christi nach dem Apostel Paulus*, Münster, 1937, p. 123.

7. In his review of E. Käsemann's *Leib und Leib Christi*, in *Jahrb. f. Lit. Wiss.*, 1933, t. XIII, p. 290 f., and in his posthumous work: *Mysterium der Ekklesia*, Mainz, 1961, p. 65 ff. and *passim*.

8. *San Pablo: Cartas de la Cautividad*, in Coll. *Christus Hodie*, Madrid, 1956. The author stresses the unique life principle that forms the spouses: pp. 205-207.

9. *Le Mystère du Corps et de l'Esprit dans le Christ ressuscité et dans l'Église (Verbum Caro*, XII, no. 45), 1958, pp. 41-42.

10. Casel's opinion was criticized by Wikenhauser, *op. cit.*, p. 231 (*vade infra* note 6). P. Benoit calls González Ruiz' opinion "less happy" (*Rev. Bibl.*, 1957, p. 615. Cf. 1956, p. 25, n. 1, 2; p. 37, n. 1). The interpretation of Martelet "does not satisfy," in the eyes of E. Schweizer, *Gemeinde und Gemeindordnung im N.T.*, Zurich, 1959, p. 82, n. 353.

masculine one. We therefore have an equation: woman = body, which is curious." [11] The scholarly writer finds a solution in the Judaeo-Christian exegesis of the creation account. Yet he does not seem to point out, or point out sufficiently, that the Book of Genesis had already likened the woman to the body. To verify it we must recall a few peculiarities of Hebrew idiom. Hebrew has no proper word for body. The term *baśar* which it uses signifies "the flesh' properly so-called, or more exactly the carnal organism, which in order to make up the body still needs bones,[12] and for the complete man, blood. Hence these stereotyped expressions: "flesh and bone," "flesh and blood." [13] Nevertheless, by synecdoche, we most often limit ourselves to the term *baśar* to denote the body or even the human person (cf. anybody, nobody). "All flesh" means each individual (*Gn.* 6: 12; *Is.* 40: 5; 49: 26; *Jer.* 25: 31; *Ezk.* 21: 9; *Joel* 3: 1).

It was natural that the specific word signifying the flesh became the usual term for expressing blood relationship. *Baśar* is a principle of solidarity rather than of individuation. This is why we like to point out the relationship we have with someone by identifying his body with our own. Judah dissuaded his brothers from killing Joseph "for he is our flesh" (*Gn.* 37: 27). Similarly in Isaiah 58: 7: "When you see a naked man cover him up, and do not despise your flesh." Laban says to his nephew Jacob: "Truly you are flesh of my flesh and bone of my bone," an expression which in this sense is met with at least eight times in the Old Testament [14] and which brings us back to the account of the formation of Eve, the root of all kinship.

Adam's spouse is called a helpmate, a person like him, literally his "face-to-face" (*kenegdo*: *Gn.* 2: 18, 20).[15]She is given the name *'isshâh* because she was taken from a man, *'ish* (*Gn.* 2: 23). For Adam, she is like the reflection of himself in whom he recognizes himself." [16] Hence his exclamation: "This at last is bone from my bones, and flesh from my flesh," body from my body (*ibid.*). Eve is shown to be Adam's body (since she issued from it) in order that she might form with him the highest conceivable unity; she is as close to man as his own body. For this reason man will cling to his wife("to both" the Septuagint adds) and they will become one flesh (2: 24) or as Paul will say, one body (I *Cor.* 6: 16).

In the *Life of Adam* (par. 3), he calls Eve "my own flesh." In line with the same reasoning, divorce is called *kérîtûth* in Hebrew (its proper sense being a "cut").[17] The man who repudiates his wife cuts her off from his flesh according to Sirach (*Si.* 25: 26).

Leviticus gives us still stronger examples of this identification, e.g., in chapter 18: "None of you shall approach the flesh of his body (i.e., of his kin) to uncover its nakedness. You shall

---

11. *Théologie du Judéo-christianisme,* Tournai, 1957, p. 332. Augustine is the chief witness for this equation: "Totus itaque Christus caput et corpus, tamquam integer vir: quia et femina de viro facta est, et ad virum pertinet" (*In Ps.* 138: 2). "Quomodo sponsus et sponsa, sic caput et corpus; quia caput mulieris vir. Sive ergo dicam caput et corpus, sive dicam sponsus et sponsa: unum intelligite" (*Serm.* 341: 9-10). Cf. *In Ps.* 74: 4. Gregory the Great, *Praef, Mor.,* 14.

12. Cf. *Job* 2: 5; *Lk.* 24: 39.

13. On this subject we may consult: É. Dhorme, *L'emploi métaphorique des noms de parties du corps en hébreu et en akkadien* (*Rev. Bibl.,* 1920, pp. 465-506); J. Robinson, *The Body: A Study in Pauline Theology,* London, 1957, p. 11ff.; J. Luzzi, *"Basar" en el contexto veterotestamentario,* in *Ciencia y Fe,* 1958, pp. 3-38.

14. *Gn.* 2: 23; 29: 14 (37: 27); *Jdt.* 9: 2; II *Kg.* 5: 1; 19: 13-14; I *Chr.* 11: 1.

15. "Wie sein Gegenüber": F. Delitzsch, *Neuer Commentar über die Genesis,* 1887, s.p. Cf. F. Zorell, *Lexic. f. Hebr. and Aram. V.T.,* 1957: "sicut iuxta eum = ei conveniens, fere 'égal' vis-à-vis de lui" (s.v.).

16. Delitzsch, *loc. cit.;* see further on, note 79.

17. É. Dhorme, *L'Ancien Testament,* vol. I. Paris, 1957, p. 580, n. 1. The equation "one's own flesh" = woman is completely Hebraic, but in the Septuagint the formula is not yet translated by "own body." See I *Cor.* 6: 18; 7: 4a, b; 15: 38; II *Cor.* 5: 10? The Septuagint translate *baśar* 145 times by σάρξ, 23 times by σῶμα. Paul prefers σῶμα, e.g., I *Cor.* 6: 16; *Rm.* 8: 13; *Heb.* 13: 11. In all likelihood Christ at the moment of the institution of the Eucharist said: "dēn biśrî ... dēn 'idhmî." These terms may be translated either by the couple σάρξ καὶ αἷμα (*Jn.* 6: 51-56: Ignatius of Antioch, *Rm.* 7, 3; *Philad.,* iv; *Trall.,* viii, 1; *Smyrn.,* vii, 1), or, as do Paul and the Synoptics, by the couple σῶμα καὶ αἷμα (I *Cor.* 10: 16; 11: 24-25; *Mt.* 26: 26-28 parall.). See J. Jeremias, *Die Abendmahlsworte Jesu,* Zurich, 1949, pp. 103-104.

not uncover the nakedness of your father which is the nakedness of your mother . . . .[18] You shall not uncover the nakedness of your son's daughter or your daughter's daughter. For their nakedness is your own nakedness. You shall not uncover the nakedness of your father's brother, that is you shall not approach his wife, for she is your aunt" (vv. 6, 7, 8, 10, 14; cf. vv. 12-13; 20: 19; 21: 2; 25: 49).

Yet in "incorporating" himself in his wife,[19] the Jew was still not monistic. These metaphors and hyperboles did not prevent him from clearly distinguishing between himself and his wife. In a word, the married man is realized in two bodies, his own and his wife's. He can call his wife's body his own since he treats it as his own.

Properly speaking this is equally valid for the wife, as Paul tells us (I *Cor.* 7: 3-5). But in reality the Jewish wife was "inferior to man in everything." [20] In many circumstances of family life, the woman was looked upon as a "thing" rather than a person. Marriage transferred her from the power of her father to that of her husband (I *Sam.* 18: 17, 19, 27). For a woman "to marry" meant "to be controlled by a master," "to be possessed by a possessor" (*be'ûlat ba'al*), the Hebrew *ba'al* (master, possessor) signifying the husband (*Gn.* 20: 3; *Deut.* 22: 22). If the husband had two bodies, the wife had to realize that she had two heads: her own and her husband's (I *Cor.* 11: 3, 5) and to manifest this she wore a veil (vv. 5, 10, 15; cf. *Gn.* 24: 65).

We find this confirmed here with the use of the word "vessel" which in the Hebrew *kelî* as well as the Greek σκεῦος (more rarely: ἀγγεῖον) represents the body in order to emphasize man's role, his subservience toward others (God, his neighbor, the devil). In this respect Paul speaks of a vessel of clay, a vessel useful to the master, and of himself as a vessel of election.[21]

Married people have two vessels at their disposal: their own body and their spouse's. Hence Peter's exhortation: "Likewise, you husbands, live considerably with the feminine vessel as being the weaker one, bestowing honor on her, as a joint heir of the grace of life" (I *Pet.* 3: 7). It goes without saying that in civil society people spoke less of man being the wife's vessel than the contrary which resulted that in popular speech men spoke only of the wife as one's vessel.[22] We must not exclude the fact that in Hebrew a play on words between *keli* (vessel) and *kalah* (wife) influenced this manner of speaking.

Whatever the case, the context will decide whether we are dealing with man's own body [23] or his wife's. The addition of the reflexive pronoun does not solve the question automatically. The expression "one's own vessel" can very well be understood of one's wife. Thus in Proverbs 5: 15 "Drink water from your own cistern (i.e., vessel), flowing water from your own well" (cf.

---

18. We are following the new translation of the *Nederlands Bijbelgenootschap*, 1951. Ordinarily it is translated: "*and* the nakedness of your mother," which makes the verse nebulous and incomplete. The *waw* here is explicative and not copulative (cf. v. 14). Homosexual sins are treated only beginning with verse 22.

19. J. De Fraine, *Adam et son lignage*: *étude sur la notion de "personnalité corporative" dans la Bible*, Bruges, 1959, p. 46 f. A. Dubarle, *La conception de l'homme dans l'Ancien Testament*, in *Sacra Pagina*, Gembloux, 1959, pp. 523-536. "For ancient Israel the descendants of one and the same ancestor form one and the same body." Even "the small society of a couple is a body like the more populated societies of the family or its extensions into the clan and the tribe" (*ibid.*, p. 530). Of this "conjugal body" man is the head (in both senses).

20. Flavius Josephus, *Ap.* 2, 201.

21. *Ac.* 9: 15; II *Cor.* 4: 7; II *Tim.* 2: 21. See É Dhorme (= note 13) p. 469 f.; *TWNT* VII, 359-368 i.v. σκεῦος (Maurer); C. Spicq, *L'image sportive de II Cor.*, IV, 7-9, in *Eph. Theol. Lov.*, 1937, pp. 209-229.

22. H. Strack-P. Billerbeck, *Kommentar z. N.T. aus Talmud u. Midrasch*, Munich, 1926, III, 632. The symbol of the wife was a wine cask, closed if she were a virgin, open if she were a widow: Strack-Billerbeck, I, 505n, 511-512. Cf. *Sg. of S.* 4: 12.

23. David is speaking of the physical bodies his soldiers when he says that the men's "vessels" are in a state of holiness (I *Sam.* 21: 5-6). Although this is in a sexual context the word *keli* is not necessarily a euphemism here for the male sexual organ. Abstaining from marriage makes the whole person pure and holy (*Ex.* 19: 15, 22) just as the use of marriage makes the whole person unclean (*Lv.* 15: 18). In the Old Testament, it was the holiness of persons and not that of bodily members that was spoken of: Maurer, *op. cit.*, 360.

Sg. of S. 4: 12, 15) we have a reference to the lawful wife. In the same sense I Thessalonians 4: 4 must be understood: "Abstain from immorality; that each one of you know how to use your own vessel (i.e., take a wife for himself) in holiness and honor." [24]

As far as the term σῶμα goes it seems to lend itself to the same twofold meaning as *kelî* and σκεῦος. Let us first point out that in the Bible, σῶμα like the Hebrew word *baśar* means not only body but also the human person in so far as it is involved with its surroundings or realizes its solidarity with creation.[25] The word can therefore replace the personal pronoun, but in this case σῶμα often has a reflexive sense: "it is the ego rather than the I," [26] it is the "object-me as distinct from the subject-I." [27] Now if according to the book of Genesis man sees himself projected in his wife, the term σῶμα with the possessive pronoun may be used to denote both a man's own body and his wife's. This is all the more the case since the Jewish wife was not only the other self of her *'îsh* but also, as we have seen, the possession of her *ba'al*.[28] She was part of the master of the house's furniture, somewhat like his σώματα, the domestics and slaves with whom she has often been confused,[29] not to emphasize her servilism but to show that she belonged to her lord.[30]

Finally, since we are not dealing with an individual woman but with a whole people — one which God has acquired for himself (*Is.* 43: 21) and which is often represented as the spouse of Yahweh — we must expect that this "corporative personality" [31] be compared to the human body and its members, a metaphor greatly popularized by Stoicism in the pagan world and one that was not unknown in the Judaism of the dispersion.[32]

It is clear that several metaphors are here superimposed. The primordial relationship of God with his entire people is compared to a marriage, but in turn the union existing between man and wife lends itself to a new metaphor, *viz.*, that of the head and the body. In this light the "body and the members" serves to illustrate the mutual relations of the members of the same organization.

Let us apply this to the New Testament and especially to Paul's thought with which we shall now be concerned.

The unity of the faithful among themselves is a consequence

of their unity with Christ. For this latter unity Paul like John (*Jn.* 3: 29; *Rv.* 21: 2, 9; 22: 17) uses the image of conjugal union in particular — and this is peculiar to him — as it was realized in the first human couple. Now it is only as a consequence of the fact that the new Eve can be called the body of the new

---

24. Exegetes are not in agreement on τὸ ἑαυτοῦ σκεῦος: "one's own vessel" (I *Th.* 4: 4), since they do not know whether it should be understood of one's own body or one's wife. B. Rigaux, after a long article, opts for the first interpretation (*Saint Paul. Les Épîtres aux Thessaloniciens,* Paris, 1956, pp. 503-507); Maurer, *op. cit.,* 365-368. opts for the second, and rightly so, it seems to us. First of all because the Rabbis spoke of the wife with the word "vessel," and then because the expression σκεῦος κτᾶσΘαι which Paul uses here makes one also think of κτᾶσΘαι γυναῖκα, the consecrated term for "to marry." We may add that the context excludes the other interpretation, not only because of ἐν τῷ πράγματι (v. 6) which (also according to Rigaux) refers to the sin of taking one's neighbor's wife, but especially because of ἀπέχεσΘαι ὑμᾶς απὸ τῆς πορνείας, which precedes τὸ ἑαυτοῦ σκεῦος κτᾶσΘαι. The term πορνεία, which really means prostitution, is used most of the time in the New Testament for "live in a married way," whether it is a question of an illicit love or of a matrimonial union in the forbidden degrees. The Jewish legislation was stricter in this area than the pagan customs. In the same manner we must understand the term πορνεία in the commandment that the Jerusalem assembly gave to the pagans regarding abstaining from every unlawful union (*Ac.* 15: 20, 29). This is why Christ taught that one could not put aside one's wife except in a case of concubinage: παρεκτὸς λόγου πορνείας (*Mt.* 5: 32). Paul calls πορνεία, the fact that someone is living with his father's wife (I *Cor.* 5: 1). In this frame of reference it is less correct to connect πόρνη, πορνεία (I *Cor.* 6: 15-18) simply with prostitution. In mind is every form of concubinage contrary to the prescriptions of the law. 7: 2 must be understood in the same sense: "In order to avoid every concubinage, let each man have his own wife." Here we have exactly the same exhortation as in I Thessalonians 4, 4, except that in the place of "wife" we have the term "vessel": "ἀπέχεσΘαι ... απὸ τῆς πορνείας ... ἕκαστον ... τὸ ἑκαστοῦ σκεῦς κτᾶσΘαι."

25. Robinson, *op. cit.,* 6. 31, 78. We refer particularly to the article σῶμα which was to appear in *TWNT*. The author, Prof. E. Schweizer, was most obliging in lending us his manuscript. We are most grateful for his deep expression of generosity and friendship.

26. R. Bultmann, *Theologie des N.T.,* I, p. 192, cited by Robinson, *op. cit.,* p. 13. Robinson does not approve this analysis which he regards

Adam that the many faithful she comprises must be considered as members of one another. The "body" metaphor then has a twofold aspect: first of all *body-spouse* and only then *body-collectivity*. This latter comparison makes up the superstructure as it were of the bride and groom metaphor. But here we need fuller evidence.[33]

As a good pupil of the Rabbis, Paul exalts the new Covenant under the marriage image.[34] Christ is the Bridegroom for his faithful in the twofold sense that the term had for the Jews: he is the Lord, the Master (*ba'al*); he is the husband, the bridegroom (*'îsh*)."Just as after her husband's death, the wife is free to remarry," St. Paul tells the Romans, "you have died to the law through the body of Christ, so that you may belong to another, to him who has been raised from the dead" (7: 1-4; cf. I *Cor.* 7: 39). Should we not also understand in the same conjugal sense expressions like "belong to the Lord, be the Lord's, live for, live with Christ" and other verbs with the prefix σύν which are so characteristic of the Apostle's style: His glory will be to have betrothed us to one sole Bridegroom, Christ, in order to present us to him as a pure virgin (II *Cor.* 11: 2). "The expression ἑνὶ ἀνδρί, which must be connected with τοῦ ἑνὸς ἀνθρώπου (*Rm.* 5: 19) hints that Paul is thinking of Adam" [35] and the virgin, tempted as she is by the serpent of paradise (v. 3), seems in the Apostle's eyes to be the new Eve.

Now Paul says in several places that this betrothed of Christ's is Christ's body. The first time that this theme appears, the text shows clearly that the body-bride simile was already well known to his readers (I *Cor.* 6: 13-20; cf. "do you not know" repeated three times). Treating of libertinage, the Apostle writes, "The body is not meant for immorality, but for the Lord, and the Lord for the body" (v. 13). Somewhat further on we meet an analogous phrase in reference to marriage: "The wife does not rule over her own body, but the husband does; likewise the husband does not rule over his own body, but the wife does" (7: 4). In 6: 13 we are therefore dealing with the conjugal fidelity between Christ and the faithful (*Sg of S.* 2: 16), and the word body can be replaced by *bride*.[36] Our bodies are members of Christ (6: 15) not because of our identification with his individual body, nor in the way that the faithful can call themselves members of one another in one and the same social body (I *Cor.* 12: 27; *Rm.* 12: 5; *Ep.* 5: 30), but only — the text is most clear — in the way man and wife are in the same conjugal body: "Shall I there-

---

as not being Hebraic, but completely "post-Cartesian." Yet he himself writes on p. 29: "It may be that Paul is using the plural σώματα in place of the reflexive pronoun (*Rm.* 1: 24; 8: 11; 12: 1; I *Cor.* 6: 15; *Ep.* 5: 28)."

27. K. Grobel, *SOMA as "Self, Person" in the LXX, in Beih. f. d. ZNTW*, XXI, Berlin, 1954, p. 58.

28. If Yahweh (*Hosea* 2, 18) no longer wishes to have the expression *Ba'ali* (my Master) used in his regard, it is not only because this name denotes the local divinity, but also because God prides himself on a more intimate relationship with his people: not one of master to handmaid but that of husband (*'ishi*) to wife.

29. Cf. *Gn.* 36: 6; *Ex.* 20: 17; *Tob.* 10: 10; *Dn.* 14: 32; II *Mac.* 8: 11; *Gal.* 3: 28; *Rv.* 18: 13. The *Berakhoth* of Jewish Morning Prayer are formulated in this way: "Blessed art thou, O Lord our God, King of the world, that thou hast not made me heathen... nor slave... nor a woman" (And the women in order to make the prayer applicable to themselves said: "...that thou hast made me according to thy will." Meuzelaar, *op. cit.*, p. 84 f.). Even a slave's members are his master's property: *TWNT*, t. II, p. 277; III p. 514; IV p. 566 ff. Cf. *Rm.* 7: 5, 23.

30. Taken in this sense there is much to be said about G. Gloege's interpretation which understands "body of Christ" as "Christ's handmaid"; *Reich Gottes und die Kirche im N.T.*, Bernau, 1928, pp. 286-296. But this is not the whole truth: Paul's idea about the body of Christ is more complex. See σῶμα = possession: Grobel, *loc. cit.*

31. De Fraine, *op. cit.*, p. 97, 103, 106, 200 ff. J. P. Udet prefers to say "incorporating personality" (*Rev. Bibl.*, 1960. p. 296 f.).

32. G. Knight speaks in his *Christian Theology of the Old Testament* (London 1959) constantly of the "body of Israel" without justifying this expression. Nevertheless K. Stendahl is wrong in asserting that the metaphor has no relationship with the idea of the people of God (*Kirche im Urchristentum*, in *RGG*, 3rd ed., t. III, 1300). Against Cerfaux who holds that in the language of the time *sôma* never had the moral sense of a society (*op. cit.*, p. 208 ff.) we make our own the opinion of P. De Fraine: "Even if we must concede that the secular sense of *sôma* is never the body social (see however S. Lyonnet, in *Bibl.*, 1951, p. 285), we should in any case be mindful of the fact that the idea of collective body is absolutely current in Judaism" (*op. cit.*, p. 206. See above, note 19). Philo gives us a very noteworthy proof of this. The high priest, according to him, prays and

fore take the members of Christ and make them members of a prostitute?" (v. 15). For the two shall become one body, one flesh (v. 16).

The quote borrowed from Genesis (2: 24) [37] prepares the way for its application to the faithful: "But he who is united to the Lord becomes one spirit with him" (v. 17). Instead of ἓν πνεῦμα, if need be it would be possible to paraphrase ἓν σῶμα πνευματικόν,[38] on the condition that this pneumatic body is clearly distinguished from the individual body of the risen Christ. Otherwise the parallel with Genesis 2: 24 does not work.[39] Paul has in mind the conjugal body which is made up either of husband and wife or Christ and the Church. If we hold to the nuptial sense of *membra Christi* we may also understand why, although every other sin man may commit is exterior to his body, he who lives in concubinage sins against his own body. In giving himself to a prostitute (vv. 13b, 16) he makes a wrong use of his physical body since it no longer belongs to him but (in the Lord: 7: 39) to his lawful wife and through her to the Lord (v. 13, 19). For, the Apostle adds, you were bought with a price (v. 20), you are his slaves (7: 22); your bodies are doubly the possession of your Bridegroom, just as the daughter of Zion was of her divine *go'el* ("Redeemer").[40] Therefore give glory to God in your body (6: 20).

Even more than the unity in marriage, it was the unity in the communities that touched the Apostle's heart. What is to be done to curb the divisions that threaten to grow even into a schism? Paul insists at length that the one with whom the faithful are united is the Bridegroom with an undivided heart.[41] It is to one man alone (ἑνὶ ἀνδρί II *Cor.* 11: 2) that we are betrothed. Just as in John's thought one Shepherd must correspond to one flock (*Jn.* 10: 16), so for Paul there must be a correlation between the one Bridegroom, the one Lord (I *Cor.* 8: 6), the one Spirit (12: 6 ff.),[42] the one Christ (12: 12?), the one Bread (10: 17), the one crucified body [43] on the one hand, and the one Bride, the one ecclesial body or the undivided community on the other (*Rm.* 12: 5; I *Cor.* 10: 17; 12: 12, 13; *Col.* 3: 15; *Ep.* 4: 4). "For although there may be many so-called "gods" and "lords"; for us there is one God, the Father, and one Lord" (I *Cor.* 8: 5-6; cf. 12: 5 ff.). If one Bread nourishes us the result should be that we are one body since we partake in this one Bread (10: 16-17). If there are divisions in the community (11: 8), that proves that we have not understood

makes offerings each day that all the parts of the people, as one body, may form one and the same community (*Spec. Leg.*, III, 131 = *Jn.* 11: 52?). Cf. *Virt.*, 103; Flavius Josephus, *Bell.*, 3, 104, 270, 279; *Ant.*, 7, 66. See Meuzelaar, *op. cit.*, pp. 66, 154, 160. From this fact it is possible that we must interpret the term σύσσωμος (*Ep.* 3: 6) by beginning with the notion Israel-body: Schlier-Warnach, Die Jirche im Epheserbrief, Münster, 1949, p. 85.

33. Is it not simplistic to call Paul's doctrine on the Mystical Body "eminently simple"? (B. Ahern, *The Christian Union with the Body of Christ in Cor., Gal., and Rom.*, in *The Cath. Bibl. Quarterly*, 1961, t. XXIII, p. 208).On this point we find the very pertinent remarks of J. Havet in *La doctrine du "Corps du Christ"* in *Recherches bibliques*, t. V, 1960, p. 209. Paul uses words like body, flesh, spirit, law, etc. in various senses, and it would be complicating the exegesis not to take account of this lack of precision and these lapses.

34. The Rabbis considered the contract of the covenant on Sinai as a marriage between Yahweh and Israel. The *Torah* was the marriage contract and Moses the friend of the Bridegroom: E. Stauffer. in *TWNT* t. I, i. v. γαμέω, 652 ff.

35. L. Cerfaux, *Le Christ dans la théologie de saint Paul* in *Lectio divina*, t. VI, Paris, 1961, p. 163, n. 2. In IV *Mac.* 18: 7 ff. the expression παρΘένος ἀγνή, according to the context is evidently connected with Eve. This would be a new indication to prove that in II Corinthians 11: 2 Paul looks upon the Church as the new Eve, and the "unique man" as the new Adam.

36. Or rather by "partner" or "conjunct." It is not yet Paul's intention to indicate which of the two is the groom, which the bride. He wishes simply to say that Christ and the faithful person are related in a matrimonial way. Whoever gives too literal an explanation to the Genesis passage (v. 16) will be brought incorrectly to the conclusion that Christ is the bride, the new Eve: "membra Christi;...membra meretricis; qui adhaeret meretrici... qui autem adhaeret Domino" (vv. 15, 17).

37. The Lord adds: "Thus they are no longer two, but one flesh" (*Mt.* 19: 4; *Mk.* 10: 6).

38. "A body that is supraterrestrial, spiritual": Wikenhauser, *op. cit.*,

the lesson of the one Bread nor assimilated its unifying force. Thus we eat and drink our own condemnation if we do not discern the body. Take the example from Israel's past: all received the same baptism, the same spiritual food and drink, but they perished in great number in the desert (10: 1-3).

Paul here plays on the double sense of σῶμα: body-Eucharist and body-collectivity, yet he still does not identify the two. Just as food is distinct from the body it nourishes, so the Apostle contrasts the one Bread with the one body, and when he underlines the analogy between the two he does so to emphasize that what in Christ is an exemplary cause has the force of law in the community. To identify the individual and ecclesial bodies of Christ the famous *crux interpretum* has been relied upon: "As the body is one . . . so Christ" (I *Cor.* 12: 12). But L. Cerfaux and J. Havet have duly proved that here as everywhere else it is a question of the individual Christ and not the collective Christ.[44] Let us concede however to the partisans of the collective sense that the copulative that can best complete the elliptic formula is the verb "to be." How then is it to be read?

The Apostle began by saying in chapter 12 that the diversity of the charisms and functions in the Church must not make us forget that it is always one and the same Spirit, one and the same Lord, one and the same God working in us all. He keeps returning to the fact that it is the work of one and the same Spirit that distributes to each his gifts according to his pleasure.[45] Paul clarifies his thought with an example. As the body is one even though it has many members and as all the members of the body — no matter how numerous — make up but one body, so Christ is one although he operates differently in all the faithful. This seems to us to be the phrase required by the context.[46] The point of comparison in verse 12 is unity in diversity and not the body's organic cohesion. This is evident only from the following verses as a consequence. But the motive of uniqueness is still heard as far as verse 20.

Instead of ". . . so Christ" we might just as well expect to read ". . . so the Spirit." [47] And Paul goes further: "For it is also by the one Spirit that we have all been baptized into one body"

(v. 13). People have wished to apply this "one body" to the personal body of the Lord.[48] But the parallels Romans 12, 5 and Galatians 3: 28, which have "in Christ" instead of "in the Spirit," prevent us from doing so. The one Spirit in whom we have been

---

p. 105. Clement of Alexandria was already of this opinion, *Stromata,* VII, par. 87, 3; 88, 2. For the exegesis, see Casel, *op. cit.,* p. 291.

39. In my opinion there is nothing here to indicate that Paul has in mind and as a reality the pneumatic body of the risen Christ as is thought by: Schweizer, in *TWNT,* t. VI, p. 416; Benoit, *Corps, tête et plérôma dans les épîtres de la captivité,* in *Rev. Bibl.,* 1956, p. 13, n. 5; J. Reuss, *Die Kirche als "Leib Christi" und die Herkunft dieser Vorstellung bei dem Apostel Paulus,* in *Bibl. Zeitschr.,* 1958, p. 106, e. a. Martelet gives ample proof how this is one of the faults on which rests the so-called inclusion or inadequate identification theory. See also S. Tromp, *Corpus Christi, quo est Ecclesia,* p. ii: *De Christo Capite,* Rome, 1960, pp. 347-349.

40. Yahweh is the *gô'êl* of his people reduced to slavery (esp. in *Is.* 41: 14; 44: 6, 24; 47: 4; 48: 17; 49: 26; 59: 20; 63: 16).

41. At least we believe that we can so interpret I Corinthians 1: 13 in connection with 7, 33-35, where the same verb form is used. There is no reason then to understand Christ in a collective sense here (against Mersch) nor to see a metaphor in this expression (against J. Havet in his otherwise excellent article, *"Christ collectif" ou "Christ individuel,"* in *Eph. Theol. Lov.,* 1947, p. 516). Instead of "put in pieces," "quartered," it might be better translated "torn in various directions"; cf. *Mt.* 12, 26.

42. The same correlation in Ephesians 4: 4: "There is one Body and (i.e., because) one Spirit." The uniqueness of the Spirit demands the oneness of the body, which is the Church. See Ch. Masson, *L'Épître de saint Paul aux Éphésiens,* Neuchâtel, 1953, p. 185; H. Schlier, *Der Brief an die Epheser,* Düsseldorf, 1958, p. 186 f.

43. The best commentators are of the opinion that in Ephesians 2: 14-16 there is the same correlation between the one body of the Crucified and the one body of the Church. Out of two peoples the Lord has made one alone. He created both in one man, reconciling them with God, both by one body sacrificed on the cross. The one Victim requires the oneness of the ecclesial body. That this is the meaning of "in one body" (v. 16) is clear after the addition "by means of the cross" and from the context: "by the blood of Christ" (v. 13), "by his flesh" (v. 14), "by himself" (vv. 15 & 16), "by one spirit" (v. 18). Furthermore, the parallel text, Colossians 1: 22: "he has now reconciled you in his body of flesh by his death" furnishes the best of commentaries. Cf. Cerfaux, *op. cit.,* pp. 184-186; Schlier, *op. cit.,* p. 134 ff.

steeped (*ibid.*) is similarly correlated with the one ecclesial body, as the Bread was earlier. Let us keep to the current interpretation then of body-community. Moreover we cannot escape from the impression that Paul in repeating "one body" (10: 17; 12: 13) connects it with the expression used for the first time when he says that man and woman are one body (6: 16) just as the faithful, the members of Christ, are one spirit. Fr. Benoit rightly points out that the theme of the body of Christ was already present in the Apostle's mind when he called the faithful individually a *member* of Christ.[49] If Paul therefore had taken this expression in the conjugal sense, as we have seen *a fortiori,* body of Christ must also be understood in this way. Now the Apostle concludes his comparison of the body with these words: "Now you are body of Christ,[50] and individually members of it" (12: 27). He can presuppose that its sense is obvious. Further, the parallel Ephesians 5: 30 is clear enough to remove any doubt.

As the new Eve, the community is the body of the new Adam.[51] In expressly calling Christ the new Adam, we do not wish to force our argumentation. The parallelism Adam-Christ holds an important, if not capital place in Pauline thought (*Rm.* 5: 12-19; I *Cor.* 15: 21-22, 45-49).[52] Some think that the same relationship is implied in the christological hymn of Philippians 2.[53] In our opinion a better example of this parallelism is I Corinthians 11: 3-16. If first of all we are dealing here with each man and each woman, we are very soon aware that the Apostle had the first couple particularly in view. Not only is the terminology inspired to a great extent by the account of the earthly paradise, but it is said twice that man was not taken from woman but woman from man (vv. 8, 12), which can directly be applied only to Adam and Eve.

Another peculiarity: man like woman can speak of his head in two senses, the proper and the figurative, and Paul uses both in a way that no commentator can be completely sure of their distinction. We should not be surprised then if the same difficulty is present in relation to the two bodies of Christ: his physical body and the body of his Church.

Why is man the "head" of the woman? Certainly not primarily

because he is her *ba'al,* her master. This is the result of a much
deeper reality: woman is subject to man and comes after him
in rank because he is the principle and the source from which
she has come; he is the model of which she is the reflection (v. 7)
and in whom she finds her purpose (v. 9; *Gn.* 3: 16). She is man's

---

44. *Op. cit.* (= note 41 and note 33 where he adopts the opinion of
Cerfaux). Let us go along wtih W. Goossens by saying that the encyclical
"Mystici Corporis" which admits the collective sense of the word Christ
in I Corinthians 12: 12 did not wish to settle this question which is solely
concerned with the terminology and not the doctrine of the Apostles:
L'Église, Corps du Christ d'après saint Paul, Paris, 1949, p. 42, n. 1.

45. Here it is the Spirit, elsewhere God (7: 7. *Rm.* 12: 3, 6) or
Christ (I *Cor.* 3: 5; *Ep.* 4: 7), who distributes to each one these gifts
in accordance with his pleasure. This puts us on guard not to carry
to the extreme the Spirit-soul image, which we are invited to do by verses
7-10 of I Corinthians. The Spirit-soul is not an integrating part nor is
Christ-the-head a co-member of the Mystical Body. The divine reality
infinitely surpasses them, the images are defective, and Paul must necessarily be inconsistent in the way he applies them.

46. Proved convincingly by I. Hermann, *Kyrios und Pneuma,* Munich,
1961.

47. It is still Hermann whom we are following (*loc. cit*) Paul willingly
varies, using one time "in the spirit" and another time "in Christ," as the
continuation of our text will show (*ibid.,* p. 142, 10). F. Neuberger has
shown to be false the opinion which give to Paul's *in Christo* a local or
spatial sense. The formula is always connected with an event which is
to be inserted into the historical development of the Christ mystery and
thereby be the result of his *kyrial* domination: *Das Paulinische "in Christo"*
(*NTS,* 1958, p. 137; cf. p. 130, -38). Has this fact not too often escaped
the attention of those who understand the formula *in Christo* as being
equal to *in corpore Christo?*

48. This is Cerfaux's opinion, *La théologie de l'Église,* p. 207 ff., which
connects with our passage from Romans 6: 3-4: "baptized in his death."
"Baptized in one body" would mean "baptized in one Christ who died
for us." Such an interpretation of "one body" (without the addition of "of
Christ") is difficult to uphold, since Paul did not previously mention the
crucified body. We do not think furthermore that "to be baptized in the
name of" and "baptized into the death of" are variants. We do think
that "to be baptized in Christ" (*Rm.* 6: 3; *Gal.* 3: 27), like "to be
baptized in Moses" (I *Cor.* 10: 2) is an abbreviation of "to be baptized in
the body etc." and designates the baptismal *rite* itself. (Cf. our article

glory and all the more so if she takes care of her appearance, her own glory (v. 6. 15).

Christ is man's head (v. 3). This is the first time that this title has been given to him. From what we have just said it is possible to deduce the meaning of this title.[54] Christ is man's head (and therefore indirectly also the head of the woman: *Ep.* 5: 22; *Col.* 3: 28), not only because he is his lord and Master, but first of all and especially because he is the origin, the Archetype, of which man is the reflection; man is [55] the image and the *glory* of the Lord (v. 7; II *Cor.* 3: 18). For the same reason God is Christ's *head* (v. 3), although this reason is not given here but elsewhere (II *Cor.* 4: 4; *Col.* 1: 15; *Heb.* 1: 37).

Obviously "everything comes from God" (v. 12) but within this provenance, there is a hierarchy of values in which each particular circle is the head of that which follows insofar as its glory is reflected in it. Inversely, we find a phrase such as the following: "All are yours; and you are Christ's and Christ is God's" (3: 23).

Head and glory seem therefore to be correlative notions. However obvious the correlation head-body may be, only the twin letters to the Colossians and the Ephesians assert it formally. All the data however is already to be found in the major epistles: we find there the equation spouse of Christ = body of Christ, and Christ in turn is called the Lord of the Body (I *Cor.* 6: 13), Heads of its glory (11: 7), Bridegroom of his Church (II *Cor.* 11: 2). If it is true that the body is for plants what the glory is for the stars (I *Cor.* 15: 37-42), and if it is true that the glory fulfills in God's regard the role which *baśar* plays for man, i.e., the exterior appearance of the person and his fullness,[56] there is only one step to be taken from *head-glory* to *head-body*.[57]

The most important passage offered to us by the captivity epistles is Ephesians 5: 22-23. The pericope is divided into two parts: 1. the woman is asked to submit to her husband because she is her head; 2. the man is required to love his wife because she is his body. "Wives be subject to your husbands as to the Lord. For the husband is the head of the wife as Christ is the head of the Church, the Savior of the body" (vv. 22-23).

By no longer designating Christ as man's head (I *Cor.* 11: 3) but as the head of his bride, the Church, Paul is on the verge of completing his comparison: the woman behaves towards her husband *as* the Church toward Christ; man behaves towards

---

Les stigmates de Jésus in Bijdragen, 1962, pp. 139-154). Nevertheless, "to be baptized in," relating not to a person but to a thing as for example Matthew 3: 6; Acts 2: 38; Romans 6: 3-4 ("to be baptized into the death"); I Corinthians 12: 13 ("... in a body") signifies the *effect* of baptism. Also "to put on Christ" (*Gal.* 3: 27 = to be a new creature: *Gal.* 6: 15; II *Cor.* 5: 17), "to be one" (*Gal.* 3: 28). The passage which interests us is parallel to *Ep.* 2: 14 ff.: "He who has made us both one that he might craft in himself one new man in place of the two, by one crucified body" (= in one spirit of I *Cor.* 12: 13. Cf. *supra,* note 42). See Meuzelaar, *op. cit.,* p. 87 ff.

---

49. *Op. cit.,* p. 13.

50. Both words are without the article, undoubtedly because they were addressed to one community.

51. "This is why in the Christian reinterpretation of Genesis body and wife are one. The Church is the new Eve because she is the body of the new Adam": L. Thornton, *Revelation and the Modern World,* London, 1950, p. 241.

52. Daniélou notes a growing importance of Adam in later Judaism (*op. cit.,* 334 ff.) and Schweizer amply proves it: *Die Kirche als Leib Christi in den Paulinischen Homologumena* (*Theol. Lit. Zeitung,* 1961, col. 163 ff.).

53. E.g., L. Bouyer, ΑΡΠΑΓΜΟΣ, in *Rech. Sc. Rel.,* 1951-1952 (*Mélanges Lebreton,* t. I, pp. 281-288). See *Mt.* 4: 9 & parall.; *Ezk.* 28: 12 ff.; *Is.* 14: 12 ff.; *Lk.* 10: 18; *Rv.* 12: 7-9). There are many other parallels to be uncovered that implicitly connect the first human couple with the eschatological couple: "Adam was formed first, *then* Eve" (I *Tim.* 2: 13) just as "those who belong to Christ" will *then rise* insofar as Christ (= the second Adam) has first risen (I *Cor.* 15: 23). What characterizes the second Adam is that he is life-giving Spirit (I *Cor.* 15: 45; cf. 22). Therefore he who unites himself with him is one spirit (6: 17; κολλᾶσθαι is used in the sexual sense in the Septuagint: *Gn.* 2: 24; *Sir.* 19: 2, but also to denote consecration to God: *Deut.* 6: 13; 10: 20; II *Kg.* 18: 6; *Sir.* 2: 2; *Ps.* 62: 9; 72: 28).

---

54. Although here the comparative conjunction of Ephesians 5, 23 is absent.

his wife *as* Christ toward the Church. *Head* in this instance means bridegroom, but in the special sense that this word already has for the man of Paradise, *viz.,* origin and archetype of the woman. Man is head of his wife because he represents our common ancestor from whom woman had been taken. Christ and the Church have the same relationship to one another. Also the Apostle at the end of the pericope will make reference once again to the creation account.[58]

In itself the notion of head is so broad and — as a metaphor — so common, that it does not necessarily evoke the idea of body. But as soon as Paul puts the two notions in correlation its symbolic sense is that man and Christ are heads of their bride just as the wife and the Church are the bodies of their spouses. All the other meanings of σῶμα, trunk and individual body, for example, seem excluded by these words: ". . . Christ, the Savior of the body" (v. 23).[59] Only with difficulty can it be said of the head that it is the savior of the physical body, any more than one would say that one were one's own savior. If in place of "body" we read "bride" the phrase is most clear. Actually, immediately afterward, the text says expressly that Christ has delivered himself for his bride in order to make her what she should be, the glory of her husband: "in splendor (i.e., in glory) . . . without spot or wrinkle" (vv. 25-27).[60] If husbands are to love their wives as their own body (v. 28),[61] as their own flesh (v. 29), as themselves (vv. 28b, 33), we have here the exact way in which Christ considers the Church to be his body. He is the body of his bride (v. 30) or as is said elsewhere: "He is the head of the *body of the Church,*[62] he is the beginning, the first-born among the dead" (*Col.* 1, 18).

Also in Colossians 1: 24 there is nothing against reading "bride of Christ" for "body of Christ." Quite the contrary. Christ has handed himself over for (ὑπέρ) his Church, wishing to present her to himself glorious and without stain (*Ep.* 5: 25-27). Now Paul feels the same divine jealously for her since he is desirous to present her to Christ as a pure virgin (II *Cor.* 11: 2). Also he rejoices at being able to suffer for her and thus complete in her flesh what is lacking in the trials of Christ for (ὑπέρ) his body, i.e., for his bride which is the Church.

But a doubly attested assertion, and one of very primary value, seems to be against our interpretation (*Col.* 2: 19; *Ep.* 4: 15-16).

---

55. For the term ὑπάρχειν, see Liddell & Scott: "being originally" i.e., "by nature as a result of one's creation." This shows once again that we are dealing here with the first man, at the very least with man in accordance with his origin.

56. *Corp. Herm.*, XIV, 7: μία γάρ ἐστιν αὐτῷ δόξα τὸ ποιεῖν τὰ πάντα, καὶ τουτό ἐστι τοῦ Θεοῦ ὥσπερ σῶμα, ἡ ποίησις quoted by Cerfaux, *op. cit.*, p. 249, who adds: "This way of speaking will seem less strange if we recall that the body manifests and exteriorizes the soul.... Metaphorically God's creative action is called his body." Knight, *op. cit.*, I, par. 8.

57. In II Clement 14: 4 we find the word pair "spirit-flesh" in the sense of the risen Christ and the Church which is still flesh until the *parousia*: "This flesh is the copy of the Spirit." This seems to us to be a more correct interpretation of Pauline thought than the opinion that the most ancient epistles of Paul would not present Christ as the Head of the body, but as the body itself as formed by its members. E.g., Benoit, *op. cit.*, p. 23 ("in the great epistles Christ is the totality of the *sôma*") and C. Moule, *The Epistles of Paul to the Colossians*, Cambridge, 1957, p. 67. — In the *Homologumena*, no less than in the *Antilegomena*, Christ is situated with regard to the Church either as the Bridegroom (I *Cor.* 6: 13), Master (6: 30; 7: 22-23), Kyrios (Hermann, *op. cit.*,), or as the eucharistic Bread (10: 17), personal Spirit (ch. 12), while the notion of *sôma* there expresses clearly an interdependence: Gloege, *op. cit.*, p. 300.

---

58. The words "of his flesh and of his bones" (*Ep.* 5: 30) are omitted by a few responsible manuscripts, but their presence in all the others and in the majority of early translations is a sufficient guarantee of their authenticity. We may even say that these words are required by the context, and in other passages of the same epistle they are understood. See for a fuller treatment: Masson, *op. cit.*, p. 214. Thornton, *op. cit.*, p. 241, n. 1. In opposition: Schlier, *op. cit.*, p. 261, n. 2, who neglects to point out that for Paul the woman, and consequently the new Eve, always comes from man as we have seen.

59. Cf. I *Clem.* 37: 5; 38: 1. By the term "Savior" Paul indicates the reason why Christ can be called the Head of the body of the Church: He is the source of her salvation and her preservation (see above, note 40).

Paul speaks of the Church as "one" in the complexity of its reciprocal services. But while in I Corinthians 12 he sees the matter as static, he now considers the dynamic character of this organism. It is from the Head that the body of the Church receives its growth; it is towards him, the Head, that the growth converges. Does the Apostle not present Christ here as co-member of the whole organism, as the head from which all the members of the trunk receive concord and cohesion?

No one will have any doubt perhaps after becoming acquainted with Tromp's studies on these passages.[63] Yet this does not prevent us from having to admit that this figurative language is very defective and, or rather because, the marriage metaphor shows through many times.

1. Let us establish one thing first. The construction of the phrase indicates that in using "head" Paul did not have the organ of the body in mind, but was rather thinking of a person instead: ἐξ οὖ instead of ἐξ ἧς (*Ep.* 4: 16; *Col.* 2: 19), as previously he had spoken of the "head and the body of *this person*" — σῶμα αὐτοῦ — and of εἰς αὐτόν instead of εἰς αὐτήν (*Ep.* 4: 15).

2. Let us go further. How can we form an idea of the physiological value of the head when it is a peculiarity of the captivity epistles to conceive the Church as the earthly body of which Christ is the Head in heaven? [64] It is difficult to admit with Schlier that the mission of the Church to grow in all things to Christ would mean that the body must grow towards the Head in heaven with the result that once the body reaches the Head, the Perfect man would be constituted.[65] If on the other hand we retain the meaning that "head" seems to have up to now then the whole passage is clear: Paul would have in view Christ as the Bridegroom-Archetype from whom the new Eve was formed and towards whom she must tend in order to be transformed into this same image (II *Cor.* 3: 18). This ebb and flow is attested to in the Paradise account and noted by Paul: "The woman is taken from the man" (*Gn.* 2: 22, 23), "and her desire will be for her husband" (3: 16; I *Cor.* 11, 8, 9, 12).

3. A. Dubarle wonders if Paul is not still alluding here to the creation account when he speaks of the *building up* of the body of Christ (*Ep.* 4: 16), in comparison with Genesis 2: 22: Yahweh *formed* the woman out of the rib he had taken from the man, since the verbs are the same in the Greek text.[66] In any

---

"Christ creates the community by the fact that he saves it": Gloege, *op. cit.*, p. 232.

60. For the term δόξα cf. I *Cor.* 6: 20; 11: 7, 15; *Ep.* 1: 6, 12, 14 and again Schlier, *op. cit.*, p. 258 ff. Παριστάνειν, the presentation of the bride to her bridegroom in our opinion also plays its part in Ephesians 1: 4, 12. According to the Rabbis the custom goes back to God himself who presented Eve to Adam: Strack-Billerbeck, *op. cit.*, t. I, p. 503 ff.

61. There is no comparison in the words: "as their own flesh." The "as" must be understood in the sense of *tamquam* = "as being their own body." Cf. Masson, *op. cit.*, p. 213, n. 6. In the Babylonian Talmud we find an identical phrase: "He who loves his wife as his body (*kegufô*) and honors her more than his body (*miggufô*) ... of him the Scripture (= *Job*. 5: 24) says: You shall know that your tent is safe" (*Yebhamôth*, 62b). As Fr. H. Renckens intended to point out to us, the term *guf* comes from post-biblical Hebrew where it has the sense of body, or again of person. It is why others have been able to translate the two expressions of our passage by "as one's self," "more than one's self" (L. Goldschmidt, *Der babylonische Talmud, neu übertragen*, Berlin, 1931, t. IV., p. 531). The feminine form *gufáh* is found only twice in Holy Scripture (I *Chr.* 10: 12) in the sense of corpse. As we have seen above, biblical Hebrew has no proper term for body in the Western sense of the word. More than *bašar*, the word *guf* seems to be closer to it because it is more "tangible."

62. If the genitive were an appositive genitive, with the meaning of "i.e.," ("He is the Head of the body, *i.e.*, of the Church"), we should have to understand "of *his* body" or else the absence of the article: Meuzelaar, *op. cit.*, p. 122; Cerfaux, *op. cit.*, p. 250. We find the same formula in Ignatius, *Smyrn.* 1, 2.

---

63. *Op. Cit.*, pp. 45-71. Also, *Caput influit sensum et motum*, in *Gregorianum*, 39, 1958, pp. 353-366. By the same, *Haupt*, in *Lex. f. Theol. u. Kirche*, 2nd ed., 1961, vol. V. In a manifestly opposite direction: S. Bedale, *The Meaning of Kephale in the Pauline Epistles*, in *Journal of Theological Studies*, 1954, p. 211 ff.; P. Dacquino, *De Christo Capite et de Ecclesia eius Corpore secundum S. Paulum*, in *Verbum Domini*, 1962, pp. 81-88. According to the latter, the word *kephale* must be conceived in a moral sense (= *qui praeest, dux, princeps*), even in the two passages in question. After having given several reasons in favor of his interpretation,

case it is striking to see that the mother of the Maccabees can speak of her body as *fashioned* from the rib (again the same verb) which she has always kept intact (IV *Mac.* 18: 7); rabbinical literature gives us more than one example of this and proves to us the extent that the formation of Eve, considered as a "building-up," was part of common tradition and emphasized.[67]

4. Finally, although the members of the body are joined by all kinds of articulations, the union between the head and the body is translated by the verb κρατεῖν (*Col.* 2: 19) which generally means "grasp, embrace" and consequently indicates a contact between persons. Cf. Song of Solomon 3: 4: "I found him whom my soul loves. I held him — ἐκράτησα — and would not let him go." [68]

Before concluding there is one final question: Christ is not merely called the Head of the Church but also "the head of all rule and authority" (*Col.* 2: 10). He is "head over all things" (*Ep.* 1: 22). Does that mean that Paul had in mind an eventual body of the universe (κοσμοῦ) over which Christ would have become the head? Not necessarily since the Apostle uses "head" primarily and especially in its primary sense of principle-archetype. It is in this way that he calls God Christ's "head" (I *Cor.* 11: 3), and consequently head of the universe: "all things are from God" (11: 12) without any allusion to the idea of σῶμα. If God became man, in other words, if God sends his son to earth, the God-Man precisely because of his divinity will be the head of the universe, the Lord of the heavenly militia. The redemption which has freed us from the yoke of the Powers will include a new title, giving this cosmic supremacy to Christ. It is therefore a signal privilege for the Church to have the Lord of the universe for its head [69]: ". . . He has made him head over all things for the Church which is his body" (*Ep.* 1: 22-23).

From the fact that her head is head of the universe, the Church must indeed conclude that her role opens out to the vast cosmos, but nothing in this impels us to see a *Weltleib*, embracing all things.[70] In fact the verb which the RSV inaccurately translates as "made" already suggests the disparity existing between the supreme head and his body. The word (διδόναι) shows also that the body is in a position to *accept* Christ as head and that consequently Paul looks upon the union of the head and the body as being the intimate encounter of two persons,[71] and not as being the cohesion of constitutive parts of the body.[72] To say that without Christ the Church is a "decapitated body" and Christ without the Church "a bodiless head" [73] seems hardly Pauline to us.

We are aware that we have only very imperfectly answered this question of the cosmic role of Christ and his Church. To treat

he adds, "Valor argumentationis adhuc roboratur eo quod in utroque loco kephale toti corpori (*pan to sôma*) cum suis membris (v. 16b) opponitur ita ut kephale non videatur in illo comprehendi posse" (p. 83). Yet this argument, already put forward by Cerfaux, *op. cit.*, p. 253, n. 2, seems to weaken through the analogous passage of Ephesians 2: 21. Actually we cannot deny that the cornerstone is a part of the whole building: *pasa* (let us add: *hè*) *oikodomè*. Even if we do not admit of a grammatical mistake here and hold to the translation "every edifice": instead of "the whole edifice," we do not understand how the foundation could very well be excluded from it. For more details, see Masson, *op. cit.*, pp. 170-171.

64. Masson, *op. cit.*, p. 156; Schlier, in *TWNT*, i. v. κεφαλή, p. 679. "Ipse Dominus desuper clamavit pro corpore suo: 'Saule, Saule, quid me persequeris?' Et ipsum nemo tangebat, sed pro corpore in terra laborante caput de caelo clamabat" (Augustine, *In Ps. 130 Expos.*).

65. Schlier, *loc. cit.*, and *Der Brief an die Epheser*, p. 90. In fact Schlier makes use in great part of the ancient "trunk" theory (p. 202). Now if we must acknowledge with Origen that Christ has two bodies, the one from the Virgin and the Church (*Comm. in Jo.*, 10: 23; PG, XIV, 380), the other fact is no less true, namely that the Church has two heads: "S. Robertus in controversia *de Rom. Pontif.*, I, 9 concludit Ecclesiam quatenus est aliquid totum sociale, etiam abstractione facta a Christo capite invisibili, gaudere quadam personalitate propria, et consequenter praeter Christum exigere caput quoddam humanum" (Tromp, *De Christo Capite*, p. 9). We are obviously not thinking here of the "Corpus cum pluribus capitibus monstruosum" rejected by Boniface VIII (*"Mystici Corporis,"* par. 39).

66. *Les fondements bibliques du titre marial de "Nouvelle Eve,"* in *Mélanges Lebreton*, I, Paris, 1951, p. 55. The agricultural metaphor (I *Cor.* 3: 9) and especially that of the building have influenced our passage:

it thoroughly we should have to deal here also with the problems of the Pleroma and the Perfect Man. But this would entail going beyond our subject which merely aims at focusing attention on the metaphor of the Bride and its significance in Pauline ecclesiology.

In brief, we have been able to point out the following:

1. It was not out of character for the Jews to identify themselves with their close kin and particularly with their wives. These two cases of identification merge in the first human couple since Eve is not only "flesh of the flesh" of Adam but also "the same flesh" with him.

2. According to a certain number of commentators, Paul in the major epistles identifies the Church with Christ, while in the captivity epistles he contrasts her with Christ in her relationship as Bride of Christ the Bridegroom. From the ecclesiological point of view we must certainly notice a difference between the two groups of epistles but this is not in the viewpoint which we have just mentioned. In the major epistles Paul treats especially the relations of Charity which unite Christians among themselves and Christ with them. In the captivity epistles, he shows especially how Christ is the principle of this fellowship and how we have come from him.

3. "Body of Christ" is a metaphor which the Apostle applies to the Church in a twofold way (vertically and horizontally, as we might say today): first in order to indicate that the Church is the Bride of Christ and secondly to say that she is the union of the faithful among themselves. This could shed new light on the way in which non-Catholic Christians belong to the Mystical Body of Christ.

4. It is not by chance that the head metaphor came to be superimposed on the image of Church-as-body. If it shows us that Christ is above the Church, above the Powers, it does not necessarily follow that this comes from a thematically different context. On the contrary, the head metaphor is imposed on the

body-bride metaphor to the extent that we translate *baśar* not by flesh but by body. It has been rightly pointed out that "it seems hardly possible that Paul used *kephalè* in an immediate *soma*-context without any conscious reference at all to the anatomical picture it brings to mind." [74]

---

cf. *Ep.* 2: 20-22 (*"built* upon the foundations... in whom the whole *structure*, etc."). While Paul indiscriminately uses the figures of building and body, in the non-Pauline writings the figures of building and wife are connected: Hermas, *Vis.*, III, 3, 3-4, 1; IV *Ezra* 3: 1; 4: 1; 7: 4; 9: 4, and especially *Rv.* 21: 1-2. Vielhauser speaks of an unimaginable architectural figure, in which the building is not yet completely constructed while the keystone is already in place and serves to unite the whole (*TWNT*, t. V, p. 148). This is to show how illogical is the translation ἀϰϱογωνιαῖος = keystone, proposed by J. Jeremias (e.a. in *TWNT*, t. I p. 792 f.) and that the usual translation, cornerstone is to be maintained. See J. Pfammatter, *Die Kirche als Bau, eine exegetisch-theologische Studie d. Ekklesiologie d. Paulusbriefe*, Rome 1960; K. Schaeffer, *Zur Deutung von Eph., 2, 20*, in *Neut. Aufsätze*, Regensburg, 1963, pp. 218-224. Here we find ourselves with exactly the same difficulty as with the head-body figure, if we take it too literally.

---

67. See Strack-Billerbeck, *op. cit.*, t. I, p. 503 ff.

68. Michaelis, in *TWNT*, t. III, i. v. ϰρατέω, p. 910 ff. F. Zorell, *Lex. Gr. N.T.*, Paris, 1931, 734γ: "ϰρατέω" hic = fideliter sequor, quod utique de aliquo duce vel principe intelligi tantum potest." For from causing an objection to our interpretation of body = wife, the passages Colossians 2: 19 and Ephesians 4: 15-16 are on the contrary an illustration of the rule formulated above: body (organism) - collectivity is a metaphor which is superimposed on the primordial image of body-wife. Let us note further that συμβιβάξειν (to bring together, reunite) is ordinarily used of persons (Masson, *op. cit.*, p. 165, n. 5). Ἐπιχορηγεῖν, according to Lohmeyer, is found frequently in marriage contracts and suits: *Die Briefe an die Philipper, an die Kolosser und an Philemon*, Göttingen, 1956, p. 125, n. 4. May we not connect "the help of the Spirit of Jesus Christ which is given us (ἐπιχορηγίας = *Ph.* 1: 19) with the fostering care of our divine Bridegroom? (Cf. *Ep.* 5: 29; I *Cor.* 10: 17).

69. Masson, *op. cit.*, p. 150.

70. Schlier, *op. cit.*, e.g., pp. 93-96; Benoit, *op. cit.*, p. 12, and *Épître aux Éphésiens*, in *SDB*, VII, col. 203. For a criticism of Schlier's work, see E. Käsemann, *Das Interpretationsproblem des Epheserbriefes*, in *Theol. Lit. Zeitung*, 1961, col. 1-8.

5. It has been asked what the reasons are that brought Paul to use this body metaphor. These solutions have been proposed: the Stoic theme of the cosmic body or the body politic, the Gnostic myth of the heavenly *Anthropos,* the Old Testament notions of corporate personality, the rabbinical speculations on the first man, the preponderant role of the crucified body of the Lord in the redemption mystery, the very special capacity of his glorified body,[75] the equation: Body of Christ = temple of the new covenant, the institution of the Eucharist, the very important place occupied by the vine metaphor in Judaism.[76] We think that all of these things may have influenced the Apostle. Yet Paul has clearly shown what the chief source of this metaphor was, namely the account of the formation of the first human couple [77] to which he refers us several times.[78]

For the Apostle Christ and the Church are two persons, or — which comes to the same thing — two bodies, united in one conjugal body. "Man's task is to explain and to justify woman; woman's task is to reveal the man. This is a question of capital importance. When it is said that the woman is the body of her husband it means that the husband has in her not his own extension but rather the way to encounter himself. In turn this is applied to understanding the Church as the Body of Christ. She is not the continued Christ, the continued Incarnation. We cannot pass from Christ to the Church. The cross stands between them. As the Body of Christ, the Church meets her Lord: she does not replace him, but she expresses him *hic et nunc.* She does not replace him, she makes him visible and manifests him without becoming herself confused with him." [79]

Adam ἐπουράνιος (I *Cor.* 15: 44 ff.) has returned to heaven with his resurrected and glorified body;[80] the body of the new Eve still lives on earth and in exile far from the Lord (II *Cor.* 5: 6). But the Lord is with her as heavenly bread and life-giving Spirit. "The Spirit and the Bride say 'Come, Lord.' And he answers, 'Surely I am coming soon'" (*Rv.* 22: 17, 20).

Egmond-Binnen   Dom Paul Andriessen
(Netherlands)   Abbot of Egmond-Binnen

71. It is in this way that God "gave" Eve to Adam. Of all the gifts granted by God to believers (*Ep.* 1: 17; 3, 2, 7, 8, 11) Christ is the greatest, because he is the source of all the others. See S. Hanson, *The Unity of the Church in the New Testament*, Uppsala, 1946, p. 156. Schlier, *op. cit.*, p. 190 .

72. Consequently we are entirely on Casel's side (= note 7) who holds that the expression "Body of Christ" derives from the idea of "Bride of Christ." Against Wikenhauser who rejects this opinion he makes us hold that the identification of the two metaphors is not restricted to the captivity epistles. It ought even less be conceived as "a linking up" ("an artificial linking up" according to Cerfaux, *op. cit.*, p. 276) of two very different figures which each in its own way aim at clarifying one and the same truth (= note 10).

73. Masson, *op. cit.*, p. 156.

---

74. St. Bedale, *op. cit.*, p. 214. But the author adds that Paul in no way elaborated it or applied it. See J. Hamer, *L'Église est une communion*, in *Unam Sanctam*, t. XL, Paris, 1962, pp. 62-63.

---

75. It is Reuss (*op. cit.*) who most strongly emphasized this capacity of inclusion possessed by the risen body of Christ.

76. A solution suggested by Schweizer, *Die Kirche als Leib Christi in den paulinischen Antilegomena*, in *Theol. Lit. Zeitung*, 1961, col. 241- 256.

77. A. Dubarle, *L'origine dans l'Ancien Testament de la notion paulinienne de l'Église, corps du Christ*, in *Stud, paul. C.I.C.*, Rome, t. I, pp. 231-256.

78. E.g., *Rm.* 5: 12-19; I *Cor.* 6: 16; 11: 3-12; 15: 21-22, 45-49; II *Cor.* 11: 2-3; *Ep.* 5: 29-33; I *Tim.* 2: 13-14. The human race came from one man (*Ac.* 17: 26; cf. *Tob.* 8: 6). Dupont's opinion, according to which the unique principle — ἐξ ἑνός, — would be God himself (*op. cit.*, p. 342 ff), agrees with difficulty with the ὁ Θεός of verse 24. See Hanson, *op. cit.*, p. 101 ff.

79. So I. Muirhead in his recension of J. v. Allmen's book, *Maris et femmes d'après saint Paul*, in *Scottish Journal of Theology*, t. VI, p. 331, cited by T. Torrance, *Le sacerdoce royal*, in *Verbum Caro*, 1958, t. XLVII, p. 258.

80. See on the other side A. Hulsbosch, *Het Lichaam van Christus* in *Het Schild*, 1960, pp. 193-205.

VI

Lucien Cerfaux

The Church in the Book of Revelation

Our time is experiencing a renewed interest in the Johannine Book of Revelation, which is becoming an increasingly unsealed book. I think in particular of the profound studies of several great friends of our biblical meetings at Louvain, Frs. Braun and Boisnard and Messrs. Feuilley and Cambier.[1] But our interest in this paper will not so much focus on the Book of Revelation itself as on the light it sheds on the notion of the Church within the community of Asia some forty years after the Pauline epistles.

The Church of Revelation is essentially a Church on the alert because of persecution. Christian tradition mentions the time of Domitian; and among holders of this opinion Irenaeus, Clement of Alexandria, Origen and Victorinus are cited.[2] There is no dearth of modern scholars who plead for an earlier date, but our subject does not require us to make any prior choice. As we proceed, however, certain reasons will arise that opt for the end of the first century.

From the methodological viewpoint — and this is so very important in any analysis of Revelation — we retain the unity of the book on the authority of its last redactor — the prophet — who made use of prior sources (in the broad sense). A Jewish underlay can be explained in many ways, and in any case by traditions of an apocalyptic type. The prophet is quite familiar

---

1. For the bibliography, see: *Introduction à la Bible*, t. II, Paris, 1959, pp. 710-742; A. Feuillet, *L'Apocalypse* (*Studia Neotestamentica, Subsidia,* 3), Bruges, 1963.

2. H. B. Swete, *The Apocalypse of St. John,* London, 1909, p. 99 ff.

with the Asiatic milieu and cannot fail to allude to it.[3] His
visions may be spread out over decades, and perhaps since the
Jewish war.[4] They have been gone over, retouched and adapted
to new circumstances. As we have it, the succession of eschatological events is merely a literary device. From the many repetitions
we may conclude that there were many visions but not that there
was a spacing out in time of distinct events. In general we shall
not be concerned therefore with the scenario, but shall concentrate
on certain major elements which to us seem to characterize the
Church in Revelation.[5]

First of all we shall consider the concrete religious situation
of the local churches, and only afterwards — conforming with
the schema of the book itself — will we have the Church Universal
in view. She is shown to us above all in her ideal and heavenly
reality, and represented figuratively. In the last analysis the
imagery comes from the Old Testament, but the persecution theme
at times embellishes it with antitheses that recall the familiar
personifications of the Hellenistic age.

I. THE LIFE OF THE LOCAL CHURCHES

Our subject is framed in the concrete situation of the churches
of Asia. In his epistle to the Colossians, Paul feared the influence
of a Judeo-pagan syncretism grafted upon a mystery cult of
angels identified with the astral Powers (*Col.* 2: 16-19). The
destruction of Jerusalem on the one hand and the extraordinary
success of Christianity in Asia on the other dug the trench between
Jews and Christians. The Jews were on their guard against compromising what they still possessed of religious and civil freedom
by sponsoring a sect which was suspect by Rome, the clergy
of Asia and the populace alike. For the prophet, the Jews were
nothing more than Satan's synagogue (*Rv.* 2: 9 and 3: 9). Yet
the threat of syncretistic infiltration was not over, and the sects
that made their appearance from this point on already are
harbingers of licentious Gnosticism (2: 6, 14 ff., 20-23). In

general the Christians have been true to their faith. They practice
charity with its various duties (2: 19). At first sight it is astonishing that hope is not mentioned, but in these threatening times
it is manifested concretely through endurance (1: 9; 2: 2, 3, 19;
3: 10). Furthermore the promises at the conclusion of the seven
letters can only arouse a living hope, enflamed by these figurative
formulas which are inspired by the manifold visions of the
prophecy: the tree of life, the crown of life, the hidden manna,
the morning star, the book of life, the heavenly temple, the new
Jerusalem, and finally, the exaltation to Christ's own throne.

From St. Paul's time persecution had profoundly modified
Christian consciences. The truce between the Empire and Christianity was broken. Christians are gnawed by anxiety. At every
corner their lives are threatened by contact with temples and
statues; they are recognized in the marketplace by their refusal
to buy sacrificial meats; [6] they are absent from public festivals,
and are obliged out of apostasy to reject the oath in the Emperor's
name; they are looked upon as godless and unpatriotic, in a
state of more or less open rebellion against Rome. The situation
is especially tense in the province of Asia where the populace
is fanatically devout from time immemorial to the worship of
the goddess Roma and the Emperors. "The very tone of Revelation
is an echo of (the) violence (of the conflict)," writes P. Touilleux,
"this daring attack against Roman tyranny, this stirring appeal

3. P. Touilleux, *L'Apocalypse et les cultes de Domitien et de Cybèle*,
Paris, 1935; W. Ramsey, *The Letters to the Seven Churches of Asia*, 4th
ed., London; P. Prigent, *Apocalypse 12. Histoire de l'exégèse* (*Beiträge zur
Geschichte der biblischen Exegese*, 2), Tübingen, 1959.

4. Cf. S. Giet, *L'Apocalypse et l'histoire*, Paris, 1957.

5. Of the two levels, scenario and visions, the latter is original. The
visions contemplated from various angles the lot of the persecuted Church
with her eschatological hopes, already anticipated in a first spiritual accomplishment which outlined the definitive realization. This viewpoint
seems essential to us for the interpretation of the book. We shall explain
what we mean in a more detailed way in the course of this brief study.

6. Cp. Pliny, *Ep.*, 10, 96, 10 (ed. R. Hanslick) with *Rv.* 13: 17.

to action and to martyrdom can be understood only in the context of open warfare." [7] S. Giet whispers: "Revelation is saturated in a battle atmosphere, but this is to bring Christians to an armed alert: it commits them to a courageous and tranquil period of waiting." [8]

Christ protects his own. For the prophet he is the glorious Son of Man standing in the midst of the seven gold candle-sticks which symbolize the seven Churches. They are golden candle-sticks because the Churches, especially in time of persecution, are Christ's visible witnesses. Now above all the lamp is not placed beneath the bushel.[9]

We should like to know a bit more about the organization of the Churches. An underlying element safely upholds the orthodox faith. This can be Christ's teaching alone, handed on by the message of the Twelve, these "twelve apostles of the Lamb" that the prophet sees at the foundations of the Church's ramparts (21: 14).[10] Unity comes from this faith, from active charity and the watchfulness of the Son of Man who holds in his right hand the angels if the Churches, *viz.,* the authorities governing them: angels of heaven and the local authorities on earth. If Revelation dates from the 90's we then have the right to suppose that the rule of faith of Clement of Rome's letter is already formed and is spreading throughout all the Churches: the Apostles, in order to preserve unity, have appointed their first disciples to govern the local Churches, and their line will continue in their successors. The absence of any explicit mention of bishops or presbyters, through whom this succession is ordinarily carried out, is explained by the disorder resulting from the persecutions. It is as a prophet, one especially accredited by the Spirit at this time, that John gives consolation and encouragement, and that he directs the other prophets (1: 1; 19: 10) as well as the "apostles" (18: 20) who are undoubtedly charismatic itinerants. Like Paul, as a "servant" of God and Christ (1: 1; 10: 7; 22: 6), he is aware of possessing an authority that permits him to express faithfully the "word of God and the testimony of Jesus Christ" (1: 2) and to require all Christians to submit to his prophecy (1: 3; 22: 18-19).

At first sight we are astonished to see an apocalyptic prophet presenting himself as supreme guide of the Churches, but we must remember that Paul himself in the captivity epistles appears as a prophet revealing the mystery of God (*Ep.* 3: 3 etc.), and, except for its emphasis on the end of time, the mystery of God of the Book of Revelation "announced by God to his servants the prophets" (10: 7) is not basically different from the Pauline "prophecy." Is that where the analogy stops? Tradition is perhaps not wrong in attributing an apostolic origin to John's book.

II. THE IDEALIZED (ESCHATOLOGICAL) UNIVERSAL CHURCH

The use of the word "church" is restricted to designating the local Churches. These, the collectivities of the "saints" to whom the prophecy is addressed, are symbolized by the seven golden candlesticks in the midst of which appears the Son of Man (1: 13, 20). They are essentially earthly. Only their angels and the 24 symbolic elders represent them in heaven. On the other hand

---

7. *Op. cit.*, p. 79.

8. *Op. cit.*, p. 177.

9. The formulas of "witness" abound throughout the book. In the vision of ch. 11, the "two witnesses" (11: 13) make a contrast with the two beasts, the political power and the religious authority of paganism. This remark, confirmed by the explicit citation of the vision of the lampstand and the two olive trees (the two Anointed Ones, the king and the high priest) of the fourth chapter of Zachariah, invite us to interpret them allegorically as a witness of the Church. A. Feuillet specifies this when he writes that the two witnesses "embody . . . the witness borne by the Church to Christ in the face of a Judaism that persisted in its incredulity" (A. Feuillet, *Essai d'interprétation du chapitre XI de l'Apocalypse,* in *New Testament Studies,* 1957-1958, t. IV, p. 191). We could also think especially of the witness of the spiritual authorities of the communities, perhaps even of that of the prophets (cf. v. 6).

10. Cf. 1: 2. The word of God and the witness of Jesus Christ bear on the visions, but these formulas make us think of the whole gospel and the entire teaching of Christ. The prophet understands that his prophecy concords with the teachings of Christ promulgated by the Apostles.

the Church Universal is so much within the divine plan of
salvation as a heavenly reality that the images of the betrothed
or of the heavenly Jerusalem situate it among the non-temporal
realities.

The themes and the imagery that we shall be examining are
conditioned, we suppose, by the anguish of the persecutions which
explains the preponderance of the eschatological element. A great
part of our concern will focus on an understanding of its exact
significance at this moment of Christian history.

1. *The struggle between the heavenly woman, mother of Christ,
and the dragon.*

The problem of the persecution of the Church by the authorities
of the Greco-Roman world did not preoccupy St. Paul. If he
did have a glimpse of a sovereign persecutor through reading the
Jewish and Christian apocalypses, he placed him at the very
end of time. He himself was conscious of living in a time of
peace, even perhaps of (temporary) benevolence of the Roman
Empire. It is not demonstrated that the "Restrainer" of the
second epistle to the Thessalonians would not be this very benevolence itself. The impression that we get from the whole of
the Book of Acts and I Peter is hardly less optimistic. Nor do
the pastoral epistles mention any Roman persecution.

Still, the first Christians, according to the prayer-hymn of
Acts 4: 24-30, see in Christ's passion and the hostility of the
Jews of Jerusalem the fulfillment of the prophecy of Psalm 2:
1 ff.: the nations, the kings and the princes of the earth, i.e.,
Herod, Pontius Pilate and the pagans, will rise up against God,
the *Despotes* and Creator, and against his Christ, and the
people of Israel will make chorus against them. The same text
of the Psalm will be returned to in Revelation with the "eucharistic"
canticle to the Lord God *Pantokrator* that ends the first part
of the book (11: 15 ff.). In this text we see in a non-figurative
way the eschatological theory of the prophet: the Almighty,

he who is and who was, has intervened and begun his Reign; the nations rage and God's wrath has decided upon the time of the judgment of the dead in order to reward his servants the prophets, the saints and those who fear his Name. We shall remember this sober outline when we read the tumultuous and often pathetic libretto that comprises practically all the rest of the book and describes the antagonism between the nations and the all-powerful God, the rewards of the martyrs and the punishments of the judgment. The interpretor therefore ought to look upon these visions as majestic amplifications of very simple assertions.

The drama will begin in chapter 12. To the war on Christianity declared by the Roman Empire, Christians answer with the proclamation of the Kingship of God and of Christ; over the course of the two and a half centuries of persecution it will never be otherwise. At this time the Emperor seems to be Domitian, the Nero *redivivus,* who had himself officially called Lord and God, *Dominus et Deus,* and required that he be given divine honors. "He sat on the throne clad in a purple toga, his head circled with a gold crown bearing the effigies of the Capitoline triad. At his side were the flamina of Jupiter and the college of Flavian priests, dressed like him, although their crowns bore his own image." [11] He was therefore the supreme God, God of gods and Lord of lords. The province of Asia was accustomed to prostrating before the goddess Roma and the Emperors. It was the one place on earth where people believed most seriously in divine epiphanies. Christians must submit.

Certainly historians understand this situation. It is their job to comprehend in a human way. The prophet sees much more. To him the lot of the Church seems against nature: the Kingdom of God was established with Christ's resurrection and now the saints, the kings of this Kingdom, are trampled underfoot by the kings of this earth. A religious explanation must be found and the visions give it to us in a dramatized way.

---

11. Tondriau, in J. Cerfaux and J. Tondriau, *Le Culte des Souverains,* Paris, 1956, p. 356.

The great vision of ch. 12 sets up the two protagonists first of all: the Heavenly Church, radiant and intangible, although on earth it will be an emigrant, and the Dragon. Actually Genesis suggests a primordial conflict between two symbolic beings. The woman who gives birth in pain—but who is at the same time a heavenly creature—first of all represents the Church under the Old Testament, the mother of Christ; the snake represents a demoniacal being set on destroying the divine work. The conflict is amplified in images and inscribed upon the vault of heaven, thus revealing the divine plan. At this point the snake assumes the shape of a primordial monster, the Dragon who is called Tiamat, Kronos or Python in the mythologies.[12]

A first eschatological combat is fought in heaven between the angelic armies commanded by Michael and the Dragon and his angels. The Dragon and his army are cast down to earth, while the son of the woman, the risen Christ, begins his heavenly Reign.

The Dragon will set himself against the woman who is also present on earth, but still unknown to him, under the protection of God (in the desert). His magic power raises two evil-working beasts from the sea, the first symbolizing the series of Roman Emperors and the second the pontiffs of pagan cults who are in league with the imperial power and impose the cult of Rome and the Emperors on the whole Greco-Roman religious world. Faced with this is the persecuted Church which possesses the divine promises and knows that the Messiah is reigning and shall reign.[13]

After chapter 12, the prophet abandons the figure of the Church-Mother and adopts that of the Lamb's betrothed. In the Old Testament the images may be confounded: the Israelites are the children of the woman, the nation that is betrothed to God.[14] This notion is less in line with the general trend in the New Testament; there, the role of the bridegroom has devolved upon Christ; since Christians are his brothers, the theme of the descendence of the Church is no longer easily applicable to them nor consequently is the line of motherhood to the Church. This is the more usual position of St. Paul [15] and that of Revelation after chapter 12.

2. *A general theme: the two cities.*

The Book of Daniel announced that after the destruction of the earthly empires the Kingdom of the Saints of the Most High (represented by the Son of Man) would be established. The Book of Revelation transposes this theme into a new perspective: the Kingdom has indeed been given to the Son of Man and the Saints of the Most High; for the moment the earthly empires concentrate all their power in Imperial Rome which carries on the policy of persecution begun by the Seleucids. Two cities are set against one another definitively and eschatologically: carnal Rome, the persecutor, destined to its own punishment, and the Church. The Church's trials are compensated for by her triumph; the prophet contemplates the people of God in its glory in eternity.

The thread of Ariadne which best guides us in the labyrinth of the last chapters of the book is not the scenario which for better or worse has been shaped to organize into a dramatic account the succession of events which proceed from a time of calamity to the glory of the end of the world. It is rather the

---

12. Cf. P. Prigent, *op. cit.*, pp. 120-124.

13. In passing, Paul used the image of the heavenly Jerusalem, the free-woman, our mother, but he did not borrow it from the same sources as Revelation. He derives it from the Sarah-Hagar allegory and the Deutero-Isaiah (*Gal.* 4: 23-27). To connect it with the proto-Evangelium would be difficult, since Paul uses this latter in the direction of Adam (anti-type of the Messiah)-Eve.

14. The heavenly character of the woman in chapter 12 is in fact suggested by the enthusiastic descriptions of the Deutero-Isaiah (cf. *Is.* 60: 1, 19-20) and probably also by the Song of Solomon (6: 10). Cf. M. Cambe, *Influence du Cantique des cantiques sur le Nouveau Testament,* in *Revue Thomiste,* 1962, t. LXII, pp. 5-26.

15. Cf. II *Cor.* 11: 2; *Ep.* 5: 23-32; the Church-body image is connected with that of the body and with the text of Genesis 2: 34.

psychological attitudes of the Seer who contemplates antithetically
the horrors of pagan and persecuting Rome and the ideal purity
of the Church, and who projects in the Church persecuted the
promises of the messianic and eschatological future. The visions
follow one another in line with this program and they begin with
the revelation of Rome.

3. *Rome, the great harlot.*

The prophet's imagination is familiar with the representations
of the Hellenistic world. His vision of the imperial city combines
with ease the characteristics of a symbolic goddess and those
of a city. The goddess, dressed as a harlot, is seated upon the
monster that the Dragon dragged up from the sea, the imperial
power (cf. 17: 8), or else on the seven hills (17: 9). In her
hands she holds a gold cup filled with her filth. She becomes
drunk on the blood of the saints and the witnesses of Jesus (17: 6).
She reigns over all the kings of the earth (17: 18). But she is
carried away in eschatological punishment (14: 8), and her
finish is the signal of God's triumph (19: 1-5).

The prophet need no longer explain to us that all of this
imperial power is a usurpation of the power of God and that
its cultual aspect is a parody of the one lawful religion. The
opposition has degenerated into this conflict whose victims are
the saints and martyrs. In addition Rome's fall really and literally
corresponds to the triumph of the Church, the marriage of the
Lamb (19: 6-10).

The literary antithesis recalls the two images derived from
the Old Testament: the Lamb's betrothed and the heavenly city.

4. *The Lamb's betrothed.*

A triumphal hymn to the Almighty God, the victorious king,
announces for the first time the vision of the betrothed. She
readies herself and dons the shining white linen. (The prophet

hastens to tell us, so that our imagination does not run away with us, that this linen symbolizes the merits of the saints — 19: 6-8.) This theme disappears beginning with 19: 10,[16] only to reappear in a fleeting comparison in 21: 2 (first vision of the heavenly Jerusalem) and then solemnly in 21: 9. But this time also the vision of the betrothed is as instantaneous as in its first description in 19: 6-8; or rather the vision corresponding to the solemn announcement of the betrothed is in reality that of the heavenly city. The description of Rome the harlot was wordy and stressed her showiness and her profligacy. About the betrothed we know only of her linen tunic, her purity and her title as betrothed of the Lamb (19: 7; 21: 9; cf. 19: 7, 9, the marriage of the Lamb). The imagery expresses an innate antagonism. Rome, the harlot, is drunk with the blood of the saints and the witnesses of Jesus (17: 6). The Church is betrothed to the bleeding Lamb who is called "the Lamb that was slain" (5: 6, 9, 12; 13 :8) [17] whose blood makes the robes of Christians white (7: 14) and renders them victorious (12: 11). He is the first "witness" and the Christian martyrs imitate him.

In this image of the Lamb's betrothed there is a sort of equivalence with the Pauline figure of the body of Christ. Revelation does not know this image since it is more faithful to Old Testament imagery. It does not suggest the closeness between the woman and the body of Christ (or rather it avoids it for it could remind us of the sacred marriages of paganism). John also is ignorant of Paul's ontological mysticism related to the Body of Christ theme. His own mysticism is more personal and more laden with sentiments of love for Christ. It is developed in the expectation of the *parousia*: "The Spirit and the Bride say,

---

16. Cf. below, nos. 6 & 7.

17. The choice of the expression ἀρνίον ἐσφαγμένον could be inspired by Jeremiah 11: 19 (ὡς ἀρνίον ἄκακον ἀγόμενον τοῦ Θύεσθαι) combined with Isaiah 53, 7. The substantive ἀρνίον expresses better than πρόβατον the idea of purity and innocence (cf. I *Pet.* 1: 19 with ἀμνός). The sense of *lamb* (not *ram*) is assured for Judeo-Hellenistic and Christian literature. We should be wrong to associate this with a sign of the Zodiac or with the sacred ram of Attis (Touilleux).

'Come' " (22: 17) with the deep sense of spiritual intimacy with
Christ Jesus that has begun on earth in the eucharistic meal:
"Behold I stand at the door and knock: if anyone hears my
voice and opens the door, I will come into him and eat with him
and he with me" (3: 20).[18]

5. *The heavenly city.*

The image of the heavenly city is developed much more at
length and its Old Testament departure points are much more
varied. The description of Rome confused the woman and the
city. Here the Bride of the Lamb and the city coming down
from heaven are, on the contrary, clearly distinct. Here especially
exegesis will have to be on guard against the scenario which
reserves the dazzling manifestation of the heavenly Jerusalem for
the end of time, after the *parousia*. In reality, just as it was the
Rome of the day that appeared enveloped in apocalyptic punishment, so it is the Church of the day that is already mysteriously
the heavenly city, enveloped in glory, which is revealed. To this
inference suggested by the antithetical character of the visions
are joined some details: the Bride of the Lamb with whom
the heavenly city is identified is clearly the present-day Church
(cf. 22: 17) and as we shall soon see, the great description of
the heavenly city (21: 9-22: 5) also in its present composition
focuses on the presently glorified earthly Church.

A preliminary description of the city (21: 1-8) is made up
of two visions. The first is very brief and is inspired by the first
creation account. It is an excellent way of sewing the composition
together (21: 1). The second shows us the heavenly city descending to earth. With the Jerusalem of the Jews is contrasted a new
Jerusalem, a truly holy city, like the Bride who is made ready
and bedecked for her bridegroom (we are therefore in fact within
the perspective of the earthly Church, cf. 19: 8). The vision
plays on the episodes of the desert, recalling the tent of the covenant
and the election of the people (21: 3). The theme of the doing
away with death and suffering recalls the fall (21: 4). God an-

nounces his will, realized eschatologically, in the short partial vision of 21: 1, to renew all things. He offers spiritual benefits and the gift of sonship to the Church (21: 7) and excludes the unbelievers from his promises (21: 8). The event of eschatological realization begins therefore in the Church of today, which from this viewpoint is already identified with the heavenly city, like the Bride readying herself for her marriage.

Despite its complications, the great description (21: 9-22: 5) does not alter the general theme.[19] It strengthens the contemporary character of the eschatological realization. With Ezekiel and the Deutero-Isaiah in particular, people contemplate the earthly messianic Jerusalem spiritualized, just as we might spiritualize traits coming from the second creation account and describing the rivers and trees of paradise. The perspective is no longer that of a Church persecuted by the pagans; her gates are open wide to the Gentiles, the kings bring her their riches and their splendor (21: 24-27); the leaves of a tree of life which gives fruit each month serve as a remedy to heal the Gentiles (22: 2). The messianic characteristics go hand in hand with a spiritualization that is more total than anywhere else. The city has no temple. God is its temple as well as the Lamb (21: 22); in it they have their throne (a reminder of the great inaugural vision) and it is there that God's servants will worship him (and worship him henceforward). They shall see his face and his Name will be upon their foreheads (all will be high priests and will wear the *petalon* [20]) (22: 3-4).

---

18. There are words from the Song of Solomon (cf. M. Cambe, *art. cit.*, pp. 5-9), but the tonality is quite different.

19. Literary similarities are not lacking between the two descriptions, cf. the formulas "bride" (21: 2 and 9), "Jerusalem" and "holy city" coming down from heaven from God (21: 2 and 10); compare 21: 8 and 27; 21: 6 and 22: 1 etc.

20. For this exegesis, cf. Andrew of Caesarea: ... ἀντὶ τοῦ χρυσοῦ πετάλου οὗ πάγαι ὁ ἀρχιερεὺς ἐφόρει (P. G., t. CVI, col. 444). For the "petalon" in primitive Christianity, cf. F.-M. Braun, *Jean le théologien*, Paris, 1959, p. 339.

6. *The earthly reign of the Church.*

A series of eschatological events separated the visions of the great harlot and the Bride of the Lamb, although they are paired. We come back at this point to this section (19: 11 — 20: 15) for the light it sheds on the notion of the Church, for the triumph of the Son of man, with which it deals at length, is also the triumph of the Church.

The Victor appears on a white charger (19: 11). He is a warrior king, the King of kings and the Lord of lords (the only true government is that of God and of his Christ). The beast (symbol of earthly government) and the kings of the earth with their armies engage in battle with him. The beast and the false prophet (to be identified with the second beast raised by Satan) are cast alive into the pool of flaming brimstone; the kings are massacred and the birds feast on their flesh.

Here is a break in the symbolic imagery. The Dragon should follow his minions into the pool of fire. But he is merely shut up in the abyss and rendered powerless for a millennium (22: 1-13). A first judgment with a first resurrection (of the martyrs) is followed by a triumphant reign on earth of a thousand years. After this Satan will emerge from his prison, resume his role as tempter of the nations and the war will begin again. Only this time the outcome is quite definitive and the Dragon rejoins the beast and the false prophets in the pool of fire.

The "construction" is obvious. The prophet's intention is not to focus on the temporal succession of the events about which he speaks, nor on the material reality of this whole phantasmagoria. The only things that concern him are the assertions that confirm the faith and hope of Christians. What are they?

Certainly and especially they are the sureness of the triumphal *parousia* and with it the triumph of Christians, and further, the future resurrection with the judgment. Must we add the reign of 1000 years and the second eschatological resurrection and judgment? Or would these things rather be a breaking up and an over-stretching of the one and instantaneous event of the *parousia*?

An earthly reign of Christ is a part of Jewish apocalyptic tradition.[21] The prophet has kept this in his imagery. Still his own principles do not permit us a literal interpretation. What would be the meaning of such an earthly reign in the essentially spiritual notion of the Bride of the Lamb, the heavenly Jerusalem and, as we shall see, the new people of God? Even the number 1000 is intended to show us another meaning, one which St. Augustine was so triumphantly to use in freeing himself from an old tradition: 1000 years is the duration of eternal things which have no time. Let us then say confidently that these thousand years of the anticipated reign of the resurrected Church cover the same real lapse of time as do the three and a half years of persecution. During the whole period of its earthly existence the Church will know struggle; but at the same time she is already triumphant, already participating in the *parousia* of her Bridegroom, and she will enjoy a spiritual power and the delights of divine grace.[22] This is the Kingdom of God about which Jesus taught, a kingdom founded by his word and one that is established and grows in the midst of trials. This also is Paul's idea of the fortunes of Christianity.

In connection with the essential principles of the faith, we still must explain the two resurrections and the two judgments, i.e., basically the privilege of Christians to have their own resurrection and their own judgment. Is this so unreasonable? Can we forget that Christians are to rise in order to accompany Christ in his triumphant *parousia?* Can we forget that they were chosen by God to be the brothers of his Son and that — to use the language of Revelation — along side the book which gives an accounting of human actions, there exists a book of life in which are written the names of Christ's witnesses from the creation of the world (17: 8; cf. 13: 8)? With their own shades of mean-

---

21. Cf. H. Bietenhard, *Das tausendjährige Reich. Eine biblisch-theologische Studie,* Zurich, 1955.

22. Compare with the 42 months that the pagan nations will ride rough-shod over the holy city, during which time the two witnesses, both invulnerable (cf. also the Church protected in the desert) and powerful, are fulfilling their ministry (11: 1-6), and then with the three and a half days that separate their death and resurrection (11: 7-13).

ing, the epistles of St. Paul and the Book of Revelation allow the same basic thought and the same distinctions that set Christians apart to show through. It is our wish that these distinctions be more formal than real, and in any case they do not prevent theology from being expressed in the category of one general judgment and one resurrection. St. Paul and the prophet of Revelation already hint at this synthesis, but with them we must preserve the mystery that is expressed in the predestination of Christians and their resurrection to share as a Church in Christ's triumph.

7. *The new people.*

An image which we have not mentioned until now shows in another way the same compenetration of heavenly and earthly realities in the person of the Church. The Church is on earth and it participates in the perpetual liturgy which is celebrated in heaven. Yet we do not therefore abandon the antithesis with the Roman empire, for the pagan priests all celebrate the liturgy of Rome and the Caesars. In the cultual praise of the sovereign absolute God, the King of the kings of earth, and in the praise of the Lamb, the reprobation by the Seer and by all of primitive Christianity for pagan worship is expressed.

Revelation opens with a hymn to the "prince of the kings of earth" pronounced by the prophet in the name of his Churches of Asia:

"To him who has loved us
and freed us from our sins by his blood
and made us a kingdom,
priests of his God and Father,
to him be glory and power for ever and ever.
Amen" (1: 5-6).

The same hymn will be returned to and put in the mouths of the four living creatures and the 24 elders. These latter — the Church already present in heaven — prostrate themselves before the Lamb; in their hands they have zithers and golden cups filled with perfume(the prayers of the saints, the Seer explains), and they chant a new hymn: "You are worthy... because you were slain... you have ransomed (men from among the peoples) and you have made them for our God a kingdom and priests, and they shall reign on earth" (5: 8-10). Together with the four living creatures and the 24 elders are united the myriads of angels in heaven, and then all creation (5: 11-14).

Priest-Kings, wearing crowns, performing the liturgical acts, singing hymns — these are the Christians on earth; within the mystery of the Church they find themselves before God's throne. So great is the exigency of holiness that the Church, embracing through her missionary power all the nations of the earth, would be restricted to the martyrs, to those who have made their garments white in the blood of the Lamb. This tension between universalism and the heroism of sanctity characterizes the people of God that is entirely new and the Israel of God.

This new people is still the people of the desert. It will live there for three and a half years — the limited and precarious time of persecution —, protected by the Son of Man and by God's power since it has access to the meeting-tent. Similarly it will from now on enter into the heavenly Jerusalem, rediscover paradise, the living water, the tree of life. Living an anticipated *parousia,* it will reign on earth for the mysterious period of 1000 years which is symbolic of its triumph with Christ at the *Parousia.*

The solidarity between the present and the future is noted in the successive visions of chapters 6 and 7. The first vision shows the souls of martyrs beneath the altar, praying while awaiting the celebration of their triumph that the number of their brother martyrs who are still on earth might reach its fullness (6: 9-11). Then there appear the 144,000 sealed on earth from all the tribes of Israel (evidently an ideal Israel) (7: 1-8). It is they who must be saved from the great trial; in this context they form the object of the subsequent vision, the immense multitude coming from all the nations. Their triumph is celebrated (after the *Parousia*) in a liturgy at which the angels assist. They worship, palms in their hands and clad in white robes which they have brought from earth; they enjoy the totally fulfilled happiness of the new Jerusalem (7: 9-17).

These are the new people: those who wash their garment in the blood of the Lamb and are nourished with the fruit of the tree of life and enter through the gates into the City ... (22: 14). They reign now and shall reign forever.

Concluding remarks.

1. Under the threat of persecutions, the seven Churches of Asia keep faithfully the Christian principles, especially charity and purity of morals. Their faith resists the first thrust of Gnosticism; the unity of the communities among themselves is assured by the fellowship of faith and charity.

2. Underneath we rediscover the notion of the Universal Church, both ideal and heavenly, as it had already been developed in Pauline literature. This time it is expressed especially in images that come from the Old Testament. The image of the body of Christ, proper to St. Paul, is no longer used in the Book of Revelation; with it there also disappears any trace of the influence of popular Stoicism of the syncretistic gnosis of the captivity epistles, as well as its corresponding vocabulary (pleroma, Powers, elements of the world).

3. The threats of persecution have strongly reinforced the apocalyptic hope, translated into themes and visions. Hope accentuates the expectation of the *Parousia* and the triumph of the Church. In the captivity epistles the earthly Church was transported into heaven. It is the same in this book with the people of God. Yet if we must define the Church of the Book of Revelation by its chief notion, we should have to mention more impressive images: the Bride of the Lamb and the heavenly Jerusalem which "comes down" from heaven at the end of time. This "coming down" begins from this moment and the earthly Church is already transformed by it — God's answer to

its expectation that was inspired by the Holy Spirit. From this we may deduce a theology parallel to that of the spiritual gifts of the great Pauline epistles. The visions possess such spiritual purity and such evocative force that they introduce us — perhaps better than abstract formulas — into the mystery of the Church.[23] The closest analogy would be with the revelation in parables of the secret of the Kingdom of heaven found in the Synoptics.

Boulevard de Tervueren, 110,   L. Cerfaux
Louvain   Professor at the University

---

23. Cf. P. S. Minear, *Images of the Church in the New Testament*, London, 1961.

VII

Joseph Coppens

The Eucharist: Sacrament and Sacrifice of the New Covenant, Foundation of the Church

In our study on the Church (*L'Église. Nouvelle alliance de Dieu avec son peuple*) we tried to show that the notion of new covenant is basic in the New Testament for an exact understanding of the idea of the Church, and consequently, that the Eucharist, the mystery celebrated by Christ to seal his covenant, is indissolubly bound up with the origin of the religious society that Jesus came to establish on earth and which he seems therefore to have definitively called into existence at the supreme hour when he was to consummate his sacrifice.[1]

It is important therefore, in this series on the Church as presented in the New Testament, to examine and scrutinize the texts dealing with the institution of the eucharistic mystery. We are all the more happy to do so since we have already treated the New Testament eucharistic doctrine [2] and one of our former students, the late Canon Werner Goossens wrote a dissertation on the subject which is still fresh.[3] Yet since the publication of

---

1. See above, chapter I.

2. J. Coppens, *L'offrande des fidèles dans la liturgie eucharistique ancienne* in *Cours et conférences des semaines liturgiques*, t. V, pp. 99-123, Louvain, 1927; *Les prières de l'offertoire et le rite de l'offrande. Origines et développement, ibid.*, t. VI, pp. 185-196, Louvain, 1928; *Le mystère eucharistique et les mystères païens. Le canon de la sainte Messe est-elle une célébration de mystère?, ibid.*, t. VII, pp. 111-134, Louvain, 1931; *Les soi-disant analogies juives de l'eucharistie*, in *Eph. Theol. Lov.*, 1931, t. VIII, pp. 238-248.

3. W. Goossens, *Les Origines de l'Eucharistie sacrement et sacrifice*, in *Univ. Cath. Lovan. Diss. ad gradum magistri in Facult. Theol.*, ser. II, t. XXII, Gembloux-Paris, 1931.

this work, important contributions to the history of the origins of the Eucharist have appeared.[4] In taking their results into account, we hope to explain our own views on a basic belief and an essential rite of the New Covenant. We shall examine successively the problem of the tenor of the eucharistic words themselves, their setting and their doctrinal background.

I. THE MOST PRIMITIVE CONTENT OF THE WORDS OF INSTITUTION

The words of the institution of the Eucharist provide the exegete with a perfect opportunity to study the *ipsissima verba Christi*. Here more than elsewhere the primordial state of Christ's words is most necessary, and broadly speaking it is possible to discover it. Actually, under the circumstances, no one will contest that the Lord's words were handed down with variants and therefore with some freedom. The eucharistic supper was not repeated by Christ.[5] Consequently there is no way to explain the textual divergences as going back to Jesus' own repetitions of the rite. Furthermore, the existence of four traditions: Paul, Mark, Matthew and Luke gives us a unique opportunity of connecting, comparing and evaluating the various literary strata, and then of disentangling from them what might possibly be the most primitive substratum. Let us add that the attempt is all the more worthwhile since one of these traditions, the Pauline, is particularly early and goes back to the year 49 or at least 53.[6] It is thought not unreasonably to be the earliest written form of Jesus' words. It is introduced by a preliminary assumption that shows us we are in the presence of an utterance that was handed down by a pre-Pauline tradition. It is composed in language that betrays a pre-Pauline vocabulary and thereby confirms its very early origin.

The rabbinically flavored formula that introduces the eucharistic section of I Corinthians opts for the historical Christ, as is almost unanimously admitted today, even if we admit with E. Käsemann (1937), H. Lessig (1953), O. Cullmann (1954) and G. Bornkamm (1959), that it also includes a reference to the exalted or pneumatic Christ.[7]

Among the words contained in the eucharistic section and which Paul does not use elsewhere, or at least hardly ever, we find *anamnêsis, deipneîn, eucharisteîn* to designate the blessing

---

4. Let us cite in particular from a Catholic point of view: H. Schürmann, *Der Paschamahlbericht Lk. 22, (7-14) 15-8. I. Teil einer quellenkritischen Untersuchung des lukanischen Abendmahlberichtes Lk. 22, 7-38*, in *Neutest. Abh.*, t. XIX, fasc. 5, Münster, 1953; *Der Einsetzungsbericht Lk. 22, 19-20. II. Teil einer quellenkritischen Untersuchung des lukanischen Abendmahlsberichtes Lk. 22, 7-38, ibid.*, t. XX, fasc. 4, Münster, 1955; *Jesu Abschiedsrede Lk. 22, 21-38. III. Teil einer quellenkritischen Untersuchung des lukanischen Abendmahlsberichtes Lk. 22, 7-38 ibid.*, t. XX, fasc. 5, Münster 1957; *Der Abendmahlsbericht Lk. 22, 7-34 als Gottesdienstordnung, Gemeindeordnung, Lebensordnung,* in *Die Botschaft Gottes. Neutestamentliche Reihe,* fasc, 1, Leipzig, 1955; *Die Semitismen im Einsetzungsbericht bei Markus und bei Lukas (Mk. 14: 22-24 / Lk. 22: 19-20,* in *Zeitschr. Kath. Theol.*, 1951, t. LXXIII, pp. 72-77; *Lk. 22, 19b-20 als ursprüngliche Textüberlieferung,* in *Biblica,* 1951, t. XXXII, pp. 364-392; *Lk. 22: 42a das älteste Zeugnis für Lk. 22, 20,* in *Münch. Theol. Zeitschr.*, 1952, t. III, pp. 185-188; *Das apostolische Interesse am eucharistischen Kelch, ibid.*, 1953, t. IV, pp. 223-231; *Die Dublettenvermeidung im Lukasevangelium,* in *Zeitschr. Kath. Theol.*, 1954, t. LXXVI, pp. 83-93; *Die Gestalt der urchristlichen Eucharistiefeier,* in *Münch. Theol. Zeitschr.*, 1955, t. VI, pp. 107-131; *Die Eucharistie als Repräsentation und Applikation des Heilsgeschenens nach Joh.*, 6, 53-58, in *Trier. Theol. Zeitschr.*, 1959, t. LXVIII, pp. 30-45, 108-118; *Joh. 6, 51c, ein Schüssel zur grossen johannesischen Brotrede,* in *Bibl. Zeitschr.*, 1958, t. II, pp. 244-262, P. Neunzeit, *Das Herrenmahl Studien zur paulinischen Eucharistieauffassung,* in *Studien zum Alten und Neuen Testament*, t. I, Munich, 1960. J. Betz, *Die Eucharistie in der Zeit der griechischen Väter*, t. II, 1: *Die Realpräsenz des Leibes und des Blutes Jesu im Abendmahl nach dem Neuen Testament*, Freiburg-am-B., 1961.

For the patristic period, cf. J. Betz, *Die Eucharistie in der Zeit der griechischen Väter*, t. I, 1: *Die Aktualpräsenz der Person und des Heilswerkes Jesu Abendmahl nach der vorephesischen griechischen Patristik*, Freiburg-am-B., 1955.

Among the many non-Catholic works we might mention A. J. B. Higgins, *The Lords' Supper in the New Testament*, 3rd ed., in *Studies in Biblical Theology*, No. 6, London, 1956.

5. Strictly, we might suppose that Christ repeated the Eucharist after

of a meal, *klân* used without an object, *metá* followed by a
verb used as a substantive, *osákis* and *paradídosthai* used absolutely. To this list some add *sôma* as designating the body of Christ
alone, whereas elsewhere this term mysteriously includes Christians
themselves, as well as the word-pair *sôma-diathéke* which would
not be Pauline. In the commentary or midrash accompanying the
account of the Last Supper Paul substitutes the couple *sarx-haîma*
for it (I *Cor.* 11: 27) which we also find in I Corinthians 10:
16 in connection with the eucharistic cup and bread. And here
is the final indication of the earliness and priority of the Pauline
passage: only this text gives us a eucharistic celebration where
a meal separates the blessing of the cup from that of the bread.[8]

We are then on good authority, it seems, to accord to
the Pauline text the privilege of ancientness. Yet we do not wish
to infer from this that it also furnishes us with the most ancient
type of the eucharistic celebration.

Closest to the Pauline tradition is Luke's text. And this brings
us to place the two side by side and to study them as more or
less independent witnesses of the same source. There is another
affinity found between Mark and Matthew which shows us the
traces of another tradition. It will be important to discover in
each of these two groups what elements appear to have preserved
the most ancient form, then to compare with the same idea in
mind the two formulas that we shall have reconstituted in each
of the two traditions with fair probability as the earliest archetypes
that can be attained by means of an historical and critical investigation.

*In our attempt to go back to the most remote past, in the
attempt to reconstitute as much as possible the* ipsissima verba
*of the Savior as he pronounced them at the Last Supper, we shall
have to take certain directives into account. It will be useful to
make them known as an introduction to our study and necessary
to weigh their importance.*

*First directive. Good method finds the elements common to
the various traditions and attributes them to the original source.*

In fact, except for manifest proof to the contrary, the rule may be followed. Yet we shall take care not to consider *a priori* every tradition proper to only one of the sources as not being capable of being original, and not to forget that certain common elements also can be the result of a harmonization process. According to Jeremias as we should be particularly wary of elements that

the resurrection on the occasion of certain appearances. We can think, for example, of the *fractio panis* in the presence of the disciples at Emmaus. But the eucharistic interpretation of the rite is not sure. Moreover it remains that at the Last Supper the eucharistic words seemed to have been uttered only once. The problem arises then of arriving at an original text and going beyond the variants in order to come as close as possible to the *ipsissima verba Christi*.

In *Das Evangelium nach Markus übersetzt und erklärt*, 10th ed. (*Das Neue Testament Deutsch*, Göttingen, 1963, p. 185), Julius Schniewind thinks that we must give up trying to rediscover the *ipsissima vox* of the Lord. Here as elsewhere we do not have any "rules of order" or "minutes" of what happened. Furthermore, he adds, we have no need for the *ipsissima vox* to establish the historicity of the real content of the action and the words attributed to Jesus. And the author enunciates a norm stamped with a strong critical sense: "Whenever a word attributed to Jesus is in harmony on the one hand with the totality of his words and their Old Testament and Jewish backgrounds, and on the other hand with their consequences: the faith of the primitive Church, the doctrine of the New Testament, then its historicity is guaranteed." This, he concludes, is the case of the *logia* connected with the Eucharist.

6. On the date of the first epistle to the Corinthians, cf. M. Goguel, *Les Épîtres pauliniennes*, in *Introduction au Nouveau Testament*, t. IV, 2nd part, Paris, 1926; W. Michaelis, *Einleitung in das Neue Testament*, Bern, 1946; A. Wikenhauser, *Einleitung in das Neue Testament*, Freiburg-am-B., 1953; E.-B. Allo, *Saint Paul. Première épître aux Corinthiens*, 2nd ed., in *Études Bibliques*, Paris, 1956; W. Marxsen, *Einleitung in das Neue Testament*, 2nd ed., Gütersloh, 1964.

7. E. Käsemann, *Das Abendmahl im Neuen Testament*, in *Beih. Evang. Theol.*, fasc. 3, Munich, 1937; 2nd ed., 1938. H. Lessig, *Die Abendmahlsprobleme im Lichte der neutestamentlichen Forschung* (Diss. Theol.), Bonn, 1953. O. Cullmann, *Die Tradition als exegetisches, historisches und theologisches Problem*, Zurich, 1954. G. Bornkamm, *Herrenmahl und Kirche bei Paulus*, in *Studien zu Antike und Christentum. Gesammelte Aufsätze*, t. II, Munich, 1959.

have changed position and context in the course of the text's transmission. *Wanderworte sind verdächtig.*[9] This is the case of the determination introduced by *huper.* Paul and John mention it in relation to the bread while Mark and Matthew use it for the wine. Luke mentions it for the blessing of both elements.[10] Yet it is not excluded that the addition itself is early and even original. It possesses a Semitic flavor and in the beginning it might indeed have been reserved to the bread alone. Later, tradition would have completed analogically the blessing of the wine. We shall see further on that there are reasons that plead for another way of looking at the matter. In fact the term *Wanderworte* is only very imperfectly verified in this instance.

Second directive. Granted that Jesus probably pronounced the words of the Eucharistic Supper in Aramaic, it is reasonable to think that the terms, expressions and turns of phrase which are of Semitic inspiration can and should win out over the Hellenisms.

For this reason we shall prefer the "for many" of Mark 14: 24; Matthew 26: 28, to the "for you" of Luke 22: 20, as well as the sequence of words in the incidental clause: "which is poured out for many" (*Mk.* 14: 24) to the more Greek word order of Luke 22: 20: literally, "which *for you* is poured out." Partially for the same reason, some hold that the adjective "new" is a secondary addition introduced under the influence of Jeremiah 31: 31, even though Mark and Matthew attest to it. An adjective placed before a substantive does not conform with the spirit of the Semitic languages.

The import of this second rule is no more absolute than the first. The fact that the rite was handed down in a Palestinian context could still have introduced Semitic inspiration and flavor even though this came after Jesus' time.

A third rule is to be handled with still more prudence. It is the invitation not to consider as original the elements that have a strong liturgical bent. This bears, as we point out, on elements that eventually came from a Christian liturgy.

The sources are actually unanimous in placing the supper in the setting of a Jewish liturgical meal — one which the majority of authors even think they can identify, without great danger of error, as a Passover meal.

To the influence of the Christian liturgy, we shall perhaps have to attribute the presence of "you" in Luke 22: 20. Let us point out however that this same pronoun does not seem to put off many of the critics when they are dealing with evaluating the ancientness of the blessing formula of the bread in I Corinthians 11: 24; Luke 22: 19. To the evolution of the eucharistic meal can also be attributed the proximity of the two eucharistic blessings, a proximity which is present everywhere except in Paul, and also the significant displacement of the particle "likewise" in Luke 22: 20, in connection with the place it has again in I Corinthians 11: 25.

The tendency to parallelism and to harmonization may also have introduced new elements. This furnishes us with a fourth criterion.

We shall be able to use it for example when we are dealing with the Lucan addition: "which for you was poured out" (*Lk.* 22: 20), or the substitution of "my blood of the (new) covenant" (*Mk.* 14: 24; *Mt.* 26: 27) for "this cup — the new covenant" of Paul and Luke.

But once again we shall be very prudent, for the use of

---

8. This would result from the place given to "likewise" (*hosaútos*). Luke (22: 20) changes the place of this particle in a way that clearly states that the two eucharistic rites came after the meal. It is for the Hellenists to decide whether too much importance has been given to this detail of the Pauline text. For some ancient data from Mark, cfr. G. D. Kilpatrick, *L'eucharistie dans le Nouveau Testament*, in *Rev. Théol. Phil.*, 1964, t. XCVII, pp. 193-204.

---

9. J. Jeremias, *Die Abendmahlsworte Jesu*, 3rd ed., Göttingen, 1960, p. 188.

10. *Ibid.*, p. 188.

parallelism can go back to Jesus himself whose language offers many examples of this sacrifice of biblical style.

It remains for us to point out one last criterion: the setting and the theological foundation of the accounts.

Actually we can consider the eucharistic meal under different aspects: a Passover meal, a covenant meal or an eschatological meal. Here we have various notions that may be completed and at the same time verified from the beginning, but they also could have pervaded Christian awareness at different stages.

A. *The tradition of Paul and Luke.*

By reason of the date of the epistle to the Corinthians let us first examine the texts of Paul and Luke. The composition of the latter, as we know, offers a special problem: are the verses 19-20 of chapter 22, the very ones which concern us, authentic? Even in 1931, W. Goossens answered affirmatively.[11] Most recent research, particularly the thorough monograph of H. Schürmann, seems to support him. Moreover the question has not very great importance for our precise point of interest. Authentic or not, verses 19-20 represent an ancient version of the eucharistic blessing, connected with the tradition from which the Pauline formula came. It is therefore to be retained as material for comparison.

These are the two texts:

I *Cor.* 11: 23-27	*Lk.* 22: 19-20
23. For I received from the Lord what I also delivered to you, that the Lord Jesus on the night when he was betrayed, took bread	19. And taking bread

24. And when he had given thanks he broke it and said: Take and eat, this is my body which is for you;
    Do this in remembrance of me.
25. Likewise also the cup after supper saying: this cup is the new covenant in my blood. Do this as often as you drink it, in remembrance of me.
26. For as often as you eat this bread and drink this cup, you proclaim the death of the Lord until he comes.
27. Whoever therefore eats the bread or drinks the cup of the Lord
	he gave thanks
	
	he broke it and gave it to them, saying: this is my body which is given for you:
	    Do this in remembrance of me.
	20. And the cup likewise after supper, saying: this cup (is) the new covenant in my blood, which for you has been poured out.

---

11. W. Goossens, *op. cit.*, pp. 101-109. On the problem, see P. Benoit, *Le récit de la cène dans Lc XXII, 15-20. Étude de critique textuelle et littéraire*, in *Exégèse et théologie*, t. I, Paris, 1961, pp. 163-203 (*Rev. Bibl.*, 1939, pp. 357-393). The author defends the long text. Although Luke presents few large-scale borrowings from Paul, in these circumstances, out of fidelity to a liturgical tradition that is anterior even to Paul, Luke took the Pauline formula but retouched it in order to obtain a more perfect parallelism either with his own context or with Mark. See also P. Neuenzeit, *Das Herrenmahl. Studien zur paulinischen Eucharistieauffassung*, in *Studien zum Alten und Neuen Testament*, t. I, Munich, 1960, pp. 101-102. A. Higgins (*op. cit.*, pp. 37-43) also considers the longer text as authentic, but he thinks that Luke 22: 15-19b gives us a form of the primitive celebration of the Eucharist. He does not however conclude from this "that Luke 22: 15-19a points to a *communio sub una.*"

unworthily, will be guilty
of (profaning) the body
and the
blood of the Lord.[12]

Let us compare the two columns from the point of view of their variants and attempt to extract those which seem closest to the *Stammform* or supposed original.

Approaching the comparison from the Pauline text, we discover first an inversion: the adverb "likewise" occupies another place than in St. Luke. The result would be that according to the tradition reported by the Apostle, the two eucharistic rites were separated from one another by the meal. If this is true then we are indeed in the presence of an early element of a primitive ordinance which was not long in disappearing.[13]

Moreover Paul has the words: "Take, eat" as words of Christ in the very beginning. With the pen of the Apostle — as happens with the re-use of the same Greek verb "to eat" in verses 26-29 — these verbs have real import. They emphasize the act of eating and tend to confer on the rite the meaning of a sacrificial meal. Did Jesus utter them himself? It is very hard to say. The Savior's gestures could have made them superfluous. Yet three texts to which we are referred by J. Jeremias: *Jerusalem Talmud,* VIII, 12a, 45; VI, 10a, 63; *Midrash Lament.,* In 1, 4, authorize us to maintain that a similar invitation accompanied the act of breaking bread.[14]

A second addition entails the invitation to repeat the eucharistic blessing of the cup. Its primordial value has been contested [15] and its introduction has been attributed to parenetic motives or the propensity for parallelism. In my opinion neither the doubt nor the opposition are justified. The repetition of the order is understood especially in the hypothesis, attested by Paul, of a separation of the two blessings. Once the two rites are juxtaposed it might be enough to give the injunction only once. Perhaps there are other reasons to explain the Lucan omission. Would it be impossible — and we should like to refer to the custom of calling the Eucharist a *fractio panis* — that in certain circumstances the primitive communities were content to repeat the eucharistic blessing of the bread alone? Wine perhaps was not always available. And furthermore, it may have been believed that the second rite, since it instituted the new covenant which was concluded once and for all, did not have to be repeated. Finally would it not be possible that the addition "as often as you drink" (I *Cor.* 11: 25) implies that in certain circumstances the blessing of the cup was omitted?

As for the presence in Paul of the copulative "is" (lacking in the Greek text of Luke) in the blessing of the cup, P. Neuenzeit thinks that it represents a primitive element. Nevertheless it does not possess any particular theological import. It does not augment the realism of the eucharistic belief. Furthermore it makes the construction of the text heavy, separating (in the Greek text) "covenant" from "in my blood," an expression which qualifies the covenant.

Finally, as for the choice of the possessive adjective (*emô*) in Paul's text (in *my* blood), P. Neuenzeit judges that it is difficult

---

12. We shall not undertake a discussion of textual variants.

13. The Passover meal, taken between the two eucharistic blessings, could hardly harm their religious import. First of all, this meal was a ritual recalling the salvific actions of God under the old law. Also it provided no danger of over-eating: those who partook could and at times had to be content with a very small piece of meat. When the Paschal meal gave way to an *agape*, i.e., an ordinary evening meal (cf. I *Cor.* 11: 17-22) it is understandable that the two blessings were brought together and that they followed as a distinct rite the secular and private meal of the Christian assembly.

14. J. Jeremias, *op. cit.*, p. 159, n. 1; p. 166, n. 3, cited by J. Betz, *op. cit.*, p. 19, n. 75.

15. On the pretended secondary character of the command to repeat the action, cf. below, note 36. H. Schürmann (*Lk. 22: 19-20 als ursprüng- liche Textüberlieferung*, p. 384) considers the Pauline repetition of the command as secondary. "Likewise," he points out, already implied it and made it superfluous. P. Neuenzeit (*op. cit.*, pp. 141-142) is content to doubt the ancientness of the Pauline addition: "as often as you drink." It is a question of a connecting sentence, destined to introduce verse 26. It is known that H. Lietzmann and W. H. Davies attributed the command to Paul's initiative: cf. A. J. B. Higgins, *op. cit.*, pp. 34-36.

to assert with certitude that it is actually Paul's word. If the Apostle is responsible for it, he did not introduce the variant for dogmatic reasons, but in order to have a composition that was more in conformity with the genius of the Greek language. He nonetheless retained the genitive pronoun (*moû*) in the blessing of the bread.

Let us proceed to Luke's text. We have just mentioned and evaluated one particular element of it, namely the position of the adverb "likewise." In our opinion this is secondary. The Lucan turns of expression where the pronoun follows the substantive in the Greek text are probably to be preferred to the Pauline text since they correspond better to a Semitic original.

Yet we should pay more attention to two Lucan additions: the participle "given" which accompanies the blessing of bread and the incidental clause: "which has been poured out for you," in regard to the cup. The first addition is retained by J. Betz for various reasons already partially mentioned above.[16] We can agree with him.

On the other hand the same author resolutely discards the second complement.[17] He claims that it is derived from a tendency toward symmetry, and that it is not needed for clarity or meaning, nor is it present in St. Paul. Most of all, however, it does not agree grammatically with the word (*haímati*) which it modifies. This latter reason alone is enough to consider it an addition.

Let us admit that these reasons do not convince us. If the grammatical construction is deficient — which is obvious — is it not just as difficult to explain in regard to an addition? To make a similar incorrect construction acceptable, we should have to suppose that we were dealing with, for example, a marginal gloss, taken over from the Mark-Matthew tradition and unhappily introduced into the Lucan text because the glosser had lost sight of the dative case of the word it modifies.[18] But why should we refuse Jesus an inclination to parallelism? Why also should we wish to minimize the importance of the fact that Mark and Matthew also have the addition? Finally, even though it may not be strictly required for the sense of the blessing of the cup, let us admit that it makes an appreciable contribution to it.

From these data, we should therefore propose the following as the primordial text of the Paul-Luke tradition:

And taking bread,
giving thanks, he broke (it)
and gave (it) to them,[19]
saying:
Take and eat: [20]
this is my body
which is given for you;
do this in remembrance of me.
Likewise also the cup
after supper,
saying:
this cup

---

16. J. Betz, *op. cit.*, pp. 15-16: 1. Separated from the blessing of the cup, the bread blessing had no clear and precise meaning without an explanatory addition; 2. This addition cannot come from Paul, for it is translatable into a Semitic language, while "for you" alone is not; 3. The Lucan formula fits in well with the most ancient apostolic kerygma. On the other side, P. Neuenzeit (*op. cit.*, pp. 108-109) hesitates to acknowledge as more primitive the addition of "given," despite the efforts exerted by Schürmann to uphold it.

17. *Ibid.*, pp. 15-16. Following H. Schürmann, P. Neuenzeit (*op. cit.*, p. 117) contests the ancientness of "which for you has been poured out." According to him, this formula likens the eucharistic rite too much to Exodus 24: 8, to the detriment of its more primitive connection with Isaiah 53.

18. Unless it is necessarily simply to connect "has been poured out" with the "cup." In this case there is no more problem and the first reason invoked by Betz is no longer present. To assert that this connection is impossible (P. Benoit, *art. cit.*, p. 169) because it supposes that Jesus poured out the cup as a libation, seems exaggerated to me.

19. The primitive character of "and (he) gave (it) to them" has been questioned under the pretext that the will and the action of giving are already included in "he broke." Agreed, but there is nothing to prevent the action of giving from being explicitly underlined by Christ.

20. The "take" is also attested by Mark 14: 22 and Matthew 26: 26. This latter text has "eat" in addition.

the new covenant
in my blood
which for you has been poured out;
do this in remembrance of me.

B. *The Mark - Matthew Tradition.*

Mark 14: 22-25	Matthew 26: 26-29
22. And as they were eating	26. Now as they were eating
Jesus, taking bread,	
having blessed (it), broke (it)	Jesus, taking bread,
and gave it to them	and having blessed (it), broke (it)
and said: Take,	and giving it to the disciples,
this is my body.	he said: Take, eat:
23. And taking (the) cup,	this is my body.
having given thanks,	27. And taking (the) cup,
he gave (it) to them,	having given thanks,
and they drank of it all (of them);	he gave (it) to them,
24. And (he) said to them:	saying: Drink of this all (of you);
this is my blood	
of the new covenant	
which has been poured out	28. for this is my blood
for many.	of the new covenant
	which for many has been poured out
	for forgiveness of sins.
25. Amen, I say to you	29. Now I say to you,
that I shall not again drink	I shall not drink again
of the fruit of the vine,	of this fruit of the vine
until that day	until that day
when I drink it new	when I will drink it new with you
in the Kingdom	in the Kingdom
of God.	of my Father.

Both texts are closely related. The divergences are not considerable. Let us try to evaluate them by comparing Matthew to Mark, a text whose composition is more ancient.

Matthew points out in passing that the eucharistic elements were distributed only to the "disciples": a superfluous specification which betrays a tradition where this term had a specific role. Matthew adds "eat" to Mark's "take." Let us say that he is justified since he rejoins the Pauline tradition. Later, Christians who were more sensitive to the mystery and more inclined to go only as far as Christ-Spirit may have been scandalized by the very realistic tone of the invitation. They may have omitted it. Paul experienced no scruple as is evident from I Corinthians 11: 26-29. For the readers to whom the Gospel of John was addressed the term was already a problem (cf. *Jn.* 6: 53-57).

If the "Take, eat" is to be retained, why should not the same order be preserved in regard to the cup, an order found only in Matthew: *"Drink* of this all (of you)" (*Mt.* 26: 27)? In these circumstances Mark seems to be more primitive. He transformed this order into a narrative statement and he has the cup and not the blood as the object of the verb "drink." Perhaps he wanted by this to avoid the direct, clear and formal invitation to "drink the blood."

Of all the witnesses Matthew is alone in adding "for forgiveness of sins" to the blessing of the cup (v. 28). This text announces the forgiveness of sins by the blood, a theological theme which we find again in Romans 3: 25; 5: 9; Colossians 1: 14; Ephesians 1: 7; Hebrews 9: 22,[21] and which is in the context of the allusions of the fourth song of the Servant of Yahweh and in Jeremiah 31: 31-34. The Roman liturgy which closely follows Matthew has taken this addition into the canon of the Mass.

The last modification: the Greek preposition which we translate "for" ("which *for* many has been poured out": v. 28) and

---

21. The theology of the purifying and redemptive blood is found developed in the epistles to the Hebrews, the first letter of John and Revelation. Cf. J. Coppens, *Les affinités qumrâniennes de l'Épître aux Hébreux,* in *Nouv. Rev. Théol.,* 1962, t. LXXXIV, pp. 128-141, 257-282.

which in the other witnesses is the word *"huper"* becomes *"peri"*
in Matthew.

For the source of the Mark-Matthew tradition then, we
shall retain the following text:

> And as they were eating,
> Jesus, taking bread,
> having blessed (it) broke (it),
> and gave (it) to them, and said:
> Take, eat:
> This is my body.
> And taking (the) cup,
> having given thanks, he gave (it) to them,
> saying:
> Drink of this all (of you):
> This is my blood
> of the new covenant
> which has been poured out for (*huper*) many.

C. *The Comparison of the two traditions.*

We therefore find ourselves faced with two traditions, one
of which, Paul-Luke, is commonly called the Antiochene. It
would go back to the Church in Corinth which would have modified
a more ancient text with harmonizations and certain adaptations
to Greek style.[22] The other tradition reflects a text that would
have been in use and circulation among the Churches of Palestine.
P. Benoit thinks it was the Church of Jerusalem, while Lessig —
pointing out a double recension — is of the opinion that one
of these recensions is of a Syriac tradition, preserved in Matthew
and the other a Roman one handed down by Mark, and that
the Church concerned was that of Caesarea in Palestine.[23] On
first sight, Mark would appear to be the most ancient form.

Let us say from the outset that it will be most difficult to
specify so strictly the places of origin. As for the recension having
priority, we have already been able to point out that original

elements are shared by the different texts. In the Antiochene tradition, certain authors feel that Paul and Luke are practically equal. But on the other hand, in Mark-Matthew, it seems to us that the so-called Caesarean or Jerusalem tradition (Matthew), if we make the exception of the use of *perí* and the addition of "for forgiveness of sins," has the priority.

Now let us try to compare from a closer vantage point the Antiochene and Caesarea-Jerusalem traditions from our reconstructions, and attempt to go beyond them in order to arrive at the archetype or *Stammform*.

The Mark-Matthew tradition authorizes us it seems to trace back to the original text two words which from their Semitic and biblical flavor betray idioms that are in no way Hellenized. It is in this light that "having blessed" (*eulogesas*) seems more archaic than "having given thanks" (*eucharistesas*). The word *eucharistein* in the sense of "to bless" is the Greek expression. It rightly replaces *eulogein* if we grant that this latter verb can hardly denote in Greek a prayer of blessing preceding a meal.[24] It is nevertheless curious that the Mark-Matthew tradition, which preserves the Semitic verb for the blessing of the bread, uses the Greek one for the blessing of the cup. Perhaps this is to introduce and point

---

22. J. Betz, *op. cit.*, p. 16. For the Antiochene origin, J. Betz (*op. cit.*, p. 10, n. 34) refers us to Schlatter (*Lukas*, 1931), H. Lessig, *Die Abendmahlsprobleme im Lichte der neutestamentlichen Forschung seit 1930* (Dissertation), Bonn, 1953, and J. Jeremias, *op. cit.*, pp. 149, 181. Antioch is the point of departure for the present form; the ultimate source would be even in this case the Palestinian Church.

23. See the references to these two authors in J. Betz, *op. cit.*, p. 11, n. 40.

24. Cf. J.-P. Audet, *Esquisse historique du genre littéraire de la "bénédiction" juive de l' "eucharistie" chrétienne*, in *Rev. Bibl.*, 1958, t. LXV, pp. 371-399. It has been pointed out (cf. P. Neuenzeit) that it is not important to stress the Semiticisms of Mark in the eucharistic words since Semiticisms are found throughout the whole of his Gospel. J. Schiewind (*op. cit.*, p. 183) thinks that we can retain the "blessing" for the beginning of the meal and the "eucharist, the thanksgiving" for the end.

out a particular shade of meaning. In addition, we shall retain in the *Stammform* a verb that is so well attested.

From the Mark-Matthew tradition we shall also borrow the term "many" (*Mt.* 26: 28) which is preferable to "you" in the text accompanying the cup, although P. Neuenzeit still considers this uncertain. Further on, we shall have the opportunity of stressing the influence that the fourth song of the *Ebed Yahweh* seems to have exerted on the doctrine of the Eucharist, and the term "many" figures prominently in it (*Is.* 53: 11-12). This expression of the Deutero-Isaiah and Mark could lead to confusion. This is why liturgical usage found it necessary to introduce "you." Yet it is not totally impossible that Jesus could have used an Aramaic pronoun corresponding to "you" in the addition modifying the eucharistized bread, while in the words relative to the shedding of his blood he preferred "many" under the influence of the allusions to the Deutero-Isaian poem. Consequently we shall also retain "which is given for you" contrary to Betz's opinion.[25] On the other hand, we shall follow this author in his suggestion to place "for you" (later variant: "for many") *after* the participle (as in Mark) in order to conform better to Semitic syntax.[26]

The phrase: "Drink of this all (of you)" which we find in Matthew, is to be preferred to the corresponding text in Mark. It may go back to the *ipsissima verba Christi*. There is nothing actually against the fact that Christ formulated the invitation. Neither the parallelism with "Take, eat" nor its liturgical flavor plead against its ancientness.

From the Pauline text it is fitting to borrow "after supper" (*I Cor.* 11: 25) for reasons mentioned above, as well as the two invitations to repeat both eucharistic blessings. The repetition of the Supper which was done almost immediately on the day after Pentecost is most naturally explained as being of a similar order. If at the Supper the two blessings did not follow one another, it is very understandable that the order to repeat them was given in two places. That this order is lacking in Mark-Matthew can be explained as the result of the fact that both Gospels recount the Supper chiefly, if not uniquely, as one of the historic episodes making up the passion account. That Luke omitted the order in reference to the cup may be purely accidental, or else, as we have pointed out, it may be because at times the Eucharist included only the consecration of the bread. Finally, in this detail of the tradition as in others, liturgical usage could and must play a part. In the Roman liturgy, the order of repetition is now mentioned but once, and concludes the words of consecration.

Various reasons plead for the keeping of "poured out for many," attested by Luke and Matthew, and in a form that is more in harmony with the genius of the Semitic languages, by Mark. The same is true of "for you" (Paul) completed by "given" (Luke) in reference to the bread. If tradition shows a certain fluctuation in regard to these two additions — the one modifying the bread being missing in Mark-Matthew, and the one relating to the cup being absent from Paul —, this may result from the fact that the participles seemed only to fit the Last Supper where Christ could announce in fact that he was to give his body and that his blood was to be poured out. On the day after Christ's death there was no longer any reason to announce these two facts but rather to remember them.

All of these texts — with the exception of a few variants — qualify the covenant, mentioned in the cup blessing, with the word "new." May some doubt be cast on the presence of this adjective — in Mark the word is possibly not preceded by the article in the Greek text — in the *ipsissima verba Christi?* As has been pointed out, it is true that in accordance with the rules of Hebrew or Aramaic the adjective ought not to precede the substantive. But should we be surprised to find the adjective changing place in the Greek versions? We may also observe that in Mark 14, 25 the adjective does not qualify the eucharistized wine but the wine of the eschatological banquet.[27] Agreed, but there is

---

25. J. Betz, *op. cit.,* p. 18.
26. *Ibid.,* p. 17.

27. Matthew 26, 29 connects the new wine with "this fruit." There is here a particular shade of meaning, perhaps.

nothing to prevent Jesus from having also qualified the covenant which was to give access to this banquet with the adjective "new."

The greatest and also only important problem arises when we compare the traditions on the words of the blessing of the cup. Mark-Matthew presents a text that veers away from the Antiochene tradition, a tradition which we might be tempted to retain as closest to Jesus' words on the grounds of the ancientness of the Pauline testimony.

Before going on to compare the two formulations, let us try to grasp the sense of the Antiochene tradition as we have attempted to reconstruct it:

> This cup
> the new covenant
> in my blood
> which for you has been poured out.

Attention is brought to the connection between the cup and the blood, a connection which the Roman liturgy explicitates by saying *calix sanguinis mei,* and which the exegetes try to explain in three ways. According to some, "in my blood" is to be connected with a copulative (is; *estin*), clearly expressed by St. Paul and understood by Luke, and it would have served to unite formally and directly the "cup" with the "covenant" in the blood.[28] But the copulative, as we already know, is not sufficiently guaranteed. The same sense is verified when, following other authors, the incidental clause is connected both with "cup" and "covenant." [29] The greatest number of exegetes still prefer to unite it directly with the covenant alone. To the already lengthy list compiled by J. Betz it would not be hard still to add other names.[30] Let us then accept this last view, which is the most difficult one for the aim that we are pursuing. Even in this case, granting that the blood is connected with the covenant and the covenant with the cup, the cup is no less governed by "in my blood" than in the other ways of understanding the construction.[31] Actually the cup can be called "cup of the covenant" only to the extent that it effects the covenant, and since the covenant necessarily involves the shedding of blood — without the shedding of blood there is neither covenant nor forgiveness of sins — the cup becomes necessarily the receptacle and vehicle of the blood. In other words, basically the Luke-Paul formula rejoins the more pregnant formula of Mark-Matthew. With this in mind, no dogmatic position invites us to prefer one or the other. We can approach the investigation of where the priority lies without the least theological prejudice.

Important authors who have specialized in the matter vote in favor of Paul-Luke,[32] although Mark-Matthew also has its partisans.[33] Let us then examine the reasons that are in favor of the Antiochene tradition and ask whether they oblige us to subscribe to it.

We must point out from the beginning that the partisans of Paul-Luke do not contest that the text of Mark-Matthew may reflect an Aramaic original. Until 1949, it is true, J. Jeremias claimed the contrary, but in 1960 he changed his opinion and

---

28. This is the opinion attributed by Betz (*op. cit.*, p. 61, n. 228) to J. Weiss (1910), Ph. Bachmann (1921), A. Schlatter (1931), E. J. Allo (1956), H. Schürmann (1955).

29. An opinion upheld by J. Behm in *Theol. Wört. N.T.*, t. III, pp. 735-736. J. Betz (*op. cit.*, p. 61, n. 24) attributes it also to W. Berning (1901), K. H. Schelke (1949), C. Fernández (1959).

30. We are referred to A. Bisping, 3rd ed. (1883), G. Heinrici (1888), W. Berning (1901), J. Knabenbauer, 2nd ed. (1905), F. S. Gutjahr (1907), R. Cornely, 2nd ed. (1909), F. Hauk (1934), J. Sickenberger, 4th ed. (1942), E. Käsemann (1947), J. Häring (1949), M. Meinertz (1950); Cf. J. Betz, *op. cit.*, p. 60, n. 222.

31. J. Betz (*op. cit.*, pp. 60-61) attempts to show it with the help of what he calls two syllogisms.

32. This is the opinion of J. Betz (*op. cit.*, pp. 24-25) and of G. Dix, 4th ed. (1949), H. Lessig (1953), H. Schürmann (1955), N. Turner (1957), G. Ruffino (1957), P. Massi (1959). F. J. Leenhardt (*Le sacrement de la Sainte Cène*, Neuchâtel, 1948, cited by A. J. B. Higgins, *op. cit.*, pp. 30-33) also defends the Pauline formula. A. J. B. Higgins rejects it.

33. J. Betz (*op. cit.*, p. 25, n. 96) refers, among recent authors, to D. Sjöberg (1951), A. J. B. Higgins (1954), E. Lohse (1955), P. Benoit (1957), J. Dupont (1958), J. Jeremias, 3rd ed. (1960).

conceded that the Marcan formula "my blood of the covenant" could be rendered in Hebrew or Aramaic. Undoubtedly it is the normal case in Hebrew that a noun with a personal suffix can no longer be followed by a genitive. But the suffix which fits the *nomen regens* may be added to the *nomen rectum* (e.g., *b^ehar qodši*). Furthermore, in Aramaic, a *nomen rectum* may be introduced by *d*. It is to this last mode of expression that G. Dalman had already appealed: *den hû idmi d^elik^eyama.* J. Jeremias himself suggests that "my blood of the covenant" may be translated in Hebrew as *dam b^erîthî,* and in Aramaic *adham q^eyamî.*[34]

Still many authors suspect the ancientness of the Marcan formula for three reasons. First of all, Mark closely connects the two eucharistic blessings and because of this he has already departed from the most ancient liturgical type. Then, under the influence of Isaiah 53: 12, he adds "poured out" to the blessing of the cup. Finally, he omits the command to repeat the action.

Of these three arguments only the first has some weight. In fact, we hesitate to follow the authors who refuse to consider the incidental clause: "which has been poured out for (*huper* or *peri*) many (or *you*)" as a recent element.[35] As for the command to repeat the rite, its absence in Mark proves nothing, especially since some authors go so far as to consider this command a secondary characteristic.[36]

Therefore, there is nothing against the fact that the Mark-Matthew formula is ancient. In order to give preference to Paul-Luke, we shall have to give some positive indications in its favor. What are they?

The word pair "body-blood," as a primary consideration, seems secondary in relation to "body-cup." Certainly Paul is also familiar with the word pair "body-blood" but he uses it only in his commentaries, in what has at times been called his midrash of the eucharistic words.[37] There should be no objection that Mark's word-pair naturally finds its place in a rite and text of sacrificial importance. Actually we may argue with that assertion adopted by J. Jeremias on the support of which the last edition of his noteworthy monograph claims to come up with new texts; Job 6: 4 (Septuagint); Philo, *De spec., leg.,* I, 231-232 (ed. F. H. Colson, The Loeb Classical Library, London, 1954, pp. 84-85); *De spec., leg.,* I, 62 (ed. cit., pp. 134-135). The sacrificial word-pair that can claim origin from the Septuagint is not body-blood, but flesh (*sarx* or *kreas*) - blood.

Another consideration in favor of the Antiochene formula is that Christ seems to be especially interested in inculcating the idea of a covenant, the new covenant which, as we shall see further on, he derives from Exodus and the Deutero-Isaiah. This idea, we must admit, is better described by Paul-Luke than by Mark-Matthew.[38]

A third reason: the clause "in the blood," characteristic of the eucharistic blessing of the cup in the Antiochene tradition is attested to in various New Testament passages (*Rm.* 3: 25; 5: 9; *Ep.* 2: 13; I *Jn.* 5: 6; *Rv.* 7: 14; 22: 14). One of them

34. Cf. J. Betz, *op. cit.,* p. 20, n. 77. The author also refers to J. Günther (*Theol. Glaube,* 1955, t. XLV, p. 47 ff.) for a less happy solution, and to J. A. Emerton (*Journ. Theol. Stud.,* 1955, t. VI, p. 328 ff.) for a Syriac parallel.

35. Cf. above.

36. J. Betz (*op. cit.,* p. 23) refers to J. Jeremias, 2nd ed. (1949), H. Lessig (1953), G. Bornkamm (1959). In support of the supposed secondary character of the command to repeat the action, it is asserted: 1. that the addition is explained more easily than its suppression; 2. that it is explained from cultual usage; 3. that it is inspired by the Hellenic *anamnesis.* In answer, it will be stated: 1. that this last explanation is hardly plausible, particularly since Hellenism did not know the formula whereas Judaism attests to it; 2. that the worship was inspired by the formula rather than the contrary; 3. that its omission in Mark and Matthew is explained by reason of the historical framework, the passion account, in which the narration of the Last Supper is found.

37. Cf. J. Betz, *op. cit.,* p. 21, n. 80. Betz follows the conclusions of H. Lessig and G. Bornkamm and rejects the view of J. Jeremias and G. Walther, *Jesus das Passalamm des neuen Bundes,* 1951.

38. J. Betz, (*op. cit.,*) does not seem to assert this reason as worthwhile.

(*Rm.* 3: 25) seems even to be part of the original apostolic kery-gma. It seems to echo a liturgical text, and specifically that of the celebration of the Supper.[39]

In addition, Betz validates a reason which is less well grounded. The addition made to the cup by the Marcan tradition, one which is even more amplified by Matthew (his opinion) puts the notion of a worship sacrifice in bold relief. This would not be the fundamental idea that Jesus intended to express. Christ would have presented himself above all as a martyr in conformity with the theology of the Servant Songs by which he was inspired.[40]

Let us add that the mention of the cup is self-explanatory. Jesus blesses the wine while he holds the cup in his hands. It is therefore natural that his words refer to it. It is so natural that the Roman liturgy, inspired by the tradition of Mark, and particularly of Matthew, felt the need of adding the cup to the mention of the blood: *Hic est calix sanguinis mei.*[41]

Furthermore, the origin of Mark's formula is easily explained. The increasingly more accentuated connection with the account of the concluding of the first covenant probably contributed to the formation of the expression: "blood of (the) new covenant" (*Ex.* 24: 8). Secondarily, the wish to stress communion in the blood may also play its part. This notion scandalized the Jews and certain Judaizing Christians to the point that primitive Christian theology felt it necessary to react to it and to inculcate it all the more strongly.[42]

The fact that Mark's formula has a clear and formal echo only in the Epistle to the Hebrews (10:29; 13: 20) could also serve as an indication in favor of a greater ancientness of the other tradition.[43]

Finally the parallelism that dominates the Mark-Matthew text and which is hardly evident in Paul-Luke invites us also — as we have already learned — to give our preference to the latter.

Still let us point out that contrary arguments are not lacking. The Mark-Matthew tradition contains more Semiticisms.[44] The mention of "cup" could have been introduced from liturgical usage, granting that the celebrant pronounced the blessing of the wine with the cup in his hands. Since the word pair "body-blood" expresses perfectly what Jesus intended to accomplish: to hand over his person (*soma*-body) and to establish the covenant in his blood. Let us also remember that the mention of the blood and the invitation to drink it are traits so characteristic of the eucharistic rite that they must be original. The procedure advanced by Betz, a procedure tending to accentuate the role of the blood in order to counter the Judaizers, cannot be demon-

---

39. J. Betz, *op. cit.*, pp. 87-92. Yet Hebrews 9: 20 is more a reflection of the Marcan formula, and this latter is also more in conformity with the text of Exodus 24: 8.

40. J. Betz, *op. cit.*, pp. 138-143.

41. This consideration is not advanced by J. Betz.

42. J. Betz, *op. cit.*, pp. 142-143. Cf. *Jn.* 6: 53-56. The idea of "drinking blood" is actually the hardest to understand in the light of the notions that were current in Judaism. Did the apostles from the outset understand the blood as an allusion to the passion and the words of Christ as an invitation to share in it? In this sense, the allusions to the cup (*Mt.* 20: 22, 23; *Mk.* 10: 38, 39; *Jn.* 18: 11) could have prepared the disciples' minds for understanding the Eucharist. For Paul, it seems that it is a question of a "pneumatic" participation in the blood of Christ. This results from the fact that the risen Christ is "spirit," and from examples of "pneumatic" participation borrowed from the Old Testament. This is also the notion of John 6: 33.

On the Jewish aversion to drinking blood, cf. also A. J. B. Higgins, *op. cit.*, p. 30; C. G. Montefiore, *The Synoptic Gospels*, t. I, London, 1927, p. 323; H. Loewe, *A Rabbinical Anthology*, London, 1938, p. 647 and J. Klausner, *Jesus of Nazareth*, London, 1947, p. 329. According to Leviticus 17: 10-12 life is in the blood, and the blood belongs to God. Let us point out that in disposing of his blood Jesus is attributing to himself, here as elsewhere, a divine prerogative and power.

43. J. Betz, *op. cit.*, p. 143. It has been observed that the epistle departs from the Septuagint text (*Ex.* 24: 8) in order to come closer to that of the blessing of the eucharistic cup.

44. On the Semiticisms of Mark-Matthew, cf. J. Betz, *op. cit.*, pp. 16-17. Cf. p. 12 n. 45. We have already noted that according to P. Neuenzeit, the Semiticisms of Mark, from the fact that we find them throughout the whole gospel, are not very convincing. Cf. also G. D. Kilpatrick, *art. cit.*, pp. 198-199.

strated with certitude.[45] The Gospel of John shows rather that it was necessary to come to the defense of the patent and clear assertions of Jesus about communion in his blood.[46] Finally, if the addition: "poured out for (*huper* or *peri*) many (or *you*)" is original, as we have attempted to show, it is juxtaposed more naturally in the Mark-Matthew formula than in Paul-Luke.

In brief, we are faced with two traditions where either one can produce valid reasons without ruling out the other completely. They might be worded in this way: "this cup, the new covenant in my blood" and "this (is) my blood which has been poured out for (*huper* or *peri*) many (*you*)." They are mutually compenetrable. The first took: "which for you has been poured out" (Luke); the second seems to have inserted "new covenant" after the fact, ending up thereby with a rather difficult series of genitives. The tendency to enlarge upon this point is found again later, particularly in the text of the Roman liturgy where we read: *Hic est calix sanguinis mei novi et aeterni testamenti.*

As we shall see below, the theological background of the Supper, i.e., all the ideas and sentiments which animated the Savior on the eve of his death, cause us to think that Jesus did in fact express simultaneously what both texts transmit to us. But tradition found it difficult to express the whole content of Christ's words in one sole formula which tended to become succinct under the influence of liturgical usage and parallelism with the first blessing (of the bread). Hence, in order to find room for all elements of tradition we are tempted to reconstitute conjecturally a more or less original text: "this cup, the new covenant, my blood which has been poured out for (*huper* or *peri*) many (*you*)." Under these conditions, the *Stammform* or basic text would be as follows:

> And as they were eating
> Jesus, taking bread,
> having given thanks,
> broke (it) and gave (it) to them and said:
> Take and eat:

This is my body
which is given for you;
This do in my remembrance.
Likewise also taking (the) cup
after supper,
having given thanks,
he gave (it) to them saying:
Drink of this all (of you):
this cup, the new covenant,[47]
my blood which has been poured out for many.
This do in my remembrance.

Until now we have retained the term "body" (*sôma*) in all the traditions preserving for us the version of the Aramaic words uttered by Jesus. It remains for us to ask first of all what is the Aramaic word corresponding to "body" what was its meaning, and finally to what extent the version "body" is more suitable than "flesh" (*sarx*) echoed in the fourth Gospel.

According to J. Bonsirven [48] the primitive Aramaic term should be *bśr*. Other words suggested by the critics are hardly suitable. We cannot retain *pègèr, pigrâ* (J. H. Bernard), nor *garmî* (A. Meyer) nor *gèšèm*, nor even *gûph, gûphâ*, despite G. Dalman's authority.[49] J. Betz came around to Bonsirven's opinion.[50] We can accept it ourselves all the more easily since in Hebrew *bśr* often expresses the "totality of the individual, what we should

45. J. Betz, *op. cit.*, p. 179. The author does not think that John introduced the term *sarx*. We may be dealing with a variant in the translation of the Aramaic original.

46. *Jn.* 6, 53-56.

47. We may ask whether another variant of the text did not exist: "this cup *of* the new covenant, my blood which has been poured out for many."

48. J. Bonsirven, *"Hoc est corpus meum": recherches sur l'original araméen,* in *Biblica,* 1948, t. XXXIX, pp. 205-219.

49. *Ibid.,* p. 218.

50. J. Betz, *op. cit.*, p. 37.

call its 'person'." [51] granting that the Semite did not possess the dichotomical Greek notion of the human being.

J. Bonsirven also thinks — and this is the answer to our third question — that the most ancient and most faithful Greek translation had the term "flesh" (*sarx*). This word is encountered in the Johannine tradition which may go back to the beginnings; [52] it is found in a few ancient Church writers like Ignatius and Justin; [53] it recommends itself all the more since "body" (*sôma*) could designate (cf. John's Gospel) a corpse,[54] and on the other hand, *sarx* can signify the "person" in biblical Greek in so far as the "body was confused in some way with the person." [55]

J. H. Bernard, if we are to believe Bonsirven, has a more subtle opinion. According to this author, *sôma* and *sarx* are two variants which the translators could have used as they wished.[56]

On the other hand, J. Betz claims to be a resolute partisan of *sôma*. In the Septuagint, he asserts, *sôma* translates the Hebrew term *bśr* 143 times.[57] Then, in Paul, *sarx* appears only in the midrash on the Eucharist. And again, *sôma* is better fitted that *sarx* to express the idea of "person." [58] Furthermore, Betz concedes that the term *sarx,* if we think it should be retained, also expresses the person of Christ in his humanity in John's Gospel.[59]

We may then conclude that the choice between *sôma* and *sarx* perhaps does not have the importance which some would want to give it.

II. THE LITURGICAL SETTING OF THE LAST SUPPER

The liturgical setting in which Christ celebrated the Last Supper is of great importance in determining the sense that he intended to give his actions. This setting has been the object of numerous investigations without any definitive solution to the problem being arrived at.

We should hardly be induced to think that the Last Supper was a completely ordinary meal. The presence of the cup of wine alone shows that under the circumstances the meal taken by Jesus and his disciples was at least out of the ordinary.

Similarly, we are in more and more agreement in not thinking of a *qiddush* or a *ḥaburah* meal as an appropriate cultual setting for the institution of the Eucharist. The *qiddush*, J. Jeremias and G. Kuhn recall, does not constitute a meal. It is only a blessing prayer which in certain circumstances was decked with special solemnity. As for the *ḥaburah* meal, the conditions customary to the Jewish milieu contemporary with the New Testament for constituting a *ḥaburah* were hardly verified in the group of the disciples, the apostles whom Jesus gathered about himself.[60]

---

51. J. Bonsirven, *art. cit.*, p. 207.

52. *Ibid.*, p. 210.

53. *Ibid.*, p. 211.

54. *Ibid.*, p. 212.

55. *Ibid.*, p. 210.

56. *Ibid.*, p. 218 ,n. 3.

57. J. Betz, *op. cit.*, p. 179, n. 668.

58. *Ibid.*, p. 37, n. 156, with a reference to K. Grobel, *Sôma as "Self, Person,"* in *Zeitschr. Neut. Wiss.*, 1954, t. XXI, pp. 52-59.

59. *Ibid.*, p. 179: "Σάρξ (V. 51c) steht demnach an Stelle des ἐγώ von 51a und meint die Person Jesu in ihrer konkreten Menschlichkeit."

60. See the opinion of G. Kuhn, in *Die Abendmahlworte, Theol. Lit. Zeit.*, 1950, t. LXXV, col. 399-408. Among the recent articles which judge that the *ḥaburah* meal should be retained as the setting of the Eucharist, we may point out *The "Hellenization" of the Gospel* of Gregory Dix, in *Teologiska Föreningens i Uppsala Förhandlingar. Acta Societatis Theologicae Upsaliensis*, I, 1951-1955, 2. 1956-1960, Uppsala, 1963, pp. 1-32. After having once held this position, the author came to accept the views of J. Jeremias. In this study he returns to his first opinion, and supports it with the following considerations: 1. The primitive form of the rite is that of the two blessings accompanying a *ḥaburah* meal; 2. For Paul, Jesus did not celebrate the Jewish Passover; he himself by his death inaugurated a new Passover; 3. The fact that the repetition of the Eucharist was not bound up with the Passover feast, not even with this Christian Passover that certain Churches celebrated, but that it was from the very beginning a weekly rite, celebrated probably in the night of Saturday-Sunday, is best explained in the framework of a *ḥaburah;* 4. When the Eucharist was separated from the meal that originally accompanied it, the eucharistic rite was called *"Eucharist"* and the meal *"agape."* These two words are derived from the *ḥaburah* vocabulary. It

E. Lohmeyer and others in his company or who follow him liken the Last Supper meal to those Jesus customarily celebrated with his disciples (*Mk*. 6: 14; 8: 6; *Lk*. 24: 30-31, 35). They give an import to these meals that they did not have, and forget that the texts in question may have been edited and not without undergoing a certain eucharistic coloration.[61]

In recent years, people have outlined certain connections with the meals of the Essenes, particularly of the Qumrân community. In the same context attention is called to a few curious passages from the apocryphal legend of Joseph and Aseneth, the Greek text of which was recently published by Batiffol.[62] These legendary accounts mention initiation rites to the Jewish religion that the Egyptian woman Aseneth had to go through: the eating of a bread of life, communion in a blessed cup containing a drink of immortality, and an anointing with an oil that was a pledge of incorruptibility (8: 5; 16: 16). In 16: 16 the three supposedly sacramental rites seem to go back to the eating of a marvelous food, the heavenly honey brought by the Archangel Michael. And in 19: 20 it is Joseph's kisses that confer the spirit of life on his bride, as well as the spirit of wisdom and the spirit of truth. We would not dare to solve the problem of the origins of the apocryphal writing but we have the impression that it is a kind of Jewish propaganda. In a roundabout way it alludes to the rites of Christian initiation. It intends to show that Judaism is not inferior in this aspect to the new religion which began to rival and supplant it among the pagans.

The most widespread and most traditional thesis situates the institution of the Eucharist in the setting of a Passover meal. Certainly not a few objections are against this. In the last analysis all of them are derived from a tradition preserved in the fourth Gospel. From reading this document it appears that Jesus was crucified on the 14th of Nisan. If this is true, he cannot have celebrated the Passover meal with his disciples.

The explanations advanced to account for the Johannine tradition are numerous. W. Goossens expounds them judiciously. Since the publication of his work — excepting the question of the Qumrân calendar — very little that is new has been brought into the debate.[63]

Various authors claim that there is nothing in John that obliges us to believe that he fixes the Savior's crucifixion on the 14th of Nisan. J. Jeremias is practically a partisan of this opinion. To support a divergent chronology in the Synoptics he retains only one passage as certain: John 18: 28.[64] On the other hand, John 13: 1 and 19: 14 do not seem to have to be accounted for.[65] Moreover, in John 19: 31 and from various clues in the Gospel, the German exegete finds proof that John is not ignorant of the paschal character of Jesus' last meal.[66]

If there are two chronologies in the Gospels and consequently two dates for the celebration of Passover in the year of Jesus' death, then — as many authors think — this actually was the case. Various hypotheses attempt to explain the dualism. Very few exegetes take into consideration J. Pickl's suggestion that attributes to the Galileans the custom of immolating the paschal lamb on the 13th of Nisan because of the inability of the temple

---

was a meal of agape, of brotherhood and began with a *berakah*; 5. The evolution of the rite and the doctrine in the Hellenized milieus kept the original characteristics of Christ's institution. Only the covenant-sacrifice notion grew dimmer. While this is in the foreground with Paul, Mark stresses the blood and Matthew the pouring out of blood. In John 6: and in Hippolytus (about 200), the notion of covenant is absent, but the later liturgical texts reintroduced it.

---

61. Cf. E. Lohmeyer, *Vom urchristlichen Abendmahl*, in *Theol. Rundschau*, 1937, new ser., t. IX, pp. 195-227, 273-312.

62. P. Batiffol, *Studia patristica*, Paris, 1889. P. Riessler, *Altjüdisches Schrifttum ausserhalb der Bibel übersetzt und erläutert*, Augsburg, 1928. The food given to Aseneth is inspired first of all, it seems, from the banquet of Song of Solomon 5, 1.

63. W. Goossens, *op. cit.*, pp. 110-127.

64. J. Jeremias, *Die Abendmahlsworte Jesu*, 3rd ed., Göttingen, 1960, pp. 13, 73-78.

65. *Ibid.*, pp. 74-75.

66. *Ibid.*, pp. 75-76.

ministers to serve everyone on the 14th.[67] Rather commonly the
authors reject another suggestion by C. D. Chwolson who thinks
that the Jews immolated the paschal lambs beginning on the 13th
when the 14th fell on Friday.[68] J. Jeremias thinks this without
foundation,[69] and he passes an identical judgment on A. Jaubert's
theory,[70] which attributes to Jesus a choice of the Essene calendar.
Jesus, Mlle Jaubert thinks, celebrated the Passover meal on Tuesday
evening — Passover Eve according to the ancient priestly calendar.
Arrested on the night of Tuesday-Wednesday, the Savior died
on Friday the 14th of Nisan and the eve of the official Passover.[71]
On the other hand, Jeremias does not radically discard the explanation of H. Strack-P. Billerbeck which appeals to two divergent ways of reckoning the 14th and 15th of Nisan in the year
of Christ's death. The Pharisees would have set the 1st of Nisan,
and consequently the 14th-15th one day sooner than the Sadducees
and Jesus would have followed the Pharisee's calendar.[72]

If we are to reject any attempt at harmonization, we shall
say with J. Jeremias that the author of the fourth Gospel transforms
a "typology" into a "chronology," [73] or that the chronological
material of the Synoptic Gospels is not to be trusted absolutely,[74]
or that Jesus anticipated the Passover on his own authority, and
even that he celebrated it in a way that cast aside various aspects —
even important ones — of the rules prescribed by the ritual.
This is the tack taken by E. Stauffer.[75] As for Jeremias, even if
he preserves the Synoptic chronology and stoutly defends the
Passover character of the eucharistic setting, he does grant that
Jesus introduced an important innovation. The German exegete
estimates that Luke 22: 15 and 18 establishes with certitude that
Jesus himself did not eat the paschal lamb and that he did not
drink the wine, indeed that in all likelihood he was fasting.[76] There
is at least every indication that Jesus did not communicate in the
eucharistized bread and wine that he distributed to his apostles.[77]

In W. Goossens, J. Jeremias and E. Ruckstuhl we can find
the various and numerous indications that plead for the celebration
of a Passover, whatever the freedom Jesus took in the observance
of the ritual. Several of these indications confirm the Synoptic

material and oblige us to retain the paschal setting of the Last Supper as duly founded and established.

Under these conditions, we may therefore ask what Passover elements there were in particular to which Jesus thought he could attach the eucharistic rites.

J. Jeremias does not hesitate to satisfy our curiosity. After

---

67. J. Pickl, *Messiaskönig Jesus,* Munich, 1935.

68. D. Chwolson, *Das letzte Passamahl Christi und der Tag seines Todes,* 2nd ed., Leipzig, 1908.

69. J. Jeremias, *op. cit.,* p. 17.

70. A. Jaubert, *La date de la Cène. Calendrier biblique et liturgie chrétienne,* in *Études bibliques,* Paris, 1957.

71. A. Jaubert, *op. cit.,* p. 107. A Ruckstuhl (*Die Chronologie des Letzten Mahles und des Leidens Jesu,* in *Biblische Beiträge,* fasc. 4, Einsiedeln, 1963) approves Mlle Jaubert's thesis. On the other side, P. Benoit has some reserves, although he does call the author's suggestion "alluring": *La Date de la Cène,* in *Exégèse et théologie,* t. I, Paris, 1961, pp. 255-261.

72. J. Jeremias, *op. cit.,* pp. 17-18.

73. *Ibid.,* p. 77.

74. This is the attitude taken, it seems, by Fr. X. Léon-Dufour, member of the Biblical Commission: *Les Évangiles et l'histoire de Jésus,* Paris, 1963, pp. 357-359; cf. esp. p. 357: "(The Gospels) differ on the date of the Passover meal.... In only considering the literary data, we should be inclined to prefer the fourth Gospel." However on page 359 he becomes more cautious and reserves his judgment: "It seems to us that only the considerations of literary criticism will allow us to trace the history of the tradition of these accounts." In the work mentioned (pp. 334-351) and in *Passion, Dict. Bibl. Supplément,* 1960, fasc. 35, col. 1419-1492, the author, relying on *Formgeschichte* and literary history, grants a certain freedom to the Evangelists in the composition of the accounts.

75. E. Stauffer, *Jesus. Gestalt und Geschichte,* in *Dalp. Taschen-Bücher,* Bern, 1956, pp. 86-90. Jesus celebrated Passover without the paschal lamb. Agreeing with Jeremias, he points out the connections between the *Deuteworte,* the explicative *logia* in use during the Passover *haggadah* (*ha lachma anja*) and the words Jesus pronounced over the bread and wine. He furnishes an explanation of this which seems to agree with that of Leenhardt and which A. Vanneste thought he could use. Cf. p. 89: "Es

pointing out the chief elements of the Passover meal as celebrated in Jesus' time, he connects the first eucharistic blessing to the prayer pronounced over the bread following the second cup and preceding the real meal, i.e., the eating of the lamb.[78] He observes that the ritual of the Passover meal did not provide for a prayer over the bread at the beginning of the ceremony. As for the blessing of the wine, it must have preceded the singing of the Hallel (*Mk.* 14: 26) and followed the eating of the main dish.[79] In other words the eucharistic words would have framed the eating of the lamb and the blessing of the wine would have been in connection with the third cup, called the *cup of blessing,* an expression used elsewhere by St. Paul (I *Cor.* 10: 16). Merx also thought of this cup, but it is known that for the blessing of the bread he proposed the morsels of bread that were served as dessert after the passing around of the third cup.[80]

At the conclusion of our investigation we must take account of the Jewish Passover ritual in order to attempt a reconstitution of the religious and theological ideas that served as a background for the eucharistic gestures of words of Jesus.[81]

III. THE THEOLOGICAL BACKGROUND OF THE LAST SUPPER

For completeness, let us recall the pseudonymous little work of Jean Pain: *Jésus dieu de la Pâque* which appeared in the collection *Christianisme. Cahiers publiés sous la direction de P.-L. Couchoud* (Paris, 1930). The anonymous author rejects the existence of a Jesus who was a miracle worker and a founder of a religion. In his eyes the Jesus of the Gospels and of the Christian faith is only a mythical being that came from a Jewish mystery rite and subsequently became the subject of a euhemerizing legend. The Jewish mystery, generator of legends and mythical personages, would dispense us from having to have recourse to the influence of the pagan mysteries: a risky but indispensable hypothesis for the historicistic notion in order for it to explain the faith in the presence of a God under the eucharistic species and in his being eaten during the course of a sacrificial meal. On the other hand, Passover would furnish all the elements we need to outline a history of the origins of the Eucharist. In the beginning it seems to have been a renewal rite that included the sacrifice of a god of vegetation. From the beginning the paschal lamb

---

geht in diesen Worten um eine Wirklichkeit 'geltungshafter' Art. Brot und Wein 'gelten vor Gott' als Leib und Blut Jesu. Es handelt sich hier um eine Realität eigener Ordnung, die durch die göttliche Vollmacht der Einsetzungsworte konstituiert ist und wieder mit materialistischen noch mit spiritualistischen Kategorien erfasst werden kann." X. Léon-Dufour (*op. cit.*, p. 359) thinks that Jesus did not celebrate the Passover rite. He intended only that his last meal would take place in "a paschal setting."

76. J. Jeremias, *op. cit.*, pp. 199-203.

77. *Ibid.*, p. 204.

---

78. *Ibid.*, p. 81.

79. *Ibid.*, p. 81.

80. Merx's opinion is reported by Ed. Schweizer, *Das Abendmahl, einer Vergegenwärtigung des Todes Jesu oder ein eschatologisches Freuden- mahl?* in *Theol. Zeitschr.*, 1946, t. II, pp. 81-101. On the Jewish Passover, we can continue to read with profit A. Edersheim, *The Temple. Its Ministry and Service as they were at the Time of Jesus Christ,* London, 1874; *The Life and Times of Jesus the Messiah,* 10th ed., 2 vol., London, 1900.

81. The object of this study is not to show in what way Jesus intended to effect his presence under the eucharistic species. On this problem we may consult two recent monographs: J. Betz, *Die Eucharistie in der Zeit der griechischen Väter,* t. II, 1: *Die Realpräsenz des Leibes und des Blutes Jesu im Abendmahl nach dem Neuen Testament,* Freiburg-im-B., 1961, and P. Neuenzeit, *Das Herrenmahl. Studien zur paulinischen Eucharistieauffass- ung, in Studien zum Alten und Neuen Testament,* t. I, Munich, 1960. Betz tries to introduce, as we know, a new vocabulary. He distinguishes what he calls an *Aktualpräsenz* of the person of Christ from a *Realpräsenz* or *Substanzialpräsenz,* i.e., the substantial presence of the body and blood of the Savior.

With even more profit, we might read the important articles of P. Benoit: *Les récits de l'institution de l'eucharistie et leur portée* in *Exégèse et théologie,* t. I, Paris, 1961, pp. 210-239; *Note sur deux études de F.-J. Leenhardt, ibid.,* pp. 244-254. P. Benoit evaluates rather severely Leen- hardt's essay which certain Catholic authors have greeted with too little discernment. In regard to transsubstantiation Benoit writes the following (*art. cit.,* pp. 233-234): "Can we penetrate more into this mystery and attempt to account for the rational thought behind it? It is inevitable that

was intimately connected with this paschal god and later was likened to the "Righteous Man." For these two reasons he would account for the divine presence and the sacramental rite. The other elements, the bread and wine, were able to contribute to the genesis of the Christian mystery, particularly by reason of the beliefs that conceived the spirit of the harvest as present in these elements.

It goes without saying that Pain's explanation, a fabric of more or less fanciful hypotheses, has not retained the attention of the historians of early Christianity. His absurd exaggerations ought not prevent us from looking into the real connections between the eucharistic mystery and the Passover rite. Even so, we must add immediately, they will not be especially obvious or enlightening.

Let us not insist upon recalling the messianic banquet. This does not formally concern the Eucharist which is a memorial of Jesus' death but the Passover which will be celebrated in heaven at the time of the definitive salvation and the establishment of the new eschatological order. It is with this order that the "new wine" mentioned in Mark's Gospel is connected.[82]

Also, let us not lose any more time over the *aphikomen* rite for an explanation of the spiritual presence of the Messiah.[83] It is a far cry from a coming or a return of the Messiah during a Passover night [84] to the belief in the presence of Jesus under the eucharistic species.

More worth our interest in explaining the command to repeat the supper and commemorate Jesus' acts is the notion of *zikkaron* which was current in Jewish milieus in connection with Passover,[85] especially if we think we are authorized to reinterpret the paschal rite not as a simple remembrance but as a "sacramental" representation of the past.[86]

R. Déaut exploits to the hilt the theology of the *aqéda*, i.e., the notion of Isaac's sacrifice as it has developed in connection with the Passover celebration.[87] But the author cited agrees with it himself: the idea of redemption is expressed in the eucharistic texts not precisely in line with Genesis 22 but with Isaiah 53.[88] And if the New Testament understands redemption under the characteristics of the three great Old Testament sacrifices (the covenant sacrifice, the sacrifice of the Passover lamb and the sacrifice of the great day of Atonement [89]) the last two do not seem to be in Christ's intention in the words of the Last Supper themselves.

---

this be done, and the effort is legitimate. With the aid of a certain philosophy it is said that the "substance" of the bread and wine was changed into the substance of the body and blood, while the appearances or "accidents" remained the same. This formulation is valid, and the Church accepted it in speaking of "transsubstantiation." Yet we should not disguise the fact that these philosophical notions themselves keep some sort of mystery. What is important is that in making use of this system we keep the sense of mystery. What they wish to say after all is that the bread and wine, consecrated by Christ's word, keep in a certain way their former being, but that they receive a deeper being which comes from the new world and transcends the old being to the extent of rendering it null; this new being, which pertains to the eschatological age as does every sacramental order, is the very being of the body of the dead and risen Christ. The traditional dogmatic statement is expressed in a natural philosophy that is not without value; yet it is permitted to rethink it and to deepen it with biblical thought, which is better perceived today, and which is more concerned with existence and its passage from the old age of sin and death into the new era of salvation and life. This passing-over which Jesus was the first to make in his person from the cross on Easter morning, is worked by him in the bread and wine in order to realize it thereby in those who will communicate in them with faith."

These reflections of P. Benoit are excellent. Only the statement beginning with "which is more concerned with existence . . ." is somewhat enigmatic and therefore not very enlightening.

Cf. also J. Coppens, *Mysterium fidei* (*Miscellanées Bibliques*, XXIV), in *Eph. Theol. Lov.*, 1957, t. XXXIII, pp. 483-506.

J. Schniewind (*op. cit.*, p. 186) understands the sense of the eucharistic words in the following way: 1. Jesus gives himself as the Messiah both in Mark 14: 25 and in Mark 14: 22-24; 2. Jesus gives himself to his disciples as the Messiah, becoming their bread of life: both the term "my body" and the word pair "body and soul" signify the "person" and therefore the gift of the person; 3. Jesus gives "his blood" i.e., his "life" to his faithful, as Messiah, in order to become their intercessor. Such a commentary still does not exhaust the whole sense of the *logia* of the Savior.

---

82. *Mk.* 14: 25. Cf. above.

One last connection with the Passover rite would consist in the formal allusion in the eucharistic rite to the concluding of a covenant. In fact, the theology of the covenant is not foreign to that of Passover.[90] Yet in this instance it is the covenant of Sinai that was more directly in Jesus' mind. The "blood of the covenant" is manifestly an allusion to Exodus 24: 8.[91]

In brief, from a literary point of view, the fourth poem of the suffering Servant and the account of the sacrificial concluding of the Sinai covenant at the foot of the mountain are silhouetted in the background of the Last Supper account much more than the texts of the Passover *haggadah*.

The "blood of the covenant," as we have just said, recalls the account of the sacrificial covenant on Sinai. So true is this that the eucharistic words have left their mark on the Exodus text in Hebrews 9: 20.

Nevertheless it is fitting to ask whether Exodus 24: 8 is the only Old Testament text to have influenced Jesus' thought during the Last Supper at the precise moment when he was interpreting his actions as the concluding of a covenant. In our opinion we cannot take exception to an allusion to Jeremiah 31: 31,[92] nor a kinship with the poems of the suffering Servant.[93]

Matthew's addition of "for forgiveness of sins" is a first reference to Jeremiah. The second and most direct is in the mention of a new covenant, granting that Jeremiah 31: 31 is the only Old Testament text to express this notion in clear terms. We have already learned, it is true, that the adjective "new" is looked upon as a later addition. Yet the reasons put forward against its authenticity are hardly pertinent. If Jesus intended to conclude a covenant, a covenant ushering in the eschatological era, a covenant conferring the forgiveness of sins, a covenant set in the background of the prophetic visions about the Servant of Yahweh, he could and should have qualified it with "new." [94]

In several places we have already alluded to the poems of the Ebed Yahweh. In fact the exegetes are more and more in agreement in saying that the Savior on the night that he was betrayed must have thought of these magnificent texts where

Old Testament revelation attained one of its most beautiful expressions.

Let us recall a few of the data on which we rely in justifying the references to the songs of the Ebed. These poems and their context give us a glimpse of a concluding of a covenant (42: 6; 49:

83. Cf. J. Pain, *op. cit.*, p. 176. Cf. W. Goossens, *op. cit.*, p. 8-13. The Hebrew term is connected with the Greek word ἀφικνέομαι, aor. ἀφικόμην, "arrive, return."

84. R. Le Déaut, *La nuit pascale*, in *Analecta Biblica*, t. XXII, Rome, 1963, pp. 279-298.

85. R. Déaut, *op. cit.*, pp. 66-71. M. Thurian, *L'eucharistie mémorial du Seigneur*, Neuchâtel, 1959. J. Jeremias (*Die abendmahlsworte Jesu*, 3rd. ed., Göttingen, 1960, pp. 229-246) suggested a very new sense for the anamnesis: "damit Gott meiner gedenke," which has not produced many followers. On the notion of memorial in the Old Testament, cf. A. J. B. Higgins (*op. cit.*, pp. 35-36) who refers to Exodus 24: 14; Deuteronomy 16: 3; Exodus 13: 3, 9; 12: 26-27; 13: 8. For J. Schniewind (*op. cit.*, p. 186), the eucharistic anamnesis is to be substituted for that of the old Passover and the idea of anamnesis is therefore derived from the old paschal rite.

86. R. Le Déaut, *op. cit.*, p. 281.

87. *Ibid.*, pp. 133-208.

88. *Ibid.*, pp. 205, 212.

89. *Ibid.*, p. 212. P. Neuenzeit (*op. cit.*, p. 148) categorically excludes that the apostolic community looked upon Jesus in the Eucharist as the paschal lamb. On the other side, J. Stauffer (*Jesus, Gestalt und Geschichte*, Bern, 1957, pp. 86-90) insists on the connections with the Passover meal although it was celebrated without the lamb.

90. R. Le Déaut, *op. cit.*, p. 79-87.

91. H. Gottlieb, *To haima tes diathekes*, in *Studia Theologica*, t. XIV, pp. 115-118. The author supposes: '*dmy slbryt*' or in Aramaic: '*dmy dy qym*' as the original text, a construction with the relative particle and a proleptic suffix (p. 117).

For. P. Neuenzeit (*op. cit.*, pp. 195-198) the allusion to Exodus 24, 8 is manifest in Mark, especially in reading "my blood of the covenant." The addition "new" is superfluous and the tendency is clear: to accentuate the character of sacrificial oblation. For Neuenzeit as for Betz, this theological notion is secondary in relation to that of voluntary oblation by way of martyrdom, conforming with the theology of Isaiah 53.

According to J. Schniewind (*op. cit.*, p. 183) we may also be reminded

8; 59: 21; 61: 8) which would be new (42: 9) and which in some way would be made in the person of the Servant (42: 6; 49: 8). They then recall the sacrificial image of the lamb (53: 7). They also teach expiation of sins through the substitution of an innocent victim, and they inaugurate, in order to account for the expiatory efficacy, a theology of martyrdom which perfectly fits the setting of Jesus' sacrificial death (53: 10-12). Finally they contain the enigmatic "for (*huper or peri*) many" [95] which figures in Matthew 26: 28 and Mark 14: 24.

Briefly, if the parallelism with Exodus 24: 8 suggests a connection with the theology of the Old Testament sacrifices, the many contacts with the Deutero-Isaiah invite us to place in the background of the eucharistic sacrifice what J. Betz calls a theology of voluntary personal oblation, i.e., martyrdom.[96] Jesus did not conceive the sacrifice of his life primarily in the setting of a doctrine inspired by traditions of worship,[97] but in that of emphasizing the sacrificial nature of martyrdom. This interpretation of martyrdom, moreover, had begun to be implanted in Judaism at the time of the Savior. The death of a righteous man and the death of the high priest were looked upon, it seems, as having the value of a sacrifice of expiation.[98] Yet we must not exclude every reference to the sacrificial ideology. Jewish thought on the sacrifice of Isaac that was more or less contemporary to the Savior shows how much these two ideologies of ritual sacrifices and of martyrdom tended to interpenetrate. This interpenetration reached its full maturity when it encountered the themes of the suffering servant in Jesus' thought.

The three literary contexts which are silhouetted in the background of the institution of the Eucharist (the sacrifice of the Sinai covenant, the oracle of Jeremiah 31: 31, and the poems of the Deutero-Isaiah) concord in furnishing the idea of a pact as the primordial and basic element of the eucharistic meal. In this light, the Eucharist is primarily a sacrifice and a covenant meal.[99] Situated as it is in the line of these Old Testament texts, this covenant could have been conceived only in close relation to them, i.e., as a pact leading to the formation of a new religious society, a new people of God.[100] In other words we find here a

most compelling reason for saying that Jesus truly founded his
Church at the Last Supper and that he founded it primarily as
an association of worship, a *Kultgemeinschaft*.

Moreover, by the very fact that Jesus founded this *Kultgemeinschaft* on the gift of his person,[101] indeed on the sacrificial gift of

of Zechariah 9, 11, where the "blood of the covenant" works liberation.

92. On the text of Jeremiah see J. Coppens, *La nouvelle alliance en
Jer.* 31, 31-34, in *Cath. Bibl. Quart.*, 1963, t. XXV, pp. 12-21. For P.
Neuenzeit (*op. cit.*, p. 197) the reference to Jeremiah 31: 31 suffices.
Jesus was to make other allusions to the words of Jeremiah in Matthew
5: 12; 11: 25, 30; 23: 8.

93. On the poems of the Servant of Yahweh, cf. J. Coppens, *Les
origines littéraires des Poèmes du Serviteur de Yahvé. Vers la solution d'une
énigme,* in *Sacra Pagina,* t. I, Gembloux-Paris, 1959, pp. 434-454. P.
Neuenzeit who insists strongly on the influence of Isaiah 53 on the
eucharistic doctrine seems nevertheless at a certain moment to wonder
whether at the Last Supper this influence had made itself felt.

94. On the new covenant at Qumrân, cf. R. F. Collins, *The Berîth-Notion
of the Cairo Damascus Covenant and its Comparison with the New
Testament,* in *Eph. Theol. Lov.,* 1963, t. XXXIX, pp. 555-594.

---

95. The sense of "many" is not easy to define. J. Jeremias (*op. cit.*,
pp. 171-174) devotees a few pages to it. He concludes: *har-rabbîm, hoi
polloi, i.e.,* the term preceded by the article, possesses an "inkludierende
Bedeutung." It consequently designates the totality. Without the article
(as in the text) this sense is no longer obligatory but it remains possible.
As proof, he mentions texts which paraphrase the *rabbîm* of Isaiah 52: 14
(cf. *Henoch eth.,* LXII, 3, 5; *Jn.* 1: 29), and various passages from the
New Testament in which, at times in the light of parallel passages, the
sense of *polloi = pantes* is obligatory: *Mk.* 1: 3 // *Mt.* 8: 16; *Lk.* 4: 40;
Mk. 10: 48 // *Mt.* 20: 31; *Rm.* 4: 17-18; II *Cor.* 1: 11; *Mk.* 10: 45 // I
Tim. 2: 6. The inclusive sense would be equally valid for *Mk.* 10: 45 as
for *Mk.* 14: 24. On *rabbîm* in *Is.* 53, cf. J. Coppens, *La finale du quatrième
chant de l'Ébèd. Un essai de solution,* in *Eph. Theol. Lov.,* 1963, t.
XXXIX, pp. 114-121.

96. J. Betz, *Die Eucharistie in der Zeit der griechischen Väter,* t. II,
1, pp. 37-43.

97. It is certain that some affinities have been found between the
sacrificial language and the eucharistic vocabulary. The anamnesis is
attested to for Passover (*Ex.* 12: 14) and the loaves of proposition (*Lv.*
24: 5-9). Deuteronomy (21: 8) stresses the efficacy of blood for the
remission of sins. Then the sacrifices imply a renewal of the covenant (*Lv.*

his person,[102] the covenant he established took on a second aspect: a pact based on the supreme witness of charity (*Jn.* 15: 13). It is with this background that the fourth Gospel in its rereading of the institution of the Eucharist rightly conceived the Church, the fruit of the eucharistic covenant, as a fraternal association. Must we recall that for St. Paul also the idea of brotherhood dominates the eucharistic doctrine, even to the extent, as has been suggested, that for the Apostle Christ's body in the Eucharist and in the Church is completely "one"? [103] Moreover is it not the same St. Paul who formulated the principle that the "gift of the body" without love (I *Cor.* 13: 3) would be only vanity and nothingness?

Finally, in instituting the Eucharist, Jesus instituted the Church, and from the beginning he gave it two characteristics which he intended to be basic and beyond any juridical organization, namely those of a worship assembly and a universal brotherhood.[104]

Place de l'Université, 3,   J. Coppens
Louvain   Professor at the University

2: 13). Finally and especially, most of the sacrifices include a communion rite. But the sacrificial word pair *sarx* or *kreas* and *haima* does not appear in the most ancient eucharistic texts where we find *body-blood* or *body-covenant*. St. Paul, we are told, uses the word pair *flesh-blood* only in his commentary on the Eucharist and it is very questionable that the Johannine terminology which is inspired by anti-Docetist tendencies is original. We might still observe however that Paul may have substituted body for flesh in the wake of his at time pessimistic views on the flesh and the importance given by him to the body in explaining the union of Christians with Christ.

J. Schniewind (*op. cit.*, pp. 186-187) admits a reference to the sacrificial language by conceding that the theology of Isaiah 53 predominates.

98. We are referred to Philo, *De sacrificio Abelis et Caini,* 121 ed. F. H. Colson-G. H. Whitaker (*The Loeb Classical Library*), London, 1950, pp. 182-183, and to the Jerusalem Talmud, *Yoma,* VII, *Makkôth,* 11b. Cf. M. Gaster, in *Enc. Rel. Eth.,* t. XI, col. 276; R. Eisler, in *Zeitschr. Neut. Wiss.,* 1923, t. XXIV, pp. 177-178 and *Revue de Qumrân,* no. 12, p. 498. See also the texts assembled by R. Le Déaut, *op. cit.,* pp. 194-200, for ex-

ample, IV Maccabees 6: 29; 17: 21-22, and especially everything that concerns the sacrifice of Isaac. This religious act which was cut short became in the first century the very type of the interior sacrifice that the Lord receives and rewards (*ibid.,* p. 200).

99. It is not required that we think of a strict pact concluded between more or less equal partners. J. Schniewind (*op. cit.,* p. 185) speaks of *Ordnung* instead of *Bund.* Thus is inaugurated the idea of "testament."

100. P. Neuenzeit (*op. cit.,* p. 197) acknowledges it: "Das Ziel der neuen Diatheke stimmt mit dem der alten überein; Jahweh Israels Gott, Israel Jahwehs Volk." See also X. Léon-Dufour, *op. cit.,* p. 437: "It is a 'new' covenant that Jesus founds in his blood . . . . Thanks to Jesus' blood, the people of God exists anew . . . Israel 'passes over' into this new people: the Church of Jesus is founded on earth in view of the Heavenly Kingdom to come." A. J. B. Higgins (*op. cit.,* pp. 32-33) contests the presence of the covenant idea in the words uttered by Jesus. To justify his opinion he alleges six reasons: a) the expression "my blood of the covenant" is hard and untranslatable into Aramaic; b) the expression "blood of the covenant" was connected in the Judaism of Jesus' time with the blood of circumcision; c) the idea of covenant is a Pauline idea (*Rm.* 9: 4; 11: 27; II *Cor.* 3: 6 ff.; *Gal.* 3: 15 ff.; 4: 24 ff.; *Ep.* 2: 12), and it was introduced into the words of the Last Supper under the influence of the Apostle; d) the reference to the blood must be understood not in the light of Exodus 24: 8 but of Isaiah 53: 12; e) Jesus could not have alluded to Jeremiah 31: 31 for this text did not provide for the conclusion of a covenant on the basis of a sacrifice.

We have already examined the greater part of these remarks: a) Certainly Paul develops a theology of covenants but the departure point may have, in part at least, been an utterance of Christ; b) Isaiah 53 did exert influence, but the mention of the "blood" does not refer to Isaiah 53 but to Exodus 24: 8; c) if Jeremiah 31: 31 does not imply sacrifice, it still does not exclude it; d) the expression "my blood of the covenant" is no longer considered untranslatable; d) the expression "blood of the covenant" to designate circumcision is secondary in connection with Exodus 24: 8. Furthermore, circumcision also implies the idea of covenant; e) finally, the idea of covenant, a new covenant, was the order of the day in Christ's time if we refer to the Qumrân texts.

J. Schniewind (*op. cit.,* p. 184) connects the foundation of the Church to the Eucharist also by having recourse to the fact that the texts speak of one broken bread and of one cup offered to all. The one cup would be contrary to the Jewish custom of the time. Through the unified bread and cup Jesus would have intended to signify that he was founding a "family" (*Mk.* 3: 35), the Assembly of God, the new people of God.

101. This gift of the person is expressed in the words of the consecra-

tion of the bread especially if we understand *sôma-gûph* as the "person" and if we accept as original the addition "which for you has been given" (*Lk.* 22: 19).

---

102. The sacrificial gift is especially evident in the words of the consecration of the wine to the extent that they allude to the shedding of blood.

103. Cf. L. Cerfaux, *Le Christ dans la théologie de saint Paul,* in *Lectio Divina,* t. VI, Paris, 1951, p. 265 and *La Théologie de l'Église suivant saint Paul,* 2nd ed., in *Unam Sanctam,* t. X, Paris, 1948, pp. 202-203.

104. See again on the Eucharist J. R. Schiefler, *Asi nacieron los Evangelios,* Bilbao, 1964, pp. 85-87, 336-340. The author makes reference to J. Schneider, *Zur Frage der Komposition von Jo. 6, 27-58,* in *In Memoriam Lohmeyer,* pp. 132-142, Stuttgart, 1951, t. XXXIII, pp. 237-239; E. Schweizer, *Das johannesische Zeugnis vom Herrenmahl,* in *Evang. Theol.,* 1952-1953, t. XII, pp. 358-361; G. Bornkamm, *Die eucharistische Rede im Johannesevangelium,* in *Zeitschr. Neut. Wiss.,* 1956, t. XLVII, pp. 161-169; N. Turner, *The Style of St. Mark's Eucharistic Words,* in *Journ. Theol. Stud.,* 1957, t. VIII, pp. 108-111; W. Wilkens, *Das Abendmahlszeugnis im vierten Evangelium,* in *Evang. Theol.,* 1958, t. XVIII, pp. 354-370; R. H. Mounce, *Continuity of the Primitive Tradition. Some Pre-pauline Elements in I Corinth.,* in *Interp.* (Richmond), 1959, t. XIII, pp. 417-424; J. C. Cooper, *The Problem of the Text in Luke 22, 19-20,* in *Luth. Quart.* (Rock Islands), 1962, t. XIV, pp. 39-48; E. J. Kilmartin, *The Eucharistic Cup in the Primitive Liturgy,* in *Cath. Bibl. Quart.,* 1962, t. XXIV, pp. 32-43.

VIII

Pierre Grelot

Ministerial Vocation in the Service of the People of God[1]

The pericope from St. Luke on the miraculous draught of fishes (*Lk.* 5: 1-11) invites us to study in its totality the theme to which it is related: the ministerial vocation in the service of God's people.[2] Actually this passage preserves not only the memory of the day that Jesus called his first four apostles to leave their fishing and follow him to become fishers of men. In Luke's account this call is bound up further with a highly meaningful episode: the miraculous draught of fishes. There is no

---

1. This article of P. Grelot appeared for the first time in *Assemblées du Seigneur*, no. 38, Bruges, Abbaye de St. André, 1964. We are grateful to the Éditions de l'Abbaye de St.-André and Professor Grelot for having authorized us to reprint the text of this study.

2. Bibliography on the subject is immense. It naturally includes the articles from the *TWNT*: *Apostellô* etc., *Diakonéô*, etc., *Doulos*, *Episkopéô* etc., *Hiérourgéô, Leitourgéô, Presbyteros*, etc. Studies on the whole question: J. Colson, *L'évêque dans les communautés primitives*, Paris, 1951; *Les fonctions ecclésiales aux deux premiers siècles*, Bruges-Paris, 1956; *La fonction diaconale aux origines de l'Église*, Paris, 1960; J. Lécuyer, *Le sacerdoce dans le mystère du Christ*, Paris, 1957. From a non-Catholic point of view: H. von Campenhausen, *Kirchliches Amt und geistliche Vollmacht in den drei Jahrhunderten*, Tübingen, 1953; Dom G. Dix, *The Ministry in the Early Church*, London, 1954; E. Schweizer, *Church Order in the New Testament*, London, 1961; F. T. Torrance, *Royal Priesthood*, Edinburgh-London, 1955. Collections: *Études sur le sacrement de l'ordre* (Lex orandi 22), Paris, 1957; *La tradition sacerdotale*, Le Puy, 1959; *Le sacrement de l'Ordre*, in *Bulletin du Comité des études* (Compagnie de St.-Sulpice), no. 38-39, 1962 (cf. *Le sacerdoce chrétien dans l'Écriture*, pp. 279-337). *Vocabulaire de théologie biblique*, art. *Apôtre, Charismes, Église, Ministères, Pastuer, Sacerdoce*.

doubt that the Evangelist sees in this a symbol of the task awaiting the fishers of men after Christ's resurrection. While the fourth Gospel sets this episode in an appearance of the risen Christ in Galilee (*Jn.* 21: 1-14), it still retains the same meaning. It also connects it with Jesus' words conferring the mission of feeding his flock to Peter. From another point of reference this presentation, so different from the symbolic catch, would still bring us back to the same theme, that of the ministry.

Still it is important here to distinguish two different but closely related planes: the apostolic ministry on the one hand and the ecclesiastical ministries on the other. Actually the continuity between the first and the second does not mean that they are identical. When the New Testament says that the Church is "built on the foundaiton of the Apostles" (*Ep.* 2: 20; *Rv.* 21: 14) it means that her faith rests on their witness, that her structures are those that they have determined and that her concrete life must retain as a norm the "deposit" which they entrusted to her. The apostolic word and the tradition that it handed on to the Church are formative of the definitive revelation and regulative for the ecclesiastical tradition that harbors them. This is a nontransmittable role that could be fulfilled only by the direct legates of the risen Christ. After them, the people of God can do no more than remain faithful to this trust, not certainly in a spirit of archaism which would obstruct the Church's real progress but in an active fidelity which would bring out all the virtual riches contained in this life-giving seed. This is the task of the ecclesiastical ministries over the course of the ages.

I. THE APOSTOLIC MINISTRY

1. *In the Gospels.*

We must not expect to find in Jesus' words and actions specifications about the ministries which only the experience of the apostolic age could bring out. During his public life and during the appearances following his resurrection, he was certainly not content with merely announcing the evangelical message; he entrusted its care to other men and set down the foundations of the institution which was to be responsible for it, his Church (*Mt.* 16: 18; 18: 17). But the way in which his intentions are made plain corresponds to the practical situation of the time. He did not leave his followers a ready-made action program whose details were spelled out in advance on all points. It is therefore through the ministerial vocation of the apostles and disciples that we must come to understand the format of the future ecclesiastical institutions.

This vocation is not merely the call to membership in the Kingdom of God, a call that is universal and allows men to remain in their prior context, their family and their work. This implies that a man leave everything to follow Jesus just as the Galilean fishermen had done (*Mk.* 1: 16-20, parall.) or Matthew did (*Mk.* 2: 13 parall.), a thing which all are not capable of doing (*Mt.* 8: 18-21 parall.). Even among those who became disciples, Jesus makes a choice: he sets the twelve apart from the others (*Lk.* 6: 13-16, parall.; *Jn.* 6: 70). A meaningful act which is of immense import. For whoever left his earthly goods for the name of Jesus will receive eternal life, but in the new world, these Twelve "will sit on twelve thrones, judging (i.e., governing) the twelve tribes of Israel" (*Mt.* 19: 27-29). In other words, the New Israel proclaimed by the prophets makes its entrance into history when Jesus establishes on earth the Kingdom of God; to this Israel he gives a framework in the Twelve. It is not they who chose their lot. It is he who chose them in order to place them in this role (*Jn.* 15: 16). And straight away their mission begins (*Mt.* 10: 5), an extension of his own and performed in his name. They are to proclaim the Gospel of the Kingdom in the cities and in the towns, and to work as he did the signs that manifest his presence on earth (*Mt.* 10: 7-8 and parall.). Is such a mission proper to the Twelve alone? Luke says precisely the contrary since he shows that it is also entrusted to the 70 or 72 disciples (*Lk.* 10: 1-20), who remind us of the 70 aides that Moses had (*Num.* 11: 16 ff., 24 ff.; *Ex.* 24: 1, 9) just as the

Twelve recall the chiefs of the old tribes. Thus the proclamation of the Kingdom goes far beyond the sole responsibility of those who were given the name apostles, i.e., preeminent envoys.

Nevertheless attention focuses on them when we see Jesus entrusting to them special functions and powers: the power of binding and loosing given conjointly to Peter (*Mt.* 16: 19) and to the whole group (*Mt.* 18: 18). Must we understand this as the power to declare what is permitted or forbidden, the power of forgiving or retaining sins as a parallel text from the fourth gospel says (*Jn.* 22: 23)? Whatever explanation we accept, it is still a question of an essential function which concerns the inner order of the community formed by those who believed in the gospel of the Kingdom. During the Last Supper there will be added the command to repeat the institutional gesture of the eucharistic meal: "Do this in remembrance of me" (*Lk.* 22: 19; I *Cor.* 11: 24 ff.). Only the Twelve, at the last appearance of the risen Lord, will receive the mission to convert all nations, to baptize and teach them (*Mt.* 28: 19 ff.); to preach the gospel to every creature and to confer baptism (*Mk.* 16: 15 ff.); to bear witness to the risen Jesus (*Ac.* 1: 8; cf. *Jn.* 15: 27). Only they will receive the gift of the Holy Spirit in order to fulfill their mission (*Jn.* 20: 22; *Ac.* 1: 8; 2: 4).

In this way the characteristics of a special ministry that Jesus himself defined in terms of service are specified (*Mt.* 10: 24; 20: 27; 23: 11; *Lk.* 22: 26 ff.; *Jn.* 13: 16: the words *doulos* and *diakonos* alternate without any notable change in meaning). This is a service of the Gospel and undoubtedly of others; but it is above all the service of Jesus who is the Master for his disciples, and the Lord for his servants (*Mt.* 10: 24 ff.; *Jn.* 13: 13-16). In addition, behind the men who exercise the ministry there is found the person of Jesus himself: "Who receives you, receives me and who receives me, receives him who sent me" (*Mt.* 10: 40; cf. *Lk.* 10: 16). And the same shepherd image which is used to define Jesus' function toward men (all of John 10) also defines the apostle's responsibility (ecclesiastical discourse of Matthew 18: 12-14) and that of Peter (appearance in Galilee reported in John

21: 15-17). Thus the Shepherd-Christ can disappear from the stage of history once he has given his life for his sheep; he will continue to act visibly in his flock through the shepherds he gave to it. To assist them in this work he will abide with them until the end of the world (*Mt.* 28: 20).

2. *In Acts and the Epistles.*

The Acts of the Apostles and the apostolic epistles show us what the ministry of these first shepherd-pastors was. After Judas' betrayal, the college of the Twelve was completed (*Act* 1: 15-16) in order to signify unequivocally the character of New Israel that colors the institution founded by Jesus (cf. *Rv.* 21: 12-14). The title *apostle* designates these men as the risen Lord's direct *envoys*. Moreover another direct envoy will soon come to take his place at their side: Saul of Tarsus, converted on the road to Damascus (*Act* 9), "an apostle not from men nor through men, but through Jesus Christ and God the Father, who raised him from the dead" (*Gal.* 1: 1). It is thanks to him especially that the thought on the apostolic ministry is enriched and made specific. Like the Twelve, even though he is the "least of the apostles" (I *Cor.* 15: 8 ff.), he was "set apart before he was born and called through grace" (*Gal.* 1: 15). This call made him Christ's ambassador (II *Cor.* 5: 19) and of his gospel (*Ep.* 6: 20). He received as a charge the "ministry of the new covenant," which is incomparably superior to that of Moses himself since it brings the lifegiving Spirit to men (II *Cor.* 3: 5-11). It is the "ministry of reconciliation" (II *Cor.* 5: 18); not in the sense that the ministers would perform rites capable of taking away men's sins but because God who reconciled the world to himself in Christ placed on their lips the words of reconciliation (II *Cor.* 5: 18 ff.). This point brings us to the core of the functions making up the apostleship. In combining the data from Acts and the epistles — however occasional and incomplete they may be — we see them develop in three related areas: proclaiming the

Gospel, ruling the Churches, and directing worship and the rites of sanctification.

The ministry of the word naturally occupies first place since everything else flows from it. In Acts it includes the proclamation of the salvation message leading men to the very significant rite of Baptism (e.g., *Act* 2: 14-41), but also the instruction of the faithful (*Act* 2, 42). For St. Paul this is the preaching of the Gospel (I *Cor*. 1: 17), this power of God that brings salvation to believers whether they be Jews or pagans (*Rm*. 1: 16), but also the handing on of a progressively deepening doctrine (*Rm*. 6: 17; 16: 17; cf. I *Cor*. 3: 1-2). This work, performed under the guidance of the Holy Spirit, makes the apostles the prophets of the new times (*Act*. 1: 15-21; cf. *Ep*. 2: 20); it thus extends into history the prophetic mission that Jesus himself assumed during his life, as he declared in the Nazareth synagogue (*Lk*. 4: 18-21). Will not the signs worked through the Word (*Mk*. 16: 17 ff. & 20) continue those which during Jesus' ministry showed concretely the presence of the Kingdom of God (*Mt*. 11: 4-5)?

This is not all. The apostles also have the power to govern the communities they founded. This governing entails organizing, overseeing (*Act* 8: 14; 11: 22), excluding the unworthy (*Act* 5: 1-11; 8: 20 ff.; I *Cor*. 5: 5 ff. & 11; I *Tim*. 1: 20) .... This is not the mere exercise of human authority, necessary for the practical operation of any group; it is the putting to work of "an authority given by the Lord to build men up" as St. Paul tells the Corinthians in dramatic circumstances (II *Cor*. 10: 8). The kingly office of the Shepherd-Christ, set up as Lord of his people through his resurrection, is manifested concretely in the pastoral function of the apostles. Finally, there remains everything that can be related in the life of the Church to the priestly role of Jesus: the rite that commemorates and makes present his sacrifice, those actions related to a certain extent to the distribution of his grace. Among them, it is certain that baptism is not reserved solely to the apostles (cf. *Act* 8: 16, 38); but the same is not true for the laying on of hands which confers the Holy Spirit (8: 17). As for the other sacramental acts, the data is too fragmentary for us to give a precise picture of it. The breaking of bread itself (*Act*

2: 42) for which we have the ritual (I *Cor.* 11: 20-27) almost eludes us. At least the one eucharistic assembly described in some detail is presided over by Paul in person (*Act* 22: 7-12).

We understand why St. Paul can proudly claim the title of servant (*doulos*: *Rm.* 1: 1), or of minister (*diakonos*: II *Cor.* 11: 23) of Christ, minister of the Gospel (*Col.* 1: 23) and minister of the Church (*Col.* 1: 25). Is not the act of representing Christ on earth in his threefold office of priest, king and prophet the most beautiful title of glory in the order of faith? The apostleship is the first of the gifts given by Christ who has ascended into heaven (*Ep.* 4: 11), the first of the charisms of the Spirit (I *Cor.* 12: 28). If Christ is the cornerstone of his Church, the apostleship is the foundation (*Ep.* 2: 20). Yet how is this role to be perpetuated in time once the apostolic generation is no more?

II. THE ECCLESIASTICAL MINISTRIES

At this point we must point out within the apostolic functions the basic distinction which will occupy the rest of our reflections. The apostleship includes something which is altogether untransferable: the fact of being a direct envoy of the risen Lord, of fulfilling in this way the role of witness, and thereby being the source of revelation for the Church of every age which will believe in the Gospel. But it also includes something transferable: the practical responsibility over the Gospel as it has been handed on, the sanctifying of worship and the various rites, and the governing of the Churches. On this precise point the New Testament makes us witnesses of the arising of new ministers appointed by the apostles themselves to provide for the perpetuity of their work.

1. *The beginning of the ministries.*

The New Testament writers have not left us any detailed list of the ecclesiastical ministries nor any elaborated theological reflection on their nature or the conditions of their exercise. Their aim was practical in their writing and they never treated the question except in passing on the occasion of some concrete problem arising in the life of the Churches. St. Paul gives us a striking example in writing to the Corinthians: "Now there are varieties of gifts, but the same Spirit; and there are varieties of ministries, but the same Lord; and there are varieties of working, but it is the same God who inspires them all in every one. To each is given the manifestation of the Spirit for the common good" (I *Cor.* 12: 4-7). In its trinitarian formulation the sentence sets up a practical equivalency among the ministries, the particular gifts received from the Holy Spirit (or charisms), and the various powers which are manifested in the members of the Church. But in the lists that follow we see activities appearing side by side even though they are obviously not of the same order (12: 7-10; 12: 28-30). This means that the problem to be resolved is not that of the ministries in general, but of the use of the personal charisms in the liturgical assemblies. On this point, speaking in tongues (so prized in Corinth) comes in last place, and prophecy in the first (14: 1-5) immediately after the apostleship (12: 28). This evaluation does not prejudge the hierarchy of ministries considered in their specific functions. We can deduce from Paul's considerations only that if there are charisms that are non-ministerial (speaking in tongues or the gift of interpretation), there is no ministry that is not charismatic. On the level of the ecclesiastical ministries therefore we see again the fact that we pointed out in regard to the apostolic ministry: the mission of the Holy Spirit in the Church is their source and is manifested through them. In addition the ministries participate in the works of service performed by the apostles: like them they are workers of the Gospel (cp. I *Cor.* 3: 3-4 and II *Tim.* 2: 15), soldiers of the good fight (cp. II *Cor.* 10: 3 ff. and II *Tim.* 2: 3). Paul looks upon them as fellow servants (*syndoulos*: *Col.* 1: 7; 4: 7), fellow workers (*synergos*: I *Th.* 3: 2; II *Cor.* 8: 3), fellow soldiers for Christ (*synstratiotes*: *Phm.* 2). In the various services they perform their social situation is therefore an extension of the apostles'; it is not merely an emanation of the society of the faithful it confers upon it an armature which corresponds with God's plans.

The apostles performed a ministry of the Word, as prophets of the new times, as doctors (*didaskaloi*) charged with a teaching (*didache*). Similarly there existed ministries of the Word: those of prophet and doctor (I *Cor.* 11: 28; cf. *Rm.* 12: 6-8), and that of evangelist (*Ep.* 4: 11). From the book of Acts we know that the corresponding tasks could be performed with other functions as well: in Acts 13: 1, Paul and Barnabas are named among the "prophets and doctors" of the Church of Antioch, while in Acts 21: 8 Philip is called an evangelist. This ministry of the Word (cf. I *Pet.* 4: 11) is evidently not left up to the un-governed initiative of individuals. As it extends into the time of the Church which appeared to us above to be the prophetic aspect of the apostleship, it is bound up with the tradition of the apostles, with the "deposit" entrusted by them (I *Tim.* 6: 20; II *Tim.* 1: 14; 2: 2; 3: 14), for this trust constitutes the very substance of the Gospel. With this in mind it can therefore be broadly exercised by those to whom God has given the talent, an Apollos for example (*Act* 18: 24-27), who like Paul himself was a co-worker of God in the proclamation of the Gospel to the Corin-thians (I *Cor.* 3: 5-9).

This is not the same for the "government" ministries (I *Cor.* 12: 28) which are more generally thought of under the shepherd metaphor (*Act* 20: 28; *Ep.* 4: 11; I *Pet.* 5: 2). For this reason, just as the ruling of the Churches by the apostles keenly signified the rule of the risen Lord, so new ministerial responsibilities come to play this role when the apostles are far away or no longer living.[3] The history of this local hierarchy unfortunately is frought with

---

3. To the general bibliography given above, we should add a few articles of competent biblicists: H. Schlier, *La hiérarchie de l'Église d'après les épitres pastorales*, in *Le temps de l'Église*, Paris-Tournai, 1961, pp. 140-156; P. Benoit, *Les origines de l'épiscopat dans le Nouveau Testament*, in *Exégèse et théologie*, Paris, 1962, pp. 232-246; *Les origines apostoliques de l'épiscopat*, in *L'évêque dans l'Églsie du Christ* (ed. H. Boussé and A. Mandouze), Bruges-Paris, 1963, pp. 13-57 (cf. pp. 341-346).

more than one obscure point. The institution of the presbyters, based on that of the elders in Jewish communities, is attested to both in Jerusalem (*Act* 11: 30; 15: 2-6; 16: 4; 21: 18) and in the Pauline communities (*Act* 14: 23; 20: 17), and it is found again in the various epistles (I *Tim.* 5: 17-22; *Tit.* 1: 5; *James* 5: 14; I *Pet.* 5: 1-5). The presbyters are to feed the flock (*Act* 20: 28; I *Pet.* 5: 2), watch over it (*episkopeo*: I *Pet.* 5: 2; cf. *Act* 20: 28), preside over it (I *Tim.* 5: 17). The recounting of these functions explains two titles found in use after the Pauline epistles: *episkopoi* (*Ph.* 1: 1) and presidents (I *Th.* 5: 12). At this very early period, episcopate and presidency are exercised collegially in each Church by the body of presbyters; at the end of the first century, the epistle of St. Clement of Rome attests to the persistence of the same state of affairs. Similarly, the Epistle to the Hebrews speaks always in the plural of the "leaders" (*hegoumenoi*: 13: 7, 17, 24). Nevertheless, convergent indications show that the presbyteral college in each Church possessed a head. In Jerusalem James clearly plays that role (*Act* 15: 13 ff.; 21: 18). Romans 12, 8 speaks of the president in the singular and the pastoral epistles mention always only one *episkopos* (I *Tim.* 3: 1-7; *Tit.* 1: 7-9). In the second century Justin will speak similarly of the president (*proestos*) of the assembly, and Ignatius of Antioch mentions a hierarchy of three degrees in which the *episkopos* (= bishop) is surrounded by a *presbyterium* (= priests).

In this way little by little the face of the local Churches becomes definitively formed. This does not come about by the spontaneous initiative of the faithful upon the death of the apostles, but as a result of an apostolic foundation. As long as the apostles were alive they preserved the authority over the communities they founded as we see from the epistles of St. Paul. They were also able to delegate this authority to personal emissaries charged with resolving questions in their name; e.g., Barnabas when he was sent to Antioch (*Act* 11: 22) and Titus and Timothy during Paul's missionary journeys (I *Th.* 3: 2-6; I *Cor.* 4: 17; II *Cor.* 7: 5-13). The pastoral epistles give an idea of the responsibilities of the powers accorded to these emissaries: they not only entail vigilance in matters of faith and tradition, but also the organization of the local Churches by instituting ministers (*Tit.* 1: 5) over whom these special envoys retain jurisdiction (I *Tim.* 5: 19 ff.).

In short, the apostolic function, as an exercise of authority in the Churches, is perpetuated by means of a local hierarchy which is to represent its permanence in the course of time. As we have already pointed out, the ministry proper to this hierarchy requires a charism from the Holy Spirit (I *Cor.* 12: 28: government; *Ep.* 4: 11: pastorate). Here again the pastoral epistles furnish supplementary particulars on the special case of Timothy: it is by the gesture of the laying on of hands that he receives his ministerial charism (I *Tim.* 4: 14; II *Tim.* 1: 6). We thereby reach a sacramental notion of the ministries that I Timothy 5: 22 applies explicitly to the presbyterate. It would be desirable to be able to have some specifications on the life and activity of these ministers. But we have to be content with some scattered facts. The presbyters "labor in preaching and teaching" (I *Tim.* 5: 17), and it is known that they have to defend their flock against false teachers (*Act* 20: 28-30). Their presidency implies that they labor for their communities and that they admonish the faithful (I *Th.* 5: 12), implying a real exercise of authority.

It is about the cultual and sacramental life of the Churches that the New Testament gives the least direct information. It mentions only the ordination of the presbyters by Timothy (I *Tim.* 5: 22) and the anointing of the sick by the presbyters (*James* 4: 13-15, with an indirect reference to the forgiveness of sins). Rather than arguing from this accidental silence (for there is no argument about something that causes no problem!) to deny that the local authority had any special power in these matters, particularly in regard to the celebration of the Eucharist, we must ask ourselves how the second century ecclesiastical tradition understood on this point the apostolic tradition whose practice it faithfully preserved. Here the texts are clear. "It is not allowed to baptize or to perform the agape without the bishop," wrote Ignatius of Antioch (*Smyrn.,* 8, 2); consider as valid only that Eucharist celebrated with the presidency of the bishop or his delegate" (8: 1). And who doubts that this "delegate" must

belong to the *presbyterium* that Ignatius describes surrounding
the bishop? Similarly, when Justin describes the Christian Eucharist
he insists on the essential role of the "president" (I *Apol.*, 65, 3;
67, 3-5). This then is the practice bequeathed by the apostolic
age. It is connected on the one hand with the charismatic character
of the ministries in question, and on the other with Christ's command observed by the apostles and left in trust to the Churches
founded by them: "Do this in remembrance of me."

Finally there is a lowlier ministry which is also organically
bound up with the apostleship: that of the deacons. Material
assistance to the poor within the fraternal community has been
one of the characteristics of apostolic activity from the beginning
(*Act* 4: 34 ff.). It remained one of Paul's permanent concerns
(I *Cor.* 16: 1-4; II *Cor.* 8-9). But to face the problem squarely
it was very soon necessary that the apostles acquire helpers for
themselves, helpers that were instituted in their function by the
laying on of hands (*Act* 6: 1-6). Among the charisms mentioned
by St. Paul there also figures "assistance" (I *Cor.* 12: 28) or the
diakonia (*Rm.* 12: 7; cf. I *Pet.* 4: 11), which has for its purpose
the distribution of goods (*Rm.* 12: 8). This is unquestionably
the task of the deacons (*Ph.* 1: 1; I *Tim.* 3: 8-12). On to this
basic responsibility may be grafted also a ministry of the Word,
for those whom Acts presents as the diaconal prototypes, the
seven Hellenists, preach and baptize like Philip, and speak as
doctors like Stephen. However that may be, their service leaves
them in a subordinate position.

2. *Spirituality of the ministries.*

It is not enough merely to point out historically this transition
from the apostleship to the ecclesiastical hierarchy with its three
degrees. This could be simply the human evolution of a society
which finds the means of self preservation in giving itself a practical organization. The theology of the ministries as found in the
occasional allusions in the epistles invite us to see here something

quite different. It is not for nought that the apostleship on the one hand and the ecclesiastical ministries on the other are charismatic functions: through them the action of the Holy Spirit is exercised in the Church. Undoubtedly from a certain point of view everything in the Church is under the motion of the Holy Spirit. No one can say "Jesus is Lord" except by the Spirit (I *Cor.* 12: 3); no one can call God "Abba, Father" except by the Spirit (*Rm.* 8: 15). The life of faith and charity is the first of his gifts to men (cf. *Rm.* 5: 5). But this very life has for its origin and its constant support a preaching of the Word of God, an exercise of the pastorate, a eucharistic worship and sacramental rites. In addition, the presence of the Spirit is manifested in the Church; it is specialized in some way in the particular charisms by which every ministerial activity manifests concretely the secret working of grace. The apostolic derivation of the ministries and the apostolic succession necessary for their lawful exercise are not simply historical phenomena without importance. Jesus had entrusted solely to the apostles the evangelization of the world and the ruling of his Church. They fulfilled their task by several interconnected means: a proclamation of the Gospel which fixed revelation, the legacy of a tradition that forever governed the thought and the life of the Churches, and the institution of ministries which were to perpetuate their own action. These various aspects of the work of the apostles are interrelated; they are also, although not for the same reason, constitutive of the Church.

If then Christian thought intends to work through a theology and a spirituality of the ecclesiastical ministries, it must not be content with going back to the New Testament texts that refer to it explicitly. It must also rediscover its features in all the passages related to the apostolic ministry, since the ecclesiastical ministries only extend its action in space and time. The first example of this way of operating is furnished for us by the New Testament itself. When the Gospels report the acts and the words of Jesus instituting the apostleship and defining the mission and powers of the apostles with an indication of the spirit in which they must be used, is the only reason for the concern to recount the

origin of the Twelve, to establish their authority and to make
known the instructions they received personally from the Lord?
Once we know how to read the texts, we note right away that
the missionaries of the Gospel, the possessors of the ecclesiastical
ministries, are intimately bound up with the apostles or the
disciples who are downstage. If Luke repeats the missionary discourse by presenting successively the sending forth of the Twelve
on their mission (*Lk.* 9: 1-6) and then that of the 72 disciples
(*Lk.* 10: 1-20), is it not to tell us that Jesus' teaching concerns
a public that is much vaster than the apostles, *viz.,* all the
preachers of the Kingdom of God whom the Master has sent as
workers in his harvest? From the time of the apostles to that
of the ministers, the object of the mission and its spirituality has
not changed. The more ample synthesis grafted by Matthew on
the same discourse of Christ is similar (*Mt.* 10); although it takes
up substantially authentic (and even at times archaic: cf. v. 5)
words of Jesus, it aims in fact at the situation of Christian missionaries who are sometimes welcomed and sometimes persecuted. This
mission charter is completed in the "ecclesiastical" discourse (*Mt.*
18) where the parable of the lost sheep concerns the attitude of
the ministers toward the "little ones" (18: 12-14). And is it not
symptomatic that we see elsewhere the same *logion* of Jesus
speak in different terminology of these envoys that the world will
not receive: "I shall send them prophets and apostles" (*Lk.* 11:
49; cf. *Ep.* 2: 20); "Therefore I send you prophets and wise men
and scribes" (*Mt.* 23: 34). The apostles have disappeared from
the horizon, but the apostleship continues .... In Luke it is
the instruction on humility and the spirit of service (cf. *Mt.* 20:
25-27) which is formulated in the language of the Christian
ministry: "Let the leader (*hegoumenos*: cf. *Heb.* 13: 7, 17, 24)
among you be as one who serves" (*Lk.* 22: 26).

This Christian reading of Jesus' words is not restricted to the
moral instructions alone. The ministers of the Churches allow
themselves to be seen beneath the apostles because the apostolic
functions and powers — with the exception of what is non-
transferable — continue to be exercised in the Church through

them. If the Gospels have kept words of Jesus on the forgiveness of sins, the Eucharist, the governing of the community, it is because they are of practical interest by reason of their timeliness. In actuality, the ministers of Christ do "bind and loose" (*Mt.* 18: 18), forgive and retain sins (*Jn.* 22: 23), not certainly in their own name but in the name of Christ; and still today Christian people "give glory to God for having given such power to men" (*Mt.* 9: 8). Similarly, the ministers celebrate the Eucharist following a rite which Paul himself had already received from tradition (I *Cor.* 11: 23). In every instance that we are involved in a ministerial activity of the apostles, the texts are applicable (in proper perspective) to the men that they have set up in their places and to those who will succeed them from then on.

If this is the case for the Gospels why would it not be the same for Acts and the epistles where the same ministerial activity is seen in operation? Even more than Paul's practical counsels to the presbyters of Ephesus (*Act* 20: 19-35) and to his envoys Timothy and Titus, his own reflections on the apostolic ministry have the value of a rule of life for all ministers. Stewards of the mysteries of God (I *Cor.* 4: 1), ambassadors of Christ (II *Cor.* 5: 20), charged with the ministry of the Spirit (II *Cor.* 3: 8), with the ministry of righteousness that saves men (3: 9), with the ministry of reconciliation (5: 18), they nevertheless must undergo all sorts of trials (I *Cor.* 4: 9-13; II *Cor.* 6: 4-10); for they must carry in the body the death of Jesus, so that Jesus' life may be manifested in them and be at work in the faithful (II *Cor.* 4: 8-12). Through their sufferings they complete in their flesh what was lacking in the trials of Christ for his body, the Church (*Col.* 1: 24). From this, the sense of honor for Christ, the selflessness, the absolute dedication, the fervor in service that Paul manifests in the exercise of his ministry appear as the ideal which no minister may ignore. We must go further. The relationship between the ministries and the Lord on the one hand and between them and the Christian people on the other are basically the same as that of the apostleship, with the exception of the tasks proper to the apostles in regard to the foundation of the Church, the establishing of normative tradition and the proclamation of evangelical revelation. This final point merits our attention for a moment.

3. *Theology of the ministries.*

Apostolic service was presented to us formerly in its relationship to Christ's threefold office of prophet, king and priest. The same is true for the ministries in this regard, taking into account their diversity. Undoubtedly the Christian people as such, the Church in its totality and in each of its members, also participates in this threefold office. This is the very meaning of the baptismal anointing whereby God signs us with his seal by placing within us the first fruits of his Spirit (II *Cor.* 1: 21-22). Because of this the "chosen race" is entirely associated with the "royal priesthood" of its head (I *Pet.* 2: 9; *Rv.* 5: 10); they are communitarily responsible for the "word of God and the witness of Jesus" (*Rv.* 6: 9; 12: 17; 20: 4), which is the "spirit of prophecy" (*Rv.* 19: 10). It may be said that this is the basic element of Christian existence. But in order for this threefold office of the new people of God to become a reality, Christ distributes justly to his own the ministries which give structure to the Church as a body social (cf. *Ep.* 4: 7-12), and the Holy Spirit confers on these ministers the charisms corresponding to their office (I *Cor.* 12: 4-11). The ministries and the charisms relative to the Word of God, to the "witness of Jesus" and to the evangelization of the world can be dispensed broadly, which is why the "prophets and doctors" are numerous in the Church at all times. But this is not true for the ministries that represent Christ in his office of shepherd or priest. In this case a particular call is necessary, a "setting apart," an adhesion to the apostolic succession and a consecration through the laying on of hands. The exercise of an authority which is not merely human, which can say with the apostles and presbyters of Jerusalem: "The Holy Spirit and *we* have decided . . ." is something which one cannot arrogate to one's self, and which is not received by delegation from the Christian people. Here we are dealing actually with an authentic re-presentation of apostolic authority, in complete submission to apostolic tradition, so that Christ the Good Shepherd will thereby continue to manifest his presence in the Church sacramentally. Likewise the action of Christ the Priest, the *one* priest of the human race, possesses a sacramental interpretation which clearly signifies the sanctification of the faithful and which permits their "spiritual worship" (*Rm.* 12: 1) to be united with the sacrifice of their Head. The corresponding ministerial tasks, which are all destined for the service of the Christian people, could not be considered to be performed in the name of this people, in its stead and by virtue of its own powers. They constitute the presence of Christ the Priest in his Church.

Here we are touching on a rather difficult point since the New Testament seems to avoid priestly vocabulary, whether pagan or Jewish, in speaking of the ministers of the Gospel. From here to a denial of the priestly character of the Christian ministry is but one step, which Protestantism has taken. In reality, we ought first to understand the reasons for this silence. The pagan priesthoods on the one hand and the levitical priesthood on the other are situated in a religious sociology which considers them mediators between man and the divinity. The New Testament is well aware of the total newness that Christ represents in this context; he is the *one* mediator (I *Tim.* 2: 5), the *one* Priest, just as he is also the one Prophet and the one King of his people. There is no longer any place in the Church for a priesthood of the same type as the former priesthoods, even Aaron's. Christ's ministers are today in a completely different situation. Yet, once we understand this, it is still true that the priestly activity of Christ is now performed in the context of ministerial tasks. This is why, in another sense, they take on a priestly dimension which the New Testament has not overlooked.

After mentioning his ministry in the service of the Philippians, St. Paul speaks in these terms of the martyrdom which he looks upon as soon to be: "Even if my blood is to be poured out as a libation on the sacrificial offering (*leitourgia*) of your faith, I am glad" (*Ph.* 2: 17). Let us not understand this as "the sacrificial offering which *constitutes your faith,*" but as "the sacrificial offering which *has had your faith as a result*"; it is therefore the apostle's own ministry which constitutes this "sacrificial offering." Similarly in Romans 15: 15 ff., Paul defines in clear terms his service of the Gospel: "I have written you ... because of the grace given to me by God of being a minister (*leitourgon*) of Christ Jesus, in the priestly service (*hiérourgounta*) of the Gospel of God, so that the offering (*prosphora*) of the Gentiles may become acceptable, sanctified by the Holy Spirit." The ministry, which has for its fruit the sacrificial offering of men, is a *hierurgy* entrusted to a *leitourgos;* words which belong to the priestly vocabulary. These elementary indications will have a much greater place in the reflection on the ministry, to the extent that Christian worship, the core of Church life, will become its pivot. For if it be true that a unique reality, the once-and-for-all sacrifice of Christ the Priest (*Heb.* 8-10), has been substituted for the figurative worship of Israel and for the levitical priesthood, this reality is made present in the Church under the cloak of a rite entrusted to ministers. If one compares the sociology of the Church to that of Israel, we can see that the ministries (not certainly in their own name, but in the name of Christ whom they represent) have replaced the former priesthood just as they also took the place of the prophetic and kingly functions.

This is why ecclesiastical tradition, beginning with the epistle of Clement (40-41) will legitimately develop a priestly interpretation of the ministries which will become the theology of Holy Orders. It could only be regrettable if the vocabulary used in this regard, with its background from the Old Testament and from the history of religions that it contains, would make us lose sight of the specific character of the Christian ministry. It is the extension of the apostolic ministry and is defined by its relationship with Christ. Unique in its type, it therefore entails a relationship with the threefold office of prophet, king and priest which is Christ's. This ministry was established not primarily for power and authority, but for service and for a function that is to be performed within the hierarchized Body; the Body, as a whole, participates in this threefold office. So that this service and this function may be carried out, it needs a proper charism which Christian theology has attempted to explain rather improperly by speaking of a priestly "character." Thus Christ continues to manifest his action in his Church, according to this sentence from St. Matthew: "Behold, I am with you always until the close of the age" (*Mt.* 28: 20).

Rue d'Assas, 21   P. Grelot,
Paris (6 e)   Professor at the Institut Catholique
de Paris

IX

W. C. van Unnik

The Ideas of the Gnostics concerning the Church

When one approaches the study of a subject with a view toward eventual publication, one's first task is to trace the limits of one's subject by asking certain questions. At times certain facts that call for clarification are observed and at times one starts out from points that are formulated independently from the documentation.

In the ever complex area of problems dealing with Gnosticism there are many obscure points still remaining that pertain to the first case. For example: what is the exact meaning of names like *Barbelo* or *Jaldabaoth?* Or again, how do we account for the formulation and evolution of writings like the preaching of the Naassenes preserved in Hippolytus? And again, what should be thought about the *Apocrypha of John?* In this article, however, it is to a problem of the second type that we must apply ourselves: what is the idea of the Church that we encounter among the Gnostics? It is certainly legitimate to ask this question. Insofar as some Gnostics even considered themselves Christians, it is normal to inquire into how they looked upon the Church.

We know that the number of sources that supply information on Gnostic doctrines is constantly on the increase. A person who is engaged in studying them will hardly be inclined to concern himself about questions relating to the Church and her organization since technical works devoted to Gnosis give very little space to this kind of problem. Could this be because up till now the important discoveries of Nag-Hamadi have received very little notice? We shall have occasion to come back to this point. But in the meanwhile, we must also point out an equal lack of interest on the other extreme, in the works devoted to the theology of the Church in the first centuries. Is this merely by chance? Or are we dealing with a kind of unconscious reticence on the part of the heirs of the Great Church toward these heretics? Whatever the answer may be, an author like Gustave Bardy who devoted a work to the ecclesiology of the second century,[1] hardly mentions the Gnostics. He does this since he relies on writers like Barnabas or Origen rather than on the Gnostics themselves.

It is therefore not so simple to plan a study of our theme. But it is possible that through examining problems that do not arise directly from the matter under consideration we may arrive at something worthwhile. As long as we do not systematically remain outside this matter, we shall find at times that our procedure will lead to rummaging about in dark corners that have been little explored and to a better look at aspects of the problem that are usually neglected.

First some observations on the vocabulary in which the object of our inquiry is framed, namely the ideas concerning the Church and the notion itself of Gnosticism.

On the first point, I should not want to hold myself to too strict a definition of the Church and therefore chose the rather broad expression: "ideas concerning the Church." We shall not be limited to the various uses of the word "ekklesia" alone, but shall also employ other expressions like "people of God," "flock," etc. We shall examine what the Gnostics eventually have to tell us about the nature of the Church, her organization and the concrete forms in which it appears. Our concern will entail both her theological structure and her sociological framework. We shall try to define her position, her aim, and what kind of a community she represented.

As regards the Gnostics, we do not intend to be restricted to the very careless use of the term which in recent years has become current in some circles, particularly in Germany. It is known that since the publication of Hans Jonas' work *Gnosis und spätantiker Geist,* Gnosis is looked upon as a current which in questions relative to human existence decidedly broke with the solutions advocated by Greek classicism and Judaism itself. Among these representatives of this dualism and this hatred for the world we should count not only those who have always been looked upon as Gnostics, but also Philo, the Neo-Platonists and Alexandrians like Origen. We certainly readily admit that phenomenological considerations do broaden our perspective somewhat, but it is not wise to commit ourselves to this path. To do so results in actually allowing what the classical Gnostics considered important to become blurry, and from another viewpoint we are forced to rule out certain important connections with men like Philo and Origen. In any event there is not enough fair treatment given to the actual historical facts. Moreover people seek to broaden the field of Gnosticism by attempting a restoration of its earlier stages by means of rather hazardous hypotheses. They begin with Mandaean or Manichaean documents in order to end up at Pauline communities. It is enough here to mention the works of Schmithals. The ease that hypotheses are piled one on top of the other is in proportion to the grave shortcomings in the criticism of the sources, and even perhaps more in self criticism. In accordance with good method, it is advisable to begin from those who traditionally present themselves as Gnostics or were looked upon as such. Only afterwards will it be possible to see if there really is a sort of pre-Gnosis in the New Testament writings. But in the present situation that research is in, we must proceed with extreme caution since the study of authentically Gnostic documents is far from being ready for a valid examination of problems relative to the New Testament. When H. Schlier, in his commentary on the Epistle to the Ephesians makes use of second and third century data to shed light on the work of Paul or one of his disciples, he lapses into a method of working and treating the sources which is historically unacceptable.

Moreover, I did not include in my investigation writings whose Gnostic origins are seriously questioned or frankly doubtful, such as the Odes of Solomon and the *Acta Apostolorum Apocrypha*. I have

---

1. G. Bardy, *La théologie de l'Église de saint Clément de Rome à saint Irénée,* Paris, 1945. See esp. pp. 167 ff.

limited myself to those authors and works which are generally considered to be openly Gnostic or which their ancient adversaries so catalogued.

Let us add that the Christianity of the second century, when Gnosticism had reached its zenith, is very varied and complex. Things are all still in a state of flux.

Jean Daniélou begins his *Théologie du Judéo-christianisme,* devoted to the Church, in these terms: "One of the most remarkable characteristics of Judeo-Christian theology is the position occupied in it by the doctrine of the Church.... At a very early date, the Church seems conscious of its existence as a theological entity." [2] In saying this, the author is not thinking of the theological doctrine nor of all the things that are involved in the organization of the Church.

Could a similar evaluation be formulated in regard to the Gnostics? We have already pointed out that the literature dedicated to the movement leaves little room for considerations regarding the Church. But we must still point out a very peculiar aspect. Bardy mentions that it was precisely "in the Gnostic systems that the theory of the invisible Church had its most complete development." [3] In writing "the Gnostic systems" he unduly generalizes and passes over an important question. Actually, when the data on which the author bases his thought is examined, we note that with one exception (to which we shall return) all his references are related to the Valentinian school.[4] Is this by chance? In any case, and whatever be the importance of this school, we may not merely speak of *the* Gnostics without further specification. The vast current that we call Gnosticism is much more diversified. There is certainly an element of truth in Hippolytus' remark when he states that Gnosticism proliferated in many directions from one and the same aberrant doctrine.[5] But we must not tone down the differences and boil everything down to mere variations of vocabulary. From the very outset it would not be very wise to reduce everything to one sole type. Quite the contrary. We must observe and recognize all the subtle shades of meaning and diversity within the heart of the same movement.

Let us note finally that in an investigation of the ideas on the Church we naturally may leave aside those forms which are foreign to Christian Gnosticism like the *Corpus Hermeticum*. But even in those Gnostic writings that are related to Christianity, the inquiry ends up with but meager results. A very prolific work like the *Pistis Sophia* gives us absolutely no information. And the Gospel of Philip is equally as miserly in what it has to say. The only exception is found in the heirs of Valentinus. But even here the documentary contribution is not terribly substantial. Indeed there is no question of attempting to integrate their concept of the "seeds of light" into our inquiry, as if we were obliged to look upon this notion as a kind of substitution for the idea of the Church. To a different vocabulary, another version of things must correspond.

In our inquiry about the Church among the Gnostics, we come up against a remarkable fact that may bolster our assertion about the modifications that came about in the very heart of Gnosticism. In Irenaeus' *notitium* on the Ophites, he mentions an imperishable *eon* which he describes as follows: *esse autem hanc et veram et sanctam ecclesiam, quae fuerit appellatio et conventio et adunitio Patris omnium primi hominis, et Filii secundi hominis et Christi filii eorum et praedictae feminae.*[6] In the version of the same myth that we find in the *Apocryphon Johannis,* the same expressions do not reappear. The comparison with other passages (which is particularly clear for the end of par. 10, ff.), a comparison that the recent publication of this *apocryphon* has made possible, shows that its citation in Irenaeus has been worked in a more Christian form. We may conclude without fear that we have here a certain adaptation to the ways of speaking

---

2. J. Daniélou, *Théologie du Judéo-Christianisme,* Tournai, 1958, p. 317.

3. G. Bardy, *op. cit.,* p. 167.

4. Cf. the testimony of Tertullian, *Adv. Valentinianos* I: "Valentiniani, frequentissimum plane collegium inter hereticos."

5. Hippolytus, *Refutatio,* V, 6.

6. Irenaeus, *Adv. Haereses,* I, 30, 2.

of Christianity (*sancta ecclesia*). We cannot fail to notice a polemical inference in the *veram*. Undoubtedly there existed the desire to go against the idea of the Church which resulted in speaking of the *ecclesia* as the assemblage on earth of those who believe in Christ.

Similar observations can be made in the case of Valentinus. Tertullian reports that Valentinus was a candidate for the episcopacy in Rome and that someone was preferred to him as being better qualified as a *confessor*.[7] The few indications in regard to Ptolemaeus, Heraclion or Theodotus allow us to conclude that they used New Testament writings and that they claimed to reveal their inner meaning in accordance with their own Gnosis. They used the Gnostic myth as a rule of interpretation of Scripture, at the same time giving it a Christian tone. There is therefore nothing astounding in the fact that those who stood against the "Great Church" still used the term Church.

But let us get back to our question and ask ourselves whether the fact that the Gnostics spoke so little of the Church is accidental. How do we account for their almost total silence? We know that the *argumentum e silentio* is very tenuous and almost never convincing. From "not mentioning" to "not knowing" is a risky jump. But the fact that in every instance we find only shifting sands, and that even in the Christianized form of Valentinian Gnosis the Church plays only a modest role are both very significant. If the *Ecclesia* did hold an important place in Gnostic thought, we should at least have found some traces of this in the *Pistis Sophia!*

Would the answer to our question depend on the nature of our sources? It is a fact that a good part of our documentation has come to us through the bias of polemical writings set down by adversaries. In this type of literature more emphasis is given to divergences than to points of agreement. But this argument bears little weight in this case since the original texts are now available to us and do not give us a different picture. Everything seems to indicate that the Gnostics did not accentuate an ecclesiological doctrine and that the polemic against them focused on doctrines about God and Christ, as we can see from Irenaeus and Tertullian.

Must we therefore give up all idea of finding any substantial notations? What practical value can we ascertain in the conjunction "Church-Gnosis"? It is not easy to furnish a general answer. Data has varied over the course of time. By the year 200 boundaries are clearly present, but before Irenaeus this was not the case. We have already seen that Valentinus had intrigued to acquire an episcopal see in Rome. For his part, Irenaeus tells us of a Gnostic, Marcus by name, who resided in the house of a deacon whose wife he seduced.[8] Yet that some Gnostics did belong to the Church is shown from the Shepherd of Hermes, at least if we agree with Dibelius and Joly in looking at this passage as referring to them: Οἱ πιστεύσαντες ... πιστοὶ μὲν δυσμαθεῖς δὲ καὶ αὐθάδεις καὶ ἑαυτοῖς ἀρέσκοντες Θέλουτες πάντα γίωσκειν, καὶ οὐδὲν ὅλως γινώσκουσιν (Sim., IX, 22; cf. VIII, 6, 5).[9] Still more explicitly, Justin declares that the Valentinians, the Bisilidians and the partisans of Saturnilus called themselves "Christians," [10] and the Valentinians complained that the members of the Church "kept them apart." [11] They therefore claimed to belong to the Church.[12] On the other hand several Church writers complained that they had been confused with the Gnostics. This was Origen's complaint in his book against Celsus.[13] The divisions were therefore far from being clear-cut. Yet, the differences were perceptible since Irenaeus notes that on his trip to Rome during the ponti-

---

7. Tertullian, *Adv. Valent.*, 4.

8. Irenaeus, *Adv. Haer.*, I, 13, 5.

9. M. Dibelius, *Der Hirt des Hermas*, Tübingen, 1923, p. 596 ff., 630; R. Joly, *Hermas. Le Pasteur*, Paris, p. 277, n. 3; see also G. Bardy, *op. cit.*, p. 167.

10. Justin Martyr, *Dialogus cum Tryphone*, XXXV, 5-6, cf. *Apologia*, XXVI.

11. Hippolytus, *Refut.*, V, 9.

12. Irenaeus, *Adv. Haer.*, III, 15, 2.

13. See for example Irenaeus, *Adv. Haer.*, I, 25: Carpocrates finds fault with the Church because he is accused of being a magician.

ficate of Anicetus, Polycarp "brought back to the Church of God many of the aforementioned heretics" (Valentinus, Marcion, etc.).[14]

Let us try to be more specific. One passage from Irenaeus is helpful. Adv. Haer. III, 15, 2. In this section he is engaged in full combat with the Valentinian theory that held that the apostles handed on only a part of their teaching publicly and that certain points they reserved to privileged individuals. Irenaeus then describes the part the Gnostics are playing: *Hi enim ad multitudinem propter eos qui sunt ab ecclesia, quos communes Ecclesiasticos ipsi dicunt, inferunt sermones, per quos capiunt simpliciores et illiciunt eos, simulantes nostrum tractatum, ut saepius audiant; qui etiam quaeruntur de nobis, quos quum similia nobiscum sentiant, sine causa abstineamus nos a communicatione eorum, et quum eadem dicant et eandem habeant doctrinam, vocemus illos haereticos.*[15] We see that Irenaeus reproaches the Valentinians for using terminology current in the Church and giving it a novel meaning,[16] thereby leading simple men astray. Relying on certain texts like Mark 4: 11 and 4: 34, they assert the existence of secret traditions. They quote particularly Mark 4: 11: "To you has been given the secret of the Kingdom of God, but for those outside everything is in parables"; or again Mark 4: 34: "He did not speak to them without a parable, but to his disciples he explained everything." [17] On this point we have a clarifying statement of Ptolemaeus made to Flora: "It will be taught later how beginning with a unique and incorruptible principle all natures proceed, and this therefore explains their diversity." [18]

One series of data shows that the Gnostics appealed to a secret apostolic tradition, had their own prophets and possessed many books of revelation. They especially stressed revelations that would come to them from Jesus.[19] The Nag-Hamadi discoveries give us several examples of this. These so-called traditions are for the most part attributed to Christ, who moreover has practically exclusively the title Doctor. Afterwards come the chief Gnostic leaders who according to Irenaeus desired to be looked upon as doctors.[20] In their peculiar teachings they made use of subtle allegorical interpretations of the Scriptures and in so doing claimed to supply deeper insights into the common doctrine of the Great Church.

In fact, it was especially a matter of secret doctrines that were transmitted only in esoteric assemblies. This is quite evident in regard to a sacrament that appears in many forms and which they called *apolytrosis*: "They say that this is necessary for those who receive perfect knowledge, resulting in a revival of the force that surpasses all things. Otherwise it would be impossible for them to penetrate into the *Pleroma,* seeing that this is what leads to the heart of *Buthos.* They add that it is Jesus' baptism, manifested (on earth) which assures forgiveness of sins, but the *apolytrosis* of Christ, descending in him, alone leads to perfection; the first is *psychikos* and the second *pneumatikos.*" [21] They cite Jesus' words about "the other baptism" (*Mt.* 20: 22) or what Paul says about "redemption in Christ Jesus." The Gnostic doctors claimed therefore to be perfect, for no one was

---

14. Irenaeus, *Adv. Haer.,* III, 3, 4.

15. Cf. also Tertullian, *Adv. Valent.,* I.

16. Irenaeus, *Adv. Haer.,* IV, 33, 3.

17. One text as an illustration: Irenaeus, *Adv. Haer.,* I, 3, 1 in regard to the Valentinians: ταῦτα δὲ φανερῶς μὲν μὴ εἰρῆσθαι διὰ τὸ μὴ πάντας χωρεῖν τὴν γνῶσιν αὐτῶν. μυστηριωδῶδ ςὲ ὑπὸ τοῦ Σωτῆρος διὰ παρα-βολῶν μεμηνύσθαι τοῖς συνίειν δυναμένοις οὕτως. I, 25, 5 on the Car-pocratians: τὸν Ἰησοῦν λέγοντες ἐν μυστηρίῳ τοῖς μαθηταῖς αὐτοῦ καὶ ἀποστόλοις κατ' ἰδίαν λελαληκέναι καὶ αὐτοὺς ἀξιῶσαι τοῖς ἀξίοις καὶ τοῖς πειθομένοις ταῦτα παραδιδόναι.

18. Ptolemaeus, *Ad Floram,* VII, 8-9.

19. An excellent compendium in R. Lichtenhahn, *Die Offenbarung im Gnosticismus,* Göttingen, 1901.

20. Irenaeus, *Adv. Haer.,* I, 28, 1: "Eo quod multi ex ipsis, immo omnes velint doctores esse." See also the important declaration of I, 11, 1 in regard to Valentinus: ὁ μὲν γὰρ πρῶτος ἀπὸ τῆς λεγομένης γνωστικῆς αἱρέσεως τὰς ἀρχὰς εἰς ἴδιον χαρακτῆρα διδασκαλείου μεθα-ρμόσας. In I, 30, 15, it is a question of the *Valentini schola.*

21. Irenaeus, *Adv. Haer.,* I, 21, cf. 13, 6.

thought able to be their equal when it came to the fullness of
knowledge. They were superior to Peter and Paul and the other
apostles, and they declared that they knew more than anyone else
for they had absorbed the whole compass of the knowledge of the
ineffable power; they were therefore superior to all the powers.[22]
One particular example of this mentality is furnished by the
Gnostic Marcus who fashioned a very successful career for himself in suggesting this way of going beyond the sacraments of the
Church.

The Valentinian Gnostics about whom these passages speak
to us did not therefore form an anti-Church, but they claimed
to constitute an elite that had "arrived at Gnosis" [23] within
the Church herself. We may recall at this point the well-
known text that shows their relationship to the ordinary run
of the faithful. They are truly spiritual men (πνευματικοί) who
τὴν τελείαν γνῶσιν ἔχοντες περὶ θεοῦ καὶ τᾶς· τῆς Ἀχαμὼθ μεμυημέ-
νοι μυστερία... ἐπαιδεύθησαν δὲ τὰ ψυχικὰ οἱ ψυχικοὶ ἄνθρωποι,
οἱ δι' ἔργων καὶ πίστεως ψιλῆς βεβαιούμενοι καὶ μὴ τὴν τελείαν
γνῶσιν ἔχοντες· εἶναι δὲ τούτους ἀπὸ τῆς ἐκκλησίας ἡμᾶς λέγουσιν[24]

The Gnosis in this very peculiar theosophical sense is presented in the myths and the allegorical interpretations of the
Scriptures. It is contradistinguished from the good works and
the commonplace faith of the Christian masses. The *pneumatikoi*
set themselves apart from the *psychikoi*. Moreover, consistent
with the Gnostic conception, all this was related to salvation.
The *pneumatikoi* are assured salvation, and immune to corruption, just as all that is purely earthly, by its very nature, is
incapable of salvation. As for the Christian *psychikoi,* they can
be saved only by good works.[25] The *pneumatikos* is holy by nature,
whereas ordinary people, the "psychic" Church, are saved by the
Savior.[26]

We are thus led to examine the theory behind this distinction.
It is not easy to develop in a few words for the Gnostics presented
it in such varied forms that even Irenaeus was tempted to give
up.[27] Moreover, our aim here dispenses us from analyzing the
differences between the systems and from deciding whether we

are dealing with differences of vocabulary or with different theories.

In the various Valentinian systems described to us by Irenaeus, we come up against the pair Man-Church (*Anthropos-Ekklesia*) in the first *Ogdoad*.[28] The question may be disputed as to whether this pair precedes the *Logos-Zoe,* or *vice versa.* Whatever the case, both pairs belong to the highest divine sphere. As a reference concerning this *Syzygia,* a sentence from Paul was quoted: This is a great mystery, and I take it as meaning Christ and the Church." [29] Rightly, it seems to me, several researchers connect this speculation and the speculations on the old woman in the Shepherd of Hermas or even the pneumatic

---

22. *Ibid.,* I, 13, 6.

23. *Ibid.,* I, 13, 1 ff.

24. *Ibid.,* I, 6, 1-2.

25. *Ibid.,* I, 6, 2 continues as follows: διὸ καὶ ἡμῖν μὲν ἀναγκαῖον εἶναι τὴν ἀγαθὴν πρᾶξιν ἀποφαίνονται (ἄλλως γὰρ ἀδύνατον σωθῆναι), αὐτοὺς δὲ μὴ διὰ πράξεως, ἀλλὰ διὰ τὸ φύσει πνευματικοὺς εἶναι πάντη τε καὶ πάντως σωθήσεσθαι δογματίξουσιν. ὡς γὰρ τὸ χοϊκὸν ἀδύνατον σωτηρίας μετασχεῖν (οὐ γὰρ εἶναι λέγουσιν αὐτοὶ δεκτικὸν αὐτῆς), οὕτως πάλιν τὸ πνευματικόν, ὃ αὐτοὶ εἶναι Θέλουσιν, ἀδύνατον φΘορὰν καταδέξασΘαι. The way of acting is not questioned; it can be libertine as well as ascetic. We do not intend to examine here the connection between these considerations and St. Paul's ideas, as they are expressed particularly in I Corinthians. It is enough to point out that if we consider these in contrast to the Gnostic teaching, we observe an enormous difference. This is what appears most clearly in the use of πνεῦμα and even more in that of the word φύσει which Paul never used in this sense. Cf. Irenaeus protestations, *Adv. Haer.,* IV, 37, 1 ff. and Origen, *Contra Celsum,* VI, 61.

26. The following passage from Irenaeus (*Adv. Haer.,* I, 8, 3) corresponds to Romans 11, 16: ἀπαρχὴν μὲν τὸ πνευματικὸν εἰρῆσΘαι διδάσκοντες, φύραμα δὲ ἡμᾶς, τουτέστι τὴν ψυχικὴν ἐκκλησίαν, ἧς τὸ φύραμα ἀνειληφέναι λέγουσιν αὐτὸν καὶ ἐν αὐτῷ συνεσταλκέναι, ἐπειδὴ ἦν αὐτος ζύμη.

27. See for example, Irenaeus, *op. cit.,* I, 18, 1. 21: 5.

28. Cp. Irenaeus, *Adv. Haer.,* I, 11, 1; Hippolytus, *Refut.,* V, 6.

29. *Ep.* 5, 32; Irenaeus, *op. cit.,* I, 8, 4.

Church of 2 Clem., 14, which gives an allegorical exegesis of Genesis 1: 27.[30] The well known notion of a preexistent Church which goes back and is connected with the Gnostic myth.

Here we have a handsome example of the "Christianization" of certain aberrant themes spoken of above. In a work as typically Gnostic as the *Apocryphon Johannis* there is no trace of the word pair Man-Church. Furthermore, we must add that we do not see the connection between these *eons* and the drama of the fall and redemption which is the object of the myth. If we overlook a few accidental variations the myth always speaks of the pride of the last "Wisdom" *eon* which is proud of its sub-product, "Jaldabaoth" who is the creator of the world. But he is hoodwinked because in his creature, most often called Adam, there is a seed of light emanating from the most high and hidden God: this is what assures his salvation through Gnosis and his entrance into the *Pleroma*. In the created reality of this world three categories of men are distinguished: those who are entirely sub-mitted to the creator of this world, the *hylikoi;* those who occupy a midway position since in them good and evil are mixed (the *psychikoi*); and finally those who possess Gnosis (the *pneu-matikoi*).[31]

There is only one text where a bond between these three different classes can be observed.[32] We note that the spiritual man who was "sown" by having been breathed into Adam (*Gn.* 2: 7) remains unknown to the demiurge. "For just as he did not know Mother, he did not know seed; and it is precisely, they add, what the Church is, as the image (*antitypon*) of the Heavenly Church." [33] According to the Gnostic Marcus, Jesus would have been formed in the image of the *eon* Anthropos, who descended upon him in such a way that He englobed the whole of the *Ogdoad,* and particularly the *Ekklesia.* Marcus is starting out from the text of Colossians 1: 19: "In him all the fullness (*Pleroma*) . . . was pleased to dwell" (see also 2: 9). But we must add that in Marcus' system, neither the Church nor the other eons play a well defined role. Words and little else.

In the fragments from Heracleon that Origen has preserved

for us in his commentary on John the Church is frequently mentioned. The Samaritan woman of John chapter 4 appears as an image of the Church which was awaiting Christ and which attests that he knows all things (ἐπίσταται) (*fragm. 25*). This does not refer to the Church in the broad sense but to the totality of the *pneumatikoi,* as *fragm.* 37 specifies. When it is said in John 4, 39 that many Samaritans came to the faith through the word of the woman, Heracleon, concludes that this means the *psychikoi* and that only the woman is named: τὴν δὲ μίαν λέγει τὴν ἄφθαρτον τῆς ἐκλογῆς φύσιν καὶ μονόειδῆ καὶ ἑνικήν. The Church is the "house of the Father" where the *pneumatikoi* reside and where the *psychikoi* who are outside the *Pleroma* find salvation. The "third day" is the spiritual day of the rise of the Church. It is the assembly of the *pneumatikoi* who adhere to the Savior, the Man.

---

30. G. Bardy, *l. c.,* p. 167; F. Sagnard, *La gnose valentinienne et le témoignage de saint Irénée,* Paris, 1957, p. 302 ff.; J. Daniélou, *l. c.,* p. 326 ff.

31. This is very clear in Clement of Alexandria, *Excerpta e Theodoto,* 56-57: τὸ μὲν οὖν πνευματικὸν φύσει σῳζόμενον· τὸ δὲ ψυχικόν, αὐτεξούσιον ὄν, ἐπιτηδειότητα ἔχει πρός τε πίστιν καὶ ἀφθαρσίαν καὶ πρὸς ἀπιστίαν καὶ φθοράν, κατὰ τὴν οἰκείαν αἵρεσιν· τὸ δὲ ὑλικὸν φύσει ἀπόλλυται. Cf. Hippolytus, *Refut.* V, 6 in regard to the Naassenes: "There are three species of beings in the world: the angelic, the 'psychic' and the material, their names are the elect, the called and the captive."

32. In Irenaeus, *Adv. Haer.,* I, 5, 6.

33. One version (in Irenaeus, *op. cit.,* I, 7, 4) reports that at the moment of the appearance of the Savior, the demiurge would have learned everything from him; he would have placed himself at his disposition as once before with the centurion (*Mt.,* 8, 9): τελέσειν δὲ αὐτὸν τὴν κατὰ τὸν κόσμον οἰκονομίαν μεχρὶ τοῦ δέοντος καιροῦ (a typically eschatological expression), μάλιστα δὲ διὰ τὴν τῆς ἐκκλησίας ἐπιμέλειανκαὶ διὰ τὴν ἐπίγνωσιν τοῦ ἑτοιμασθέντος αὐτῷ ἐπάθλου, ὅτι εἰς τον τῆς μητρὸς τόπον χωρήσει. We are dealing here then with a sort of recuperation of the demiurge. Since he has submitted to the Lord, the care of the Church is entrusted to him. It does seem that the concrete Church is meant and therefore this is a return to the idea that the world was created because of the Church (cf. Hermas, *Vis.,* I, 1, 6 and Dibelius' annotations).

Here then we have a way of expressing things that is different from Irenaeus' (Adv. Haer., I, 8, 4), where Mother *Achamoth* was considered to be outside the *Pleroma* in the form of the lost sheep. This must be tied up wtih the fact that the Church was dispersed (ἐξ ἧς τὴν ὧδε Θέλουσιν ἐσπάρθαι ἐκκλησίαν).

This is not, as Sagnard [34] felt, a return to an opinion that was current in the Church, for the texts on which he thought he could rely lead in quite another direction, as I had the occasion to show elsewhere.[35] Both begin with the concrete fact of the dispersion of the Church in many places throughout the world: she finds herself in a dangerous state of diaspora.[36]

In the section "on the three natures" in the Jung Codex, which possibly comes from Heracleon,[37] there are few passages relating to the Church. I have had access to these documents thanks to the kindness of my colleague M. Quispel and Doctor Zandee of Utrecht. As Quispel and Puech have already demonstrated, it is remarkable that *Ekklesia* is present immediately after the Father and the Son as existing from the beginning, while in other Valentinian systems it is bound up with *Anthropos* and only a subordinate part of the first *Ogdoad*. The love of the Father and the Son is translated into kisses and produces the "Church of many men, the Church existing for *eons,* and which is therefore called the *'eons* of *eons'*." [38] The Church is composed of those who have overcome the illness of "womanliness" and reached "manliness" (fol. 94). Undoubtedly what is meant here is the womanliness of the fallen Sophia and the manliness of the Redeemer. In describing the work of redemption of the Logos, the author emphasizes that he effects the final destiny of the *pneumatikoi*: paradise, joy, the *Pleroma;* then the kingdom, i.e., the Church, which unites them and has the form of the Church "in the *eons*" (fol. 97), i.e., the Church of the earth which is the image of the heavenly Church as we have already seen. From it will be distinguished "the place of faith and obedience through hope, prayer and supplications" (fol. 97, 9 ff.); this Doctor Zandee identifies, and not without reason, with the final destiny of the *psychikoi*.[39] Finally there is mention of the plaguing of the enemies (fol. 122 ff.), of those wicked men to whom the Church has been handed over, defenseless, like her Lord (cf. *Jn.* 15: 20). We read also of the *pneumatikoi* who are united with the Savior, for it is for them that Christ came. As for the *psychikoi,* they rejoice at this union of the bridegroom and the bride in their expectation of full restoration of the *Pleroma,* "when all the members of the body of the Church will have found their place." Here we discover the figure of the body and its members, within the background of the diaspora from which the reunion is brought about.[40] The terminology used here is well known to us through the *Excerpta e Theodoto.* It is typical of Valentinian Gnosis.

After going through the the totality of available material we are compelled to conclude that there are very few usable elements which would aid us in constructing a genuine ecclesiology. Only the Valentinians were somewhat concerned about this. For them the Church is an *eon* which is part of the *Ogdoad.* Together with the Man, it forms a pair, although it is sometimes considered a masculine entity. As for the earthly reality we call "Church," very little is said about it. Mankind is divided into three groups,

---

34. F. Sagnard, *l. c.,* p. 393 f.

35. W. C. van Unnik, *"Diaspora" en "Kerk" in de eerste eeuwen van het Christendom,* in *Ecclesia. Een bundel opstellen aageboden aan Prof. Dr. J. N. Bakhuizen van den Brink,* The Hague, 1959, pp. 38, 43.

36. Irenaeus, *op. cit.,* I, 10, 1, 2.

37. See in this regard H.-Ch. Puech-G. Quispel, *Le quatrième écrit gnostique du Codex Jung,* in *Vigiliae christianae,* 1955, IX, pp. 65-102, esp. p. 95 ff.

38. Cp. *Exc. e Theod.,* 21, 3, a text in regard to which F. Sagnard, *Clément d'Alexandrie. Extraits de Théodote* (Paris, 1948, p. 99, n. 7) recalls Heracleon, fr. 5.

39. Letter of 11 July 1962.

40. But this is very different from John 11, 52, where the background is that of the Jewish diaspora. This is not found in Christian ecclesiology. Cf. my article cit., p. 185, n. 2.

the *pneumatikoi,* the *psychikoi,* and the *hylikoi.* The first who
are the Gnostics constitute the real Church; the second also
live in the Church and are not the without hope even though they
occupy a place inferior to the *pneumatikoi.* In fact, all of this is
typically individualistic, even though the individual is only a
specimen of his species. Jesus is the Redeemer to whom the
Church is united.

There is therefore not enough material to build a good
ecclesiology. We shall find very few elements proper to Gnosticism
integrated into a classical treatise. Their whole interest centers
around the "eonic" aspect of the Church. Everything about her
essence, her characteristic marks, her government and her earthly
tasks is not even considered. Their sole interest is to determine
the characteristics of those who belong to her, since they are
so preoccupied with the species of men who possess or do not
possess the "seed of light." The connection "Church" and "Kingdom of God" is blurry, and all that is left is a catalogue in which
New Testament formulas are classed in a certain order. In any
case, there is no notion of a people of God bearing witness or
assuming a mission in the midst of the world.

In this light, there is a considerable difference between Gnostic
ideas and not only Christian theology but also the Qumrân and
Jewish apocalypses. I must emphasize this because in recent
times there has been a trend to proclaim the affinities between
Jewish religion and Gnosticism. Jewish thought is concerned with
the lot of God's people and its struggle to remain holy and
faithful to the Law. This is a far cry from what we find in the
Gnostics. Even more to the point, the Jewish contribution to
the point we have been examining is practically null..[41] The
Gnostics use words borrowed from the New Testament to which
they give an esoteric meaning, known so well to Irenaeus.[42]

To go back to the question we raised in the beginning: why
did the Gnostics leave us so few elements concerning the doctrine
of the Church and why did they do so in such a lamentable fashion,
we can give a clear answer. They were simply not interested. They

were concerned with God the unknown and not with the One who has revealed his will. The Gnostics stressed anthropology and not ecclesiology. This was the price they paid for abandoning the Old Testament and allegorizing the New.

Utrecht-Bilthoven   W. C. van Unnik
Schwerlinchlaan, 4   Professor at the University of
                                                         Utrecht

41. Cf. my article: *Die jüdische Komponente in der Entwicklung der Gnosis,* in *Vigiliae Christianae,* 1961, XV, pp. 65-82.

42. Irenaeus, *Adv. Haer.,* III, 12, 12: *Scripturas quidem confitentur, interpretationes vero convertunt.* See also Tertullian, *De praescriptione haereticorum,* 33, 7 ff.

X

Rene Marle, S.J.

The Church in the Exegesis and Theology of Bultmann

During one of the pleasant interviews that Bultmann kindly granted me in his country house at Marburg, he pointed out to me the place held in his theology, in contradistinction to other Protestants, by realities that Roman Catholic theology considers basic: in particular, the Church, the community and tradition . . . . However, he added immediately, "that does not mean obviously that I see these realities in the same way you do."

A short time ago, on the occasion of the preparation for the coming Council and the Assembly of the WCC at New Delhi, a journalist came to interview Bultmann about what he thought of the ecumenical task, and in general of the problem of Christian unity. Bultmann answered that this unity was very dear to him, that it was in line with the message of the New Testament, but that, in his opinion, the integration of all Christians within one single organization ought not to be confused with *the* Church.

What does Bultmann say about the primitive Church in his exegesis, and what place does it hold there? What is, more generally speaking, the theology of the Church that he thinks is founded in the New Testament? These are the two questions to which we should like to give a summary response before formulating a critical judgment in the third section of our essay.

Strictly speaking, as we know, for Bultmann the New Testament does not begin with the manifestation and preaching of Jesus, but with the Easter event which is understood above all as the beginning of the apostolic *kerygma*. In his *Theologie des Neuen Testaments,* he emphasizes that Jesus' preaching — and what interests him in Jesus is essentially his Word — comes from "presuppositions" of the New Testament theology of which it is not properly a part.[1] This theology is a development of the Christian act of faith and can become a reality only from the moment that a person who formerly was a "bearer of the message" himself becomes its "essential content." [2]

Thus Bultmann deliberately sets the New Testament in a context where it was loved, preached, believed, understood and formulated, namely the primitive community. This he had already done, following the then new *formgeschichliche Methode,* in his *History of the Synoptic Tradition.* In his Theology of the New Testament he does it more completely and more synthetically.

In this latter work, where he brings together in a very well-knit whole the totality of his investigations and intuitions, he gives us the opportunity of assisting at the history of this primitive community; the history of its formulas and its representations, but also through these, the history of the understanding it comes to have of itself, its faith, the message from which it is conscious of living, and the mission it is to fulfill. He gives us a history of the variations in place and in time of this *Selbstverständnis* which eventually came to take its place in the New Testament. We ourselves can certainly retrace only very schematically this Bultmannian history of the primitive community (or communities), and it is only within it that the New Testament finds its real meaning.

The very first community, in the days that followed the Easter event, continued to exist primarily according to Bultmann in order to live and reflect to a great extent within the framework of Jewish apocalypticism. As an extension of Jesus' preaching, it proclaimed not his return but the fact that he came as the Messiah, the Son of Man. It already includes and proclaims the resurrection of Jesus as proof of the raising of the crucified to this messianic role of Son of Man. Moreover this resurrection event very soon appears to it more and more as *the* decisive event, and the primitive community itself becomes increasingly aware (even if this awareness is more lived and practical than reflective) of being the eschatological community, animated by the Spirit and already living under the radiance of the authority of the one whom God has glorified. It does not waste any time in looking upon this glorified person as the "Messiah," the "Son of David," the "Son" or "Servant of God." Its being assembled at Jerusalem, the practice of baptism, of the eucharistic meal . . . give very certain evidence of this awareness that the first community very soon had of its being the "eschatological community."

A capital moment in the history of the primitive community is the propagation of the faith and the *kerygma* in a Hellenistic context. This propagation was also very early, obviously, since it is primarily from this beginning that Paul developed his own *kerygma* and theology. The preaching of Hellenistic Judaism, furthermore, had paved the way for Christian missionaries in a pagan world and it had already made necessarily certain borrowings from the system of thought of the world it was penetrating. The new communities so constructed had not only the problem of their relations with the pagan world but also of the attitude to be taken and the judgment to be brought to bear in the face of the still clearly Judaizing tendencies of the first Palestinian community. It was Paul's task to resolve these problems in all their depth, and by so doing to clarify what in reality is the new faith and the community which it defines.

Still, the Hellenistic communities, without waiting any longer specified their faith within the context of the cultural world about them. This left its mark particularly on the presentation made of the person and work of Jesus. Jesus thereby became the *Kyrios,* the object of worship. His title "Son of God" is understood as a characteristic of nature. The sacraments of baptism and the Eucharist are interpreted by analogy with the mysticism and the worship of the mystery religions. Finally, on a more speculative plane, the young Christian communities, confronted with the important Gnosis movement, could not help but take notice of it, and the radical originality of their own message caused them

---

1. *Op. cit.,* p. 1.

2. *Ibid.,* p. 34.

in the face of it to make substantial borrowings, at least on the level of expression and vocabulary.

According to Bultmann, Paul, as we said, furnished a brilliant expression of this *kerygma* which was worked out little by little in the heart of the Hellenistic communities. Similarly John furnished somewhat later an ingenious expression of the worked out *kerygma* (he undoubtedly contributed a great deal to its formulation) in the Christian communities of the East.

However, we need not treat these two great theologies separately in the systematic presentation Bultmann proposes. Let us merely say that he sees here, especially if one knows how to interpret them and make the necessary distinctions between *was gesagt und was gemeint ist,* the marvelously developed expression of the genuine eschatological faith, that faith which corresponds to the New Testament accomplishment of the Word of grace and salvation. Of necessity we shall return to these two great theologies in our second part, when we will attempt to specify what our author considers to be the authentic ecclesiology of the New Testament. But before we do this we must still point out a final stage in this evolution which we have undertaken to describe.

In Bultmann's view, this faith took some time to evolve in all its purity and in the full sense of its newness, and its formulation culminated in the Pauline and Johannine theologies. Yet it was not long before it became fatally degraded, falling back more or less into the carnal level of Judaism or the pagan religions. Bultmann does not hesitate to see in the New Testament itself evidences of the world's revenge. More than one book of the New Testament shows the progressive corruption of this eschatological *Selbstverständnis* that is explained in the Pauline and Johannine theologies. This corrupting movement represents what Bultmann calls the "evolution toward the old Church" (*die Entwicklung zur alten Kirche*), which is the subject of the third part of his Theology of the New Testament.

Bultmann considers it obvious that as it grew the Church was to define more resolutely a certain juridical order regulating its phenomenal existence. But the most urgent question that then arises for the Church is what is the proper significance of this order. Must it be granted only a "regulating" character, was it only to be the result of the power of faith, or rather should it have a "constitutive" character where the Church would then be conceived as the organism through which grace is communicated, an organism that becomes the *Heilsanstalt,* the institution of salvation? Undoubtedly the question is rarely asked with such clarity, and it is possible actually, with the practical answers given in the New Testament itself, to see every possible shade of meaning, follow all sorts of changes in emphasis, or point out undeniable contradictions.

Moreover the direction of this simultaneous evolution causes no doubt for Bultmann. The charism is more and more bound up with function, and it is thought that it can be transmitted by a rite. The title *Apostolos,* which originally designated (as it still does with Paul) all the missionaries of the Gospel, becomes quickly reserved to the Twelve; they are the guarantors of tradition and heads of the Church. The continuity of this tradition as well as the unity of the Church no longer seems to be assured simply by the power of the Spirit, and both are made to depend on an institutionally regulated succession. Simultaneously sacraments and ecclesiastical regulations are more and more looked upon as organs or means of transmitting the benefits and truths of salvation. The final stage of this evolution, which marvellously manifests its direction, is represented by the institution of penitential discipline. Considered as a repetition of baptism, it will receive sacramental value for no other reason than that it expresses the exercise of the jurisdiction of the Church.

All these transformations correspond to the alteration in the Church's *Selbstverständnis* that we have already mentioned. The "eschatological" character of this Church is no longer understood as a relationship, constantly renewed by the marvellous working of the Word of reconciliation, with the God who comes to bring us life; it is now an actual "possession" of institutions which of themselves communicate the blessings of heaven. The *tension* that was characteristic of the primitive eschatology becomes less and less and, since the end of time seems to have

withdrawn into an indefinite future, men were only too naturally
drawn into compromising with the world. In more than one
respect faith has already begun to change into "middle-class
Christian piety." Christianity is looked upon as a new religion,
in the wake of or side by side with Judaism and the various pagan
religions. The history of salvation continues and becomes confused with the history of the Church. Luke already gives rather
good evidence of this new view. Yet, in order to illustrate this
point, together with the New Testament authors Bultmann also
willingly appeals to the works of the first Christian authors (Ignatius of Antioch, Clement of Rome, the Didache, etc). This
is a supplementary proof that his primary concern is the Church
and her representatives, and that on this point at least he in no
way agrees with those who play off the Scriptures against the
Church.

How does Bultmann understand this Church to which he
constantly refers, or rather how does he think it should be understood in relation to the New Testament? The New Testament,
it is true, does give us rather varied notions of the Church and
we can discern in it undeniable lines of evolution. However in
its core, or in its summit where we see the purity of its message,
Bultmann maintains that the New Testament evidences a well
determined understanding of the Church which we must now
specify more clearly.

The idea which undoubtedly best permits us to sum up all
that the true Church of the New Testament means for Bultmann
is the "eschatological" community. To assert that the Church
is the eschatological community is to assert that her reality exists
at the "end" of the world. As such, the Church is in no way
the work of men. Never can she be possessed by them. Never
can they in any way have her in their command. She is present,
by God's grace, wherever the "word of reconciliation" is proclaimed.

This is why she becomes a reality above all in a "worship
community." For it is in worship that the Lord is present. This
presence becomes effective, in the power of the Spirit, by the

proclamation of the Word which both contains the Church and proceeds from her. Even if the Christian community can be called a Church outside the context of its worship meetings, it is still the worship assembly that manifests its true essence, and the entire life of the community is dominated by it.

Therefore, since the Church is always brought together by the Word of her Lord, proclaimed and understood in the faith during the worship meeting, she also understands herself (a third basic characteristic) as the "community of God's elect." She is not, although she will quickly and always be tempted to look upon herself in this way, a society of people possessing the truths or the means of salvation; she is the community of those whom the Word of God has brought together and will continue to bring together always.

Is the true Church of the New Testament then merely an invisible Church in Bultmann's view? She is both visible and invisible. For this Church which proceeds entirely from the Word of God and his grace becomes very truly a reality in our world and our history. The Lord whom she venerates in her worship is not simply "he who is to come" but, at the same time, he who has already come, the very one who has called into existence the whole community which is assembled in his name. But this historical realization must never be isolated from the transcendent "eschatological" act which is expressed in it and would be incapable by nature of subsisting in the world. The invisible character of the Church in her essential reality is not that of an "idea" but of "the eschatological event which, since it is only intelligible to faith, is constantly renewed within history." Bultmann goes on to explain that like the Cross of Christ which is her foundation, the Church is an "ambiguous phenomenon" (*zweideutiges Phänomen*): "visible as a fact of the world, invisible — though at the same time visible for the eye of faith — as the greatness of the world to come."

What Bultmann intends to explain by this is that the Church, according to the most authentic message of the New Testament, is always essentially constituted from on high by God's continual (or rather unceasingly renewed) intervention which is perceived and received only in faith. This transcendence — what Bultmann calls the "eschatological" character, or the relationship to the future — is preserved only to the extent that the Church is understood as the Church of the Word, the bearer of the Word, because she is at first constituted by it.

We have already emphasized that Bultmann is very far from opposing Scripture to the Church. And even less does he oppose Church and Word (which he does not fail to distinguish from Scripture). Not only does he not oppose them; he thinks that they may never be considered in their truth independently from each other. The Church is constituted by the Word which salvation continually makes present, and which the true community of the faith builds for itself as the new Israel. But inversely, and just as really, the Word is constituted by the Church. For it is what it is "not through its meaningful and timeless content, but as the authorized preaching which has been handed down by tradition." The preacher is both "server" of the Word and "server" of the Church. Both are the expression of the same "eschatological intervention of God."

If Bultmann's thought is dominated by an opposition it is not between Word and Church, but between a Church of the Word and a Church of sacrament. We do not mean to imply that Bultmann is unaware of the place of the sacraments in the life of the New Testament communities, although he does tend to minimize it particularly in his interpretation of the Gospel of John. But in the parts of the New Testament where, according to him, they are envisaged in their true significance, they are understood only as *verbum visibile,* in the strict sense of the word: "They do nothing other than what the Word does; like it they actualize the act of salvation . . . . Therefore Paul is able to designate the celebration of the Lord's supper precisely as a 'proclamation' " (I *Cor.* 11: 26) (G.V., I, 181). What Bultmann is fearful of and what he sees already outlined in the New Testament itself is, as we have already seen, the notion of the Church as an "institution of salvation" (*Heilsanstalt*), whose sacraments would in some sense be organs and modes of administration, sources of grace at the disposal of the Church herself.

The Pauline notion of the Church as the "body of Christ," through which the Apostle sought to express the unity and the transcendence of the Church in Hellenistic terms, does not seem to him to be exempt from grave dangers in this regard. Undoubtedly this doctrine can be correctly interpreted, if we still see in it the conviction that the Church is always constituted by her Lord, that he precedes every reunion of those who find themselves again "in him," just as the great Church always precedes the particular Churches where she is manifested and finds her realization. But there is a great risk that this Church will be purely and simply identified with Christ and be thought of as possessing the benefits of salvation, which in reality can come about anew always and only through the Word and the grace of God. A Church of the Sacrament for Bultmann is a Church that has lost the sense of the "eschatological" character of salvation. A Church which, instead of allowing herself to be lifted up by the God who comes and reserves to himself the calling of his faithful, thinks she is right in having his Spirit and his benefits at her command, becomes — or remains — by that very fact a mere manifestation of the sinful world.

As we can see, it is the whole of Bultmann's theology and at the same time his whole interpretation of the New Testament which is involved in his remarks or expositions concerning the Church. For an efficacious critique of his theories, we should have on this point as on most of the others both to go in detail into his exegetical analyses (on which he bases and illustrates his view), and to discuss the historical, philosophical and denominational presuppositions of his whole exegesis. Competence as well as time prevent me from ever engaging in the first undertaking. As for the second, I have already done so elsewhere, and it would be beyond the scope of this article to sum up the Bultmannian debate in all its complexity, were one only to limit one's self to a few general propositions. I prefer to stay with a brief summary of what is of interest for me to retain in Bultmann's intuitions on the Church, and what in my opinion is his most serious deficit.

Bultmann seems more and more to be criticized for what

he overlooks or leaves out than for what he stresses. It seems to me that we do not have to reject this eschatological dimension of the New Testament Church on which he places so much emphasis and which Catholic theology has possibly too often neglected. The Church is not only "Jesus Christ continued," she is not only in "possession" of the Holy Spirit, built once and for all upon the rock, equipped, if I may say so, with everything necessary to bring men to salvation. She remains also in a sense "at the mercy" of God, even though she cannot doubt the fulfillment of the promises within herself, and does not cease to be sustained by the one who remains her Head and her Savior. She is a visible society with clearly defined boundaries. The divine Call from which she proceeds and the Holy Spirit who animates her are still unfathomable mystery and indefeasible liberty. Nor could she ever separate herself from the Word, who increasingly calls her to a new beginning and who builds her on the faith. All these aspects of the mystery of the Church are attested in the New Testament. For our part we should not give the impression that our whole theology of the Church is based on Matthew 16: 18.

Undoubtedly it is also not impossible to admit certain differences of emphasis in the ecclesiology of the various books or authors of the New Testament which show certain lines of evolution. Fr. Benoit has well demonstrated, for example, the existence of such an evolution, or rather of such a development within the Pauline doctrine of the Church as the Body of Christ. Similarly, in his remarkable study of biblical theology, *Gottes Herrschaft und Reich,* R. Schnackenburg admirably analyzes the incontestable evolution of New Testament eschatology in regard to the idea of Lordship, Reign or Kingdom of God. Bultmann can urge us on to be more and more careful in our presentation of New Testament ecclesiology.

But what we do refuse him is the right to set up certain aspects of this ecclesiology as an absolute norm and to consider pure bastardization what in reality merely represents complementary viewpoints. Why should the concrete and eminently complex mystery of the Church have had to be revealed and constituted all at once and be adequately expressed only in certain Pauline perspectives? It is known that Bultmann considers the words about the Church attributed to Jesus by the Gospels as obviously redactional. Without even appealing to the prophetic awareness of Jesus, what we know from the religious world of the time, especially since the Qumrân discoveries, is enough to convince us that these declarations have nothing impossible or aberrant about them. And instead of degenerating, why would the Church as she continued to persist and to spread not have merely enriched and perfected her *Selbstverständnis* with the result that, for example, the evidence of the Pastoral Epistles or Revelation would of necessity have to be integrated into a total presentation of New Testament ecclesiology? Integrated, not merely juxtaposed, but grasped in a sufficiently "comprehensive" view of the various data so that it will be evident that it is always the same mystery which is given to us under different aspects or at different "moments" of its manifestation. This is a more difficult task undoubtedly — and one that may never be completed — than the attempt to systematize everything around one aspect, but this task is a requisite for any one who intends to remain faithful to the New Testament.

The sense of the systematization worked out here by Bultmann might perhaps be explained partially by the anthropology, or, if you will, by certain of the philosophical views that are immanent in his interpretation. I personally feel that Bultmann starts out with too individualistic a notion of man in history to be able to account for the mystery of the Church satisfactorily. Yet he knows that Paul himself to whom he especially refers — like Jesus before him, in his preaching — "never sees man as an isolated individual. . . . For Paul, man is found in the very beginning and always in an historical context. . . ." And this is why he is unwilling to consider the Word of God and the working of grace independently from the Church and from a certain condition. Yet he always tends to consider this reality as a simple "matter" on which only the individual can confer any meaning.

Nevertheless, in regard to the Church, more perhaps than in any other area, I think that it is especially his denominational background that gives this particular decisive bent to his thought. Not only because today it is unquesionably around the Church that the most unyielding denominational oppositions revolve, but also because, perhaps still more basically, Bultmann's theology of the Church is dominated by a certain idea that is specifically Protestant: the mode of God's presence and his action in his revelation and his grace.

I should be willing to call this mode exclusively prophetic. We have seen with what insistence Bultmann defends a Church of the Word in contradistinction to a sacramental Church. There again, it does not seem to be a question solely of a native and even relatively external repugnance of a Protestant theologian for the hierarchical and sacerdotal institution which concretizes primarily for him an image of the Roman Church. Bultmann's ecclesiology is, may we say, predestined in its Christology. In accord with this, from the point of view of salvation history, Jesus is actually identified with his Word; he *is* nothing more than the "eschatological" Word of reconciliation. From this viewpoint, his fleshly body, born of a woman of the human race, as well as the whole length of time during which he carried on his mission, lose if not all significance, at least a large part of their profound sense. The same thing happens to his *acta et passa in carne* upon which the sacramental organization is built, as well as to the apostolic ministry. For this ministry is not only the ministry of preaching the Easter kerygma; it is also a ministry of those men whom Jesus himself chose and *established,* after having made himself known to them through a long familiarity, so that they would remain faithful witnesses and guardians of his memory and his work: a work that did not begin on Easter day but whose bases he laid down during his mortal life before ratifying it on the Cross.

Beginning from a limited notion of the work and person of Jesus, Bultmann is led to give only a narrow and partial presentation of the New Testament Church. The multiplicity of the images through which the mystery of the Church has been revealed to us in Scripture has been pointed out more than once: Temple of God, Body of Christ, Bride, Vine, etc., a multiplicity